Books about Welfare State International
Engineers of the Imagination
ed. Coult and Kershaw

EYES ON STALKS

JOHN FOX

Methuen

Published by Methuen 2002

10 9 8 7 6 5 4 3 2 1

First published in 2002 by
Methuen Publishing Limited
215 Vauxhall Bridge Road
London SW1V 1EJ

Copyright © John Fox 2002
Woodcuts and drawings © John Fox

John Fox has asserted his right under the Copyright, Designs and Patents Act, 1988,
to be identified as the author of this work.

Methuen Publishing Limited Reg. No. 3543167

A CIP catalogue record for this book is available from the British Library.

ISBN 0 413 76190 8
Designed and typeset by Alan Beck
Printed and bound in Great Britain by
St. Edmundsbury Press, Bury St. Edmunds, Suffolk.

Caution

List of Illustrations

Foreword

Once upon 1968, I found myself in a Lancaster park swinging a baby alarm loudspeaker round my head and chanting into its microphone Williams Blake's *Proverbs of Hell*. 'Enough – or Too Much!' and 'The Road of Excess leads to the Palace of Wisdom' were two of the holy slogans. Trying hard to look avant-garde, I was taking part in Welfare State International's very first gig – *The Marriage of Heaven and Hell*.

1968 was the year when the Angel Bohemia spread her fiery wings. I was chanting for Blake's sake, but also because I was fascinated by the artists, musicians and poets who were creating Welfare State International (WSI) – which later became my favourite theatre group in the world.

WSI has always been made up of extraordinary people creating imaginary palaces for everybody even when wet, cold, soaked, hungry, mocked and insulted by some of the most mudheaded Hooligan Heritage Committees and Aesthetic Bureaucrats in the land. Brave people with big eyes. Many visionary shows, both great and small, were generated as these extraordinary people worked together – hairy folkies, keen-eared electronic wizards, firework space-walkers, dragon painters, stegosaurus actors, patient stone-carvers, galloping one-man-bands, acrobatic poets and prophets in all sizes – a great deal of love giving birth to tiny and gigantic images of flame.

I never ran away to join this circus – I had too many people to support financially. But I wrote for them when I could and ran workshops and sometimes sent new recruits, two of my daughters included. What sort of people did WSI need? Years ago I was running a project at Dartington College of the Arts – a Mud Fair. On the floor, making a costume for himself, sat one of the best students I ever met in my life. As a boy he had taught himself stage magic. He could sing, act, play any instrument you could name – and he looked at the world through big round innocent eyes. I was worrying about some big props we needed for the Fair and asked him, 'You know we need some ten-foot-high sticks with ghosts at the top we can swing around over the heads of the audience? Well, how many of our group do you think can make them?' My student looked at me in surprise; 'Oh I think we all can' he said, teaching me one of the greatest lessons of my life. His name was Andy Burton and he went on to be one of the State's finest creators and then went further on to found, with his wife Jill, a shining and surviving small travelling company called The Satellites. It's a joy to work with people like that and John Fox pays tribute to them.

Foxy himself is a poet, painter and maker with enormous imaginative energy. A phone call to him is like a bumpy magic-carpet ride, the ideas and images are torrential. I usually hang up determined to accomplish Seven Impossible Tasks before breakfast. *Eyes on Stalks*, which must be read alongside the very practical and inspiring *Engineers of the Imagination*, is an account of a personal journey as one of the chieftains of the WSI tribe. It's full of stories – exhilarating accounts of gigs in Australia and Japan and the raising of the *Titanic* in London docks, clashes with arrogant cultural bureaucrats and delicate descriptions of naming ceremonies.

Now, it seems, John and the company have settled down in their purpose-built palace in Ulverston, birthplace of the great Stan Laurel. Maybe the Road of Excess led them to the Palace of Wisdom. But I don't think that road's seen the last of them.

Adrian Mitchell
April 2002

Overture

Eyes on Stalks is about two families, the Fox family and the Welfare State International family, travelling on an interconnected journey.

I was born in December 1938 in Kingston-upon-Hull. An only child, my ancestors came from Yorkshire: my father, a Merchant Navy sea captain, my mother a schoolteacher. After thirteen years of dull education, I was called up for National Service in the Royal West African Frontier Force. In Ghana, I came to dislike missionaries and their Christianity, and preferred camping in the jungle, letting off explosives and dancing all night to Hi-life music.

After this, Philosophy, Politics and Economics at Oxford, and Fine Art at Newcastle University seemed tame. However, I discovered art at the Ruskin School of Drawing in Oxford, and in 1963 wanted to be Cézanne or Graham Sutherland. But I swung to thoughts of taking art into the streets, or indeed, finding ways of making society itself more creative and celebratory for more people. At Newcastle University in 1967 I provoked a 'happening', a memorial service for a young artist who 'passed away suffering artefact suffocation, over-exposure, disillusion, self-indulgence and deep lack of purpose'. The search for something different has gone on ever since.

In August 1962 I married Sue Robinson, who became Sue Fox, who became Sue Gill after changing her name by deed poll. Daniel our son was born in November 1968 and Hannah our daughter in January 1971. Sue and I, plus Roger Coleman and Alison Fell and others, founded Welfare State International in December 1968. Sue and I are still the artistic directors. Over the years we have worked with hundreds of people. Many of them have become friends and I guess I am no longer an only child!

The process of describing our journey of three and a half decades has itself been a journey: unpredictable and stimulating, arduous, but rewarding. It has taken about a year and has been a rite of passage in itself. My original intention was to lasso the thoughts and notebooks of many artists who had been or were working with us. This was the method we had used successfully with our other book, *Engineers of the Imagination*, and it would demonstrate again that Welfare State International is nothing without the consortium of people who have given so much to make the work and establish the company's reputation. The reason the names and mini-biographies of so many artists appear in the footnotes at the end is because my editor's advice was to keep the story moving. Please be sure to read them. Working with the company is like being on an idiosyncratic train; on average there always seem to be about thirty people in the carriage. Some get on. Some get off. Some you never see again. But for a time you share whatever turns up.

Once my own journey had gained momentum, however, I found I needed to simplify and to lay bare the points and crossroads. With the benefit of hindsight (Daniel is now thirty-three and Hannah thirty – and the mother of our grandson Reuben), I found a pattern which lent itself to a narrative. I have had to omit a huge amount and much of the work directed by other chieftains. This is no reflection on them, or the quality of their work, but rather an indication of my own wish to illuminate the interlocking stepping stones of the art, the family and the company.

The writing was complicated. I should have taken a sabbatical but there were demands of servicing a programme in a new building with eight staff and many visiting artists, students and public. As it was, all my colleagues in Lanternhouse were extraordinarily understanding and generous, as were my family at home, who had to put up with a certain obsessional, and sometimes grumpy, withdrawal. It doesn't seem quite fair to the potentially huge dramatic personae of the years to single out individuals, but on this particular carriage a number of people have been a real help and anonymity doesn't seem fair either.

So, in the production of the book, thank you to Sue Gill, my wife and best friend, who has read it all and offered strong advice, and as always, phenomenal support when I couldn't see a way out; to Gilly Adams, who despite being overworked herself, also read it and gave constructive criticism, especially when I got to carping. Heartfelt thanks to Elizabeth Ingrams my editor, for her diligence and editorial authority. At Methuen, Michael Earley, Eleanor Knight and Eugenie Boyd helped facilitate the contract. Al Beck, the inventive designer, straight from his course at Cumbria College of Art and Design, put in hours and hours good-humouredly, sorting and framing my piles of sketchbooks, photographs and ideas. Dot Queen, my assistant at Welfare State International, put in hours and hours, and even came back from holiday to type and make sense of reams and yards of unkempt manuscript and Trish Tyson volunteered for extra proofing.

Thanks also to the Theatre Archive at The Department of Drama, Bristol University, in particular Frances Carlyon, Victoria Newton and Martin Hall, who dug out information, often at short notice, but particularly Dr Gillian Hadley, whose invaluable preliminary research was a good starting point for my writing. Northern Arts, and in particular Mark Mulqueen, were very helpful too, as were many photographers and artists who, where possible, have been credited on the appropriate page. By chance, some important artists and colleagues from the early days, such as Lois Lambert, Wendy Meadley and Janet Benham, have not been described. Some I have forgotten and others crop up at random. Here is a selection of the many, some of whom are mentioned in more detail in the book: John Angus, Rachel Ashton, Jon Atkins, Rakie Ayola, Mike Beaumont, Alec Bell, Claire Benbow, Janet Benham, Jon Bielstein, Bill Blaikie, Josie Bland, Roger Bloomfield, John Bolton, Gill Bond, David Boyd, Gary Bridgens, Martin Brockman, Ian Broscomb, Andy Burton, Gill Burton, Simon

Byford, Neil Cameron, John Carroll, John Chapman, Terry Chinn, Kuljit 'Kooj' Chuhan, Susan Clarke, David Clough, Chris Coates, Steve Cochrane, Josie Coggins, Roger Coleman, Duncan Copley, Lol Coxhill, Peter Croskery, Julian Crouch, Naheed Cruickshank, Mo Cumbo, Di Davies, Sharon Dippity, Jez Dolan, Kathleen Doody, Lynda Doyle, Gail Dudson, Graeme Dunstan, Jane Durrant, Mandy Dyke, Avril Ellis, John Faulkner, Kevin Fegan, Alison Fell, Lord Peter Feversham, Tim Fleming, Patsy Forde, Dan Fox, Hannah Fox, Bob Frith, Gill Gill, Graeme Gilmour, Lou Glandfield, Celia Gore-Booth, Mark Greaves, Kay Greer, Steve Gumbley, Gill Hadley, Ben Haggerty, David Haley, Jules Hammerton, Steve Harris, Lynda Hebbert, Art Hewitt, Rob Hill, Sue Hill, Dave Hillman, Chris Hobbs, Dave Holland, Mark Hopkins, Jonathan How, Boris Howarth, Maggie Howarth, Peter Huby, Hilary Hughes, Liam Hughes, Tim Hunkin, Albert Hunt, Alex Hutt, Phil Hyde, Therese Johnston, Alison Jones, Jasmine Jones, Chris Jordan, Jo Kelly, Sheena Kelly, Baz Kershaw, Catherine Kiddle, Tom Kiddle, Dermott Killip, Alice King, Juginda Lamba, Conrad Lambert, David Lambert, Lois Lambert, Florence Lawson, Stuart Lawson, Nigel Leach, Amanda Lebus, Liz Leyh, Gavin Lewery, Mary Lewery, Tony Lewery, Liz Leyh, Tony Liddington, Val Liebowitz, Ted Little, Lizzie Lockhart, Peader Long, Chris Lurca, Elizabeth Lynch, Ken McBurney, Duncan McGregor, Ruari McNeill, Dave Martin, Wendy Meadley, Caroline Menis, Fran Menis, Miklos Menis, Luk Mishalle, Adrian Mitchell, Beatty Mitchell, Celia Mitchell, Sasha Mitchell, Stuart Mitchell, Rick Morgan, Lord and Lady Moser, Pete Moser, Vivien Mousdell, Gerry Mulgrew, Dougie Nicholson, Maddi Nicholson, Joan Oliver, Peter Oliver, Richard Oyarzabal, Bob Palmer, Naomi Parker, Claire Parr, John Pashley, Derek Pearce, Tanya Peixoto, Simon Pell, David Penn, Hugo Perks, Matthew Pike, Andy Plant, Jo Pocock, Jamie Proud, Liz Pugh, Alice Purcell, Amanda Quigley, Nicki Rathbone, Anthea Rathlin-Jones, David Rennie, Ali Rigg, Ros Rigby, Ozzie Riley, Mary-Anne Roberts, Mary Robson, Max Rosin, Sam Samkin, Pam

Sandiford, Henni Schwarz, Pierre Schwarz, Caroline Scott, Adele Shank, Ted Shank, Les Sharpe, Mette van der Sijs, Pippa Smith, Mike Snalam, Catriona Stamp, Peter Stark, Sue Stark, Howard Steel, Marcel Steiner, Greg Stephens, Ian Stephens, Eileen Strand, Simon Strand, Rikki Tarascus, Clive Tempest, Taffy Thomas, Chris Timms, Rosemary Timms, Dave Turner, Bryan Tweddle, John Vogdt, Zosin Wanda, John Wassell, Jodi Watson, Angus Watt, Shona Watt, Doreen Webster, Malcolm Webster, Warner van Wely, Ken West, Mike Westbrook, Becky Whatley, Dave Whatley, Dave Wheeler, Greville White, Mike White, Elaine Whitewood, Faridah Whyte, Jim Wilkinson, Diz Willis, Peter Wilshaw, Jenny Wilson, Chris Wolverson and Ali Wood.

This book is dedicated to all these people, and all the others with whom we have connected in temporary celebration. Celebrations can unite us in a joyful community cohesion. They can liberate energy and demonstrate wonder in sensual style. Outside the walls of playhouses, educational institutions and commercial leisure centres, they balance on the tips of the elemental and mythic. At best they provide a sense of heightened being and seeing.

And where is the real world? In our age of increasingly expensive distractions we are becoming obsessed with this word 'real'. The real world is where we try to live with our daily dreams, perpetual stresses and fears and fulfilment. It is the place where we try to grow ourselves and rear our families while our imaginations and abilities are continually bombarded, controlled and undervalued by outside agencies.

One aim of this book is to pass on information. Many of us at Welfare State International have learned much and made many mistakes. Younger people tend to ignore their elders, which is healthy, but I have found a few handy friends in books, and maybe following paths on other people's maps can save the toil of repeated exploration of the same ground. We invented the slogan 'Eyes on Stalks, Not Bums on Seats' in 1982 because our primary motivation was and still is, to create wonder.

Reuben, our grandson, was born to Hannah Fox and Duncan Copley on Hallowe'en 2000 and like all grandparents we find the elastic of mortality being stretched. As we learn from Reuben, we constantly think about his future. I worry about this English country and world culture he is growing up in, especially its violence, greed, manipulation, destruction of the imagination, ignorance of what art is and the inability to think of generations ahead.

When I started writing (in June 2001), I was in a hut by the sea. The horizon had been obliterated by rolling white mist. It is similar to that in a favourite film, *The Incredible Shrinking Man*. A man on a motor cruiser at sea is overwhelmed by such a mysterious white cloud. The wife is down below (cooking the tea!). She escapes, but he is poisoned by this unexplained force.

Thereafter he grows smaller each day and keeps shrinking. He is nearly lost down a sink in his cellar. Cheeses are ten foot high. Cats are monsters. Eventually he is the size of a sequin and still growing smaller. He walks through a mouse hole to his garden, where the night sky is full of stars. To him and the cinema audience the stars are apparently as small as him. He is becoming as tiny as an electron. In a way, he has to start all over again. Guess I feel something like that. Like all our work, *Eyes on Stalks* is designed to be a catalyst to inspire and provoke imaginative action from the reader. May your eyes wobble in their sockets, your creative juices boil over and your bum never ache.

1

New Lamps for Old

Welfare State International is a diverse group of artists, musicians and eventmongers which, since it began in December 1968, has earned a living from the fruits of its imagination. Over a dozen of us,[1] teachers and students working in and around Bradford Art College, took our art into the street in order to reach an audience who wouldn't normally cross the thresholds of elitist theatres and galleries. Over a pint in a pub in Bradford, we borrowed the tag 'Welfare State' from the real welfare state ('International' came in 1979), recognising participatory socialism, where art would be as available and accessible as free dentures, spectacles and coffins. Since then, we have swung between the poles of populist performance art and applied anthropology. In 1972, our earliest manifesto, heavily influenced by the ideas of the Situationists and Marcuse, printed on silver paper hijacked from an elitist theatre, proclaimed:

An Entertainment, an Alternative and a Way of Life
We make images, invent rituals, devise ceremonies, objectify the unpredictable and enhance atmospheres for particular places, times, situations and people. We are artists concerned with the survival and character of the imagination and the individual within a technologically advanced society.

Once we lived as outsiders on an ex-rubbish-tip in Burnley. From there, for ten years we toured widely in caravans, producing street theatre and pageants in bizarre forms with a circus tent. Then, we had the trappings of a tribe, with fierce make-up and alienating costumes to reinforce our identity. Thirty-four years later, our original intentions still hold, although we now have a more global and environmental perspective, and are more integrated with our town community. Now we are more apparently respectable, with a customised headquarters in an old Victorian school called Lanternhouse. Recently refurbished with a £1.6 million Arts Lottery award, Lanternhouse is located on the Furness Peninsula in Cumbria, in the centre of Ulverston. It has studios, exhibition spaces, accommodation, a library, coffee shop, courtyard, gardens, towers and bridges, and a separate warehouse, computers, a database, a well-staffed office (with business, marketing and centre managers), brass plaques, burglar alarms, and architectural awards, the only tent being a miniature one for the office cat. All these are a long way from the trailers of 1968, although my office is a garden shed on the roof.

Now, there is also a considerable network of hundreds of like-minded people, some of whom worked with us years ago, some of them running extraordinary visual theatre companies. Many others have been part of the UK celebratory arts movement, regularly documented in MailOut,[2] which has also spread to communities and institutions world-wide.[3]

Eyes on Stalks, however, is not about wallowing in the past. Every era courts the myth of a lost Golden Age. Nostalgia dulls reality. Most of the interpretations of Lake District history give us only what is comfortable and sterile, with little mention of rural poverty or the slave trade. In terms of satire and social comment, it refuses to venture beyond the Toby jug. Ulverston chooses the safe theme of Dickens for its winter festival, suppressing most of his social and artistic relevance and reducing him to an icon of the heritage industry – top hats and starched mobcaps, fantasies that prop up tourism, shopping and the Christmas market, with not a beggar in sight. At Brantwood, on the shore of Coniston Water, despite the efforts of the dynamic curator of his home, John Ruskin is still mainly a museum and tea shop. At the nearby architectural treasure Blackwell, influenced by William Morris, there is none of his radical socialism. Wordsworth's once revolutionary zeal is not obvious even at Dove Cottage. Nostalgia can be a tool of authoritarian centralism which maintains the old order and demonises the dissenting underbelly. So, if I look back, it's not in nostalgia, but only to offer tools, models and lessons for the future.

In the sixties, everything seemed simpler. You could literally afford to be radical. We weren't paying back student loans, unemployment was rare and with legwork you could earn a wage if not a living. Optimism, hope and the right and need to change everything was in the consciousness of a small but vocal, active and committed minority. If we were all in any case about to be annihilated instantly in a nuclear war, what had we to lose? If we were to change everything, though, we had first to survive. Targets were straightforward – Americans in Vietnam and racial equality in South Africa and the USA. The Cold War and the threat of nuclear annihilation, the two big sticks keeping most people in order, also triggered change.

The totalitarian post-industrial world with its 'comfortable, smooth, reasonable democratic unfreedom', as Marcuse put it in his *One Dimensional Man,* maintained by the very technology that could free us from toil and ignorance has not gone, despite the lessening of the threat of nuclear war.[4] In 2002, 20 per cent of Britain's population is still marginalised, existing on sink estates, with poor schools, work that is non-existent or menial and exploitative, and thousands are deprived of the fashionable technological, social and financial skills necessary for a lucrative career. The kind of lucrative career in which Tony Blair can award himself a 41 per cent pay rise, from £116,000 to £163,000. An increase equivalent to nearly five years' pay for anyone on a minimum wage but not unusual for hundreds of top managers, and small change for a few professional footballers. Socialism and protest in 2002 may not be dead, but it is looking even more anaemic than in 1968, especially for Carlo Giuliani, the twenty-three-year-old dissenter killed in Genoa during the G8 summit in 2001.[5]

We are offered a dazzling array of apparent choice, but even political radicalism, alternative religions, drugs, pornography, sadism, tourism and art products are cogs in a cultural machine. The argument continues that the new big sticks (now wielded by multinationals, the media and information technologies) dominate our imagination with money, branding, packaged care, gratuitous entertainment and the scratch-card fix. In our kind of democracy many people, particularly young people, believe their voice is unheard. Tony Blair, speaking in Genoa about street protest, said that 'normal people' should be back at home with their families, leaving it to their elected representatives to bring about change – this after the election with a 40 per cent turnout, one of the lowest in recent British elections.

Isolated in front of the telly, we are fed so-called 'reality' TV and soap voyeurism with no possibility of exchange or gift relationship. Our dreams and open-ended imaginations are stolen from us to be sold back as closed, expensive and manufactured fantasies. Some people are more liberated sexually, morally and financially than in the sixties, but there is a legacy of fear, a perception that violent crime is rising, considerable depression and loneliness linked with the breakdown of family, universal credit-card debt, confused value structures and the purely hedonistic use of drugs and sex. Commercial football is increasingly gaining the power and role of a dominant and expensive religion.[6] As if all that were not enough, we are now encountering the 'double-edged' sword of technology.

Television, information technology and mobile phones isolate us physically, if not mentally. We communicate excessively, about less and less, and generate stress for ourselves with information overload. At the same time, though, the world-wide web and e-mail has also facilitated the anti-globalisation movement. *Subcomandante insurgente* Marcos's words were picked up by the electronic picture desks of colour supplements as radical chic.[7] The media may be insatiable and amoral, but video pictures of massacres in Bosnia, Rwanda and East Timor, as well as world-wide famines and floods, have also made us aware of wars, debt repayments and climate change. Our awareness is not powerless. Contrary to popular belief, the numbers of wars and their scale and length are decreasing.[8] The breakdown of institutionalised church-going we are experiencing in England could be fuelled by media images of the ascendance of religious fundamentalism which seems to fuel hatred, terrorism and war in the USA, the Middle East and Northern Ireland.

Eyes on Stalks is undoubtedly political, but I hope it is not a tract. It is primarily about experiments in theatre, performance, community art and rites of passage that have sprung from the momentum of a rollercoaster of issues. Welfare State International has increasingly moved away from models of theatre and performance of the spectacle, however inventive, to models with a different social purpose. Always balancing on a seesaw between a social agenda and aesthetics, we have researched ways of making art work in a community context, connecting patterns of living with aesthetic and stylistic invention, maintained playful and imaginative modes of seeing (and being); looking for ways to make work itself more creative. In the process, we have stumbled across a few life-enhancing prototypes. Despite the large outcast underclass and the increasing gap between rich and poor people in Britain (and between nations of the world), some aspects of our culture have improved. We have contributed a tiny amount but it has been significant for a few people.

The fifties were dull. We were still recovering from World War II. In the sixties, racism, sexism and bullying were rife. Women and young people in particular were often oppressed by the nuclear family structure. Empire and National Service went. The Pill came. Abortion and gay rights were legalised and university education widened. Half a century on, some things are better. Now it is rare for street performers to be arrested, as was common in the early seventies. Far from it. Today, clowns, jugglers, stilt-walkers and carnival troupes are avidly hired. They are all-Dayglo, all-dancing doorknobs that open every shopping festival in every lookalike mall from Barrow to Milton Keynes. Now there are hundreds of excellent entertainment and music festivals, local authority play buses, community art agendas, lantern parades, fire shows, pyrotechnic turn-ons, an increasing number of alternative rites of passage (namings, funerals and weddings) and even one or two established but imaginative undertakers designing attractive coffins. Today the concepts of 'access', 'multigenerational' and 'diverse' participation are built into every arts-funding guideline. Although these concepts have become institutionalised, with politically correct agendas, the overall picture for artists and communities has improved.

The issues of today may seem less overt. Maybe we are anaesthetised by inertia, while our vision is channelled through consumerism, linear education, too much fake choice and a residual cynicism and insecurity left over from Thatcher's Grocerism and Greed, but the issues are no less real or urgent. They include environmental degradation, global warming, the domination of multinational brand logos, the marginalisation and relative poverty of 20 per cent of the UK population, the exploitation of economically poorer countries and people, AIDS, uncontrolled population growth and inevitable terrorism.[9]

Our journey has always been informed by these agendas.[10] We have made many practical experiments (and mistakes). I hope we continue to learn lessons and that the questions we have asked and the prototypes we have discovered are of use to others. If, as André Breton put it in 1928, 'The poet of the future will make dreams concrete', then it is a privilege to pass on the fruits of our labours.

Cheap Art

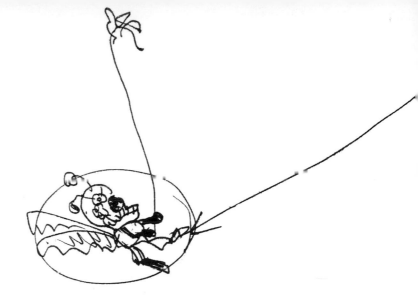

Long before anyone thought of the famous West Indian carnival in Notting Hill, Peter Schumann and his Bread and Puppet Theatre from New York were enacting *A Man Says Goodbye to his Mother*. In 1965 on a grey street corner, working in drizzle and against traffic noise, the company engaged passers-by with a tough five-minute fable about the Vietnam War. I had never seen anything like it. John Arden and Margaretta d'Arcy[1] and the Olivers[2] at Oval House were responsible for the visit. It was the trigger that inspired me to start Welfare State International.

Simple, direct, monochromatic backdrops painted on white sheets depicted an Asian village. A narrator with a skull mask carried a bag of props. There was a trumpeter, also in a skull mask, and a mother in black with a silver-grey face mask. The son marched to war to the time of a drum and was shot in the arm. The narrator replaced the mother's mask with that of an oriental woman. She became a woman from the village. As the land was dangerous, the narrator explained, the son needed weapons and he gave him a gun, a gas mask and an aeroplane.

He whirled this round his head on a string while the cast imitated the buzzing sound of engines. The woman looked to the sky. The narrator gave the woman a plant, but the son poisoned the crops (a cloth was dropped over the plant). Then the son first tore up a cut-out of the woman's house and finally killed her child. Carefully the woman placed the dead child on the ground, pulled out a pair of scissors and stabbed the son through the heart. Standing over the dead son, the narrator covered his face with a sheet and, after a long pause, he and the woman, now both wearing skull masks, carried off the dead boy's corpse.

The audience of twenty-odd were stunned. Even the traffic seem stilled. Here was truth and risk and simplicity and necessity. Every word that Peter Schumann has ever said about his work is thought-provoking:

> We don't necessarily have to revolutionise theatre. It may be that the best theatre will develop from the most traditional forms. A theatre is good when it makes sense to people . . . I feel that art in the modern world is generally superfluous. Either we should find a true need for it or give it up. We named our theatre the Bread and Puppet Theatre because we felt that theatre should be as basic as bread![3]

Peter is a saint. Over the years, our paths have crossed occasionally and I never feel I am up to his moral stance. In the autumn of 1999, Pete Moser and I were invited to a conference in New England. After our efficient and dutiful presentations to rows of suited administrators and a few professional artists, we escaped to Vermont, to the farm where Peter fed us on maple-syrup pancakes.[4] The trip was liberating. Boys in a Cadillac with Buddy Holly on the sound system, big empty roads and even emptier hills burning golden in the fall. 'Why are we doing what we do?' we kept asking ourselves in our usual dialogue about Art and Society. And the Bread and Puppet Theatre yet again showed us the way to our next adventure.

Peter and Elke Schumann and their dedicated family and followers had had a difficult year. After more than a decade, their famous Domestic Resurrection Circus had stopped. They were traumatised. Their gathering had been a huge influence on generations of theatre practitioners who regularly made the pilgrimage to Vermont, where Peter and his family had settled on a farm and had created a powerful, colourful and political pageant every summer, workshopping it with hundreds of performers in a huge landscape arena, for an audience of thousands. It was said that 50,000 regularly came to visit. As with all big crowds, there were factions and different agendas and tensions between locals and visitors.

But, after years of extraordinary and original poetry, Peter's circus had run into trouble – not from the work, but from the crowd. An incident when a man with a weak skull was accidentally killed in a scuffle forced Peter to rethink the scale of his work. He was reducing its size and when we arrived he was conducting a charming tiny vaudeville political puppet circus, with and for local children in his theatre barn. My hero, now in his late sixties, was dancing as energetically as ever, leaping one-legged on stilts, twenty feet up. Round a camp-fire that night, as his golden-haired grandson cuddled up to the great man and we passed round the whisky, I was reassured.

There is an enormous puppet museum on the farm. Barns and floors filled with tableaux, mammoth and miniature wonders from decades of shows, posters and props, scenery and scripts, a cornucopia glowing and creaking in a rickety, resinous cathedral of wood. It is extraordinary and all free. There is no supervision, just a moneybox, and you can gather armfuls of posters, books, images and poetry. We collected many treasures, but the catalyst was a pamphlet about Cheap Art written by Peter in about 1986.[5] Back in England in time for the Year of the Artist, we planned a homage to the Schumanns and produced our own manifesto. Weeks of anxiety, preparation making poems, posters, books and postcards – then, suddenly, we were off!

In Chorley Market in April 2001 there are fifty stalls and we can't believe it. It's 7.30 a.m. We've started and are a bit scared. Up at six to chug along the motorway in Howie Steward's battered Merc living van. It fits in well. With our scalding tea in a steel Thermos, our padded check shirts and early morning faces, we nearly look the part, too.[6] Half the market traders have been there for an hour already. Setting up scaffolding stalls just like ours. Draping white 'tarps' against the chill wind, which smells of rain. They will probably hate us. There's the routine, which is to find the superintendent, haggle over permits and location. Erect the stall with printing, books, sample images, CD and recording machine. (It takes about an hour at first.) Today, we are between Pet Food Man and Nylon Nighties.

Eventually we grab a bacon-and-egg butty (there's always a market food outlet) and wait for the first customer. We learn to hustle. 'A greeting card or song for you, madam. It's the Year of the Artist. We are artists bringing woodcuts and songs and books to your market today.' The cry is too dull, so we have to improve – we have to look people in the eye and talk them in. Pete's accordion is too loud and my spiel can't be heard. Passers-by, even those who put money in our bucket, won't shop with us. Why should they entrust us with writing an original greetings card or commission a song when you can buy perfectly good cards from Gordon Fraser or CDs from Woolworths? In Chorley as elsewhere, working-class people have little time to spare and are on routine speed patrol for bargains. Here, in a raw market economy, you are as good as your last deal.

At least the market traders like us. On the first day, we work mainly for them, selling little, but writing a song for the baby of the nightie man next door, and for Tokyo Joe, who brings us regular tea with the score on a slate. He donates fortune cookies in return. Mine says 'Don't cross the future'. Pet Food Man asks me to mind his huge dogs, so we must be accepted. But not yet by the dogs, which howl at us. In the afternoon, a trio dances past, as though from a painting by Watteau. One small girl, whilst balancing herself on the shoes of her big sister, is balancing a tiny teddy bear on her toes. Slipping from entrepreneur to observer, I hunt for charcoal to draw them when all three dance into our booth to make potato prints of blue hearts for the bear's birthday. Big sister, all of twelve, tells Radio Lancashire how good the project is (how assured children are with the media), while Pete instantly composes and sings a jingle in praise of local radio. This draws an audience for the rest of the tour. One joy of gigging is that you can never predict what will drop in. Our last customer is Jack, a big-eyed seven-year-old. His exhausted mum, very pregnant, parks on our high stool. Dressed in voluminous black, she rocks like an egg, explaining that Jack thinks his mother is indeed an egg and will soon burst open. His prototype drawing is therefore of a cracked egg. I suggest that by the magic of printing he can make an egg stamp in two parts, to crack and open on order, depositing in many pictures any appropriate chicken, ostrich or dinosaur.

This is fine by Jack, but as he also desires a white egg on white paper, we have to invent invisible chicks, which can only be located via their raucous crowing. I have an emergency piece of black card. 'Egg by night?' I suggest. So Jack prints, very firmly, one cracked white egg in its bottom corner. Three runny yellow stars, the yolks of a New World, complete the composition. Jack and his mother giggle with delight and pay us our fee of one pound. Two satisfied customers and a picture and a half – indeed, a whole universe – to end a rich twelve-hour day.
The tour gets better and better. In seven more markets in Cumbria and north-west Lancashire, we continue to learn our new trade. With many small transactions, we even cover the cost of our printing. The commissions and the stories pile in, and we make dozens of instant greetings cards and scores of very particular songs.

This huge man, Luggy, with a beer gut, from Burnley, loves the freedom of being on the road. Selling anything from paper towels to plastic crates. His song is called 'Wild Salmon'. He named his first child Sam and when his wife was pregnant with the second one, he threatened to call it 'Paste' so they would have 'Sam and paste'! His friend is a Pakistani selling shoes. We make a card for him showing how the Great Golden Shoe landed in a hot air balloon on Clitheroe Castle on May Day. At the end of their day, the two men comically insult each other, each mimicking the other's accent in a bizarre double-take. 'You are robbing me. I offer you one hundred per cent, and you take one hundred and fifty. You just capitalist.' 'You capitalist too' – and so on. It's a tonic for race relations and a good example of the generous camaraderie and welcoming we found amongst all these traders. One boy, aged eight, wrote his first song for his adopted mother. We know the woman. She continually rescues damaged children from dysfunctional relationships. She has brought this boy to our Welfare State concerts and he has lain on the floor, inches from the band, mesmerised by our samba drummers. Now he has written his first song. We photograph him with the words in his hand: 'My mum, my other mum, is an angel with long hair down her back'.

Long overdue and deeply felt songs for mothers, for a boyfriend arriving from Australia, a letter to 'my tiger in Nepal', a certificate for the best egg butty of the tour, 'for my husband, who is taking his accountancy exams', for 'my son, who is good at sheep dipping, but loves football', for 'my husband who is a supporter of Leeds playing Valencia tonight'. 'For my friend in Wales, who makes quilts and whose house has just been flooded', for 'our grandchildren', to illustrate my haikus, for 'my sister who is in a home, to remember her cats, they died seven years ago', for the fortieth anniversary of the Citizens Advice Bureau (who were so moved, they wanted Pete to perform it at their subsequent birthday party) and a bereavement card for 'my sister, whose daughter (22) was killed in a car crash in Canada a month ago – I don't know what to write. The police said it was a complete freak accident.'

John Fox and Peter Moser at the *Cheap Art* stall, 2001

Rehearsing Utopia

Welfare State was born on 6 December 1968. Our first gig, *The Marriage of Heaven and Hell* (with a poster based on William Blake's painting and a scenario based on his proverbs of heaven and hell), was a strange pot-pourri of stilt-walkers, fire-eaters, speciality performing bear, Punch and Judy, trade-union banners and radical student dissent. All gathered in a park above Lancaster on the Ashton Memorial (a kind of Parisian Sacré-Coeur wedding cake). These days, it is a venue for the Duke's Playhouse, who create respectable summer promenade performances such as *A Midsummer Night's Dream* or the *Arabian Nights*, but in 1968 a gaggle of anarchic artists arrived by buses from various northern art schools. Garbed in masks and primitive costumes, we performed simultaneous interpretations of the proverbs.

As evening came, the whole patchwork of artists and audience heaved its way from the park to the town centre. Chanting liberation slogans at institutions such as a boarding-school, a prison and a stranded police car on the way down, there was no doubt that Art had broken out of the frame. Al Beach of the famous John Bull Puncture Repair Kit (a radical performance-art troupe) was arrested for collecting scrap material on railway property.[1] Only the dancing bear refused to emerge from its van (except for thirty seconds, to collect a bottle of milk) as it was too cold. Ten days earlier, our son, Dan Fox, had been born, on 27 November 1968 in Manningham Lane, Bradford. His middle name – which is probably an embarrassment to him – is Blake. From 1968 until the present, our art and view of life have been inextricably enmeshed.

In 1971 we were living in Leeds in a huge, cold Victorian house in Chapeltown, a poor area of the city. Every spare room was filled with students (one of them, the original Lancelot Quail, is now the Chair of our Executive Committee).[2] Our daughter Hannah was born here on Australia Day (26 January). We had no privacy or warmth inside the house. In desperation, we moved into a 6-metre caravan in the garden. So began the mobile village. It is always hard to know what comes first – is it the manifesto or expediency? I suppose it starts with pragmatism and the philosophical rationalisations follow.

By 1972, a single-decker kitchen bus, another trailer, an ambulance, a circus tent and a hearse were parked in our small garden and the landlord quite rightly lost his patience. Fortunately, Jenny Wilson and Ruari McNeill courageously invited us over the Pennines to become Theatre Fellows of the Mid-Pennine Arts Association.[3] So we planned to move the whole shebang for a full residency on Heasandford Quarry, a reclaimed council rubbish tip in Burnley. The house in Leeds subsequently became the northern base for the Divine Light Mission – an extreme religious sect. Nothing to do with us. In fact, after a polish and a paint by them, the property was unrecognisable. Our Burnley site was to become the base from which we toured for the next five years.

When we arrived in Burnley in 1973 in our trailers and showmen's wagons on the wrong side of the ring road, we were amongst the poor of Europe. With no inside running water or sanitation and very limited accommodation, the statistics were accurate; but in a mutually supportive community of by now fifteen artists all creating together, we were usually happy and fulfilled. We could even survive away from the more lucrative post of senior lecturer in Fine Art which I had held in Leeds Polytechnic, where art teaching for me, despite the calibre of such colleagues as Jeff Nuttall, Roland Miller and John Darling, had become like trying to grow turnips in a hot house.

But those working-class people immediately across the ring road were unhappy at our presence. Caravans, travellers and men with long hair were seen as a threat. Indeed, the mayor was not encouraging to real travellers who had camped in the town. Female public-bath attendants locked the door in our faces when we took our tribe of grimy offspring for their afternoon shower. A good lesson for us 'middle-class' intellectuals experiencing how the apparently dispossessed can be abused and how the 'working class' in England hate artists, although the community arts movement had done a lot to change this perspective.

Even the official recipients of our sojourn, Nelson and Colne College of Further Education, panicked when they discovered that, as part of a cross-departmental exercise in lateral thinking (between hairdressers and engineers), we had welded twenty bicycles together, stuck twenty students on top of them, sporting outrageous sculptural hair-dos, and were riding around the playground. Everyone was looking out of the windows. As the principal maintained we knew nothing about engineering or art or perms (and demanded we go back to the classroom), we left.

The material of our early performances was very basic with rough street styles and influences from circus, fairground, carnival and pantomime. From life-size Punch and Judy, Superman and the Fleas (a mad scientist injects fleas so that they grow into giant monsters), The Humpbacked Jester (who dies from a bone stuck in his throat after no one will take responsibility for removing it) and *The Sweet Misery of Life* satirical variety show about the hypocrisies of England, we rose to more mythic packages. Eventually our own anti-hero, Lancelot Handyman Quail, initially feeding on the repression which surrounded us in Burnley, emerged to caricature the Establishment, the Devil and any incarnate dullness or oppression along the way. Gradually, confrontational satire gave way to more imaginative flights of fancy.

We evolved a processional style of theatre which had one particularly memorable climax in 1972 with a month-long ironic comic pilgrimage through south-west England. We described it as 'The First Going Away' (as opposed to 'The Second Coming'); we went from Glastonbury Abbey in Somerset to Marazion in Cornwall, reversing the mythical route of Joseph of Aramathea.[4] Along this ancient religious trail, marked by leylines, as well as a number of surprisingly well-aligned red telephone boxes, Quail (Jamie Proud), dressed in a ludicrous gold lamé woman's swimming costume (in his guise as a white-faced hermaphrodite strongman), led his flock. We were dissident clowns urgently seeking for meaning in an England where the whole pattern of work was shifting away from heavy industry to the service sector.

The heady symbolism of waywardly interpreted Christian and Arthurian legends bundled together with our own myth-as-real-life envelope in a touring 'terrace street' of yellow caravans (with twenty-five members now, earning £5 a week each, and bringing their children on the road) led to creative mayhem. Preceded by the hearse, a cavalcade of trucks and trailers wound across the country to their final sunset near Land's End. Periodically, we stopped at towns to erect our circus tent and act out a miniature version of the tour in a pantomime pageant. Points of our hero's journey (loosely based on the tarot) were shown in theatrical tableaux which were linked with events in the actual landscape. Some of these were private rites of passage, bonding exercises, with no attendant audience. Eight of us, for instance, made a dangerous crossing of Dartmoor at night; a ritual naming of Jamie's (and Jane's) son Billy and other babies was performed on Bodmin Moor with an invited audience/congregation; and firework explosions were enacted at other times for their own sake in obscure quarries.

Other instant provocations occurred more publicly. Miniature processions of strange fools (Demon Buskers) spiralled into shopping precincts. Judge Jeffreys held court on a weir in Taunton. An elusive mermaid sailed past in a cardboard rowing boat piloted by the Astronomer Royal. Finally, on the day after the autumn equinox, our Blood Stained Colonial Brass Band (in singed white jackets plus sola topi helmets with ostrich feathers) played as the sun set on Marazion Beach.

Her Majesty's submarine HMS *Andrew* (the one used in the film of Nevil Shute's *On the Beach*, now a training vessel with its torpedo tubes full of catering-size Heinz beans tins) was waiting offshore. Was this an ultimate incarnation of King Arthur's Black Bride of Lyonesse, a demonic female icon I dreamed up from the same roots and with as much reality as the cardboard elfin queens of Tolkien?

As naval helicopters circled overhead and twenty local Hell's Angels exploded twenty big white weather balloons full of hydrogen, a small boat of clowns dressed as bourgeois idiots set off from the shore to board the submarine.

The show was a linear odyssey in which Quail was continually trying to escape the conformity of the nuclear family and a conventional job. Although hectored by the Devil with propaganda about joining the military industrial complex, Quail and another Fool (me) pushed the boat out but escaped from the repository of Armageddon – as we saw it – to play at building sand castles. Inside a circle of toy windmills, we built a sand submarine topped by a radar tower of wire coathangers.

A manic peace descended. A pair of fifties moquette armchairs sat on the beach, facing the sunset. As a final beacon, I set one on fire and settled in the other. At which point a coastguard took my name and address. The South-west Tour was over. We had (just) survived. We had had one abortion, one nervous breakdown and at least a couple of love affairs, a hill set on fire and a major alert for a sunken submarine, but most significantly we had had an adventure and a bonding rite of passage for the company of artists.

★

Poster for the *Marriage of Heaven and Hell*, December 1968

In future, we would take more notice of health and safety regulations, carry more fire extinguishers, work (slightly) less maniacally, take days off, rehearse and always double-check that the coastguards, the police and the fire authorities knew what we were doing. Submarine coincidences have followed us. Seven years later we ended up near Barrow-in-Furness, near where Trident submarines are manufactured. I had, in the meantime, given a lecture somewhere entitled 'One Less Driver', explaining how the the captain of HMS *Andrew*, Tim Honnor, had left the navy to go to art school (he now makes hand-lettered books in Scotland). Unexpectedly one of the audience stood up and said he too had been on that submarine and had also left for an art career. Looking back on those early stages today, it seems a bit dated, romantic, indulgent and too confrontational, but perhaps I underestimate our achievements. As with so many other early events, these intuitive experiments contained useful seeds which have variously come to fruition.

We broke out of the confines of narrow experimental theatre and did on occasion reach a wide audience with fearsome and sometimes beautiful images. We refused clear boundaries between what was and was not performance. With our public playfulness, construction, music and dancing in real time, we could energise an environment, taking theatre beyond the proscenium and beyond illusion. We embraced carnival notions of clowning irreverence, humour and reversal as an opposition to status and authority. We established the journey and the processional form (metaphoric and actual) as central to our own work.[5] Indeed, it continues with this book. We explored ways of living in our own community. We made ceremonies and rituals. We fused life and art. We learned the value of living outside and off our wits. Camp-fire, and caravans beat the institutionalised art school any day. We also learned our trade. Where could you do it today in the UK in such a fashion? Even if you could prove your convoy and your gathering was legal, how many arts associations would fund such risky and provocative experiments?[6]

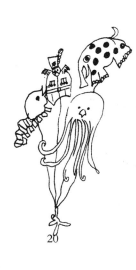

We started to explore the idea of a two-way gift relationship of exchange as opposed to that of a consumer or money economy. The circus tent was offered as an open space for the use of local community groups. The notion of barter, similar to Eugenio Barba's, providing opportunities for communities to show off their bands and choirs and 'exchange' their work with that of a travelling theatre company, was instigated, if hardly fulfilled. With hindsight, the most radical aspect of our early work (and the best thing we did for our children, nine of them under nine years) was to keep them out of school for those early formative years. The full educational tale is told by Catherine Kiddle.[7] The children learned through a life of play and work which were at times indistinguishable. They learned in a 'real' environment. Mathematics was counting gallons of diesel, geography and history was crossing through Checkpoint Charlie on the way to Poland: 'Why did the soldiers put Alsatian dogs into the back of the trucks, Daddy?' Domestic science was cooking on a barbecue, metalwork was blacksmithing at the forge, and physics was turning on the water supply, digging trenches for sewers and repairing generators. Above all, the children created art, performed and played music every day with adults who encouraged and respected them.

In their primary education, our children were not separated and timetabled into school to be trained for the shipyard armaments factory (as was the case later in Ulverston when they went to the secondary school), but learned in responsible partnership with adults in a mutual learning environment where creativity was valued and problems were solved on the road. When they did end up in school and learned to be naughty, they and we couldn't believe the destructive pettiness of some manipulative teachers. We had to suggest that they should observe their teachers and not be confrontational. So they acquired their GCEs with an objective view of grown-ups and power politics. During this period we occasionally enacted naming ceremonies for the children of our tribe (see Rites of Passage). At the time, this was something we just did instinctively as we went along and they weren't usually part of our professional theatre inventions, as they are today.

Caravans on the South-west tour, 1972

Inventing the Language

In this chapter, I describe some of the experiments we made in the first decade of the company, 1968–78, when we experimented with prototypes that were to become core elements of our work in the future. As there was no spare time or money for detailed preparation or extensive rehearsal, making discoveries was never systematic; we just went for it on the road and on our feet in a blaze of practical energy and adrenalin building. We built our events around the next area of research. This might be fire technology or sculptural procession, for example. Very often, these forms were combined. In fact, we rapidly became the victims of our own success and shows grew longer and longer, lasting many hours, with very rich scenarios. By 2002, we have become more selective and shows are usually shorter, but we do still stand by the early forms and are continually re-embellishing them.[1]

Processions

In the early seventies, we made innumerable small-scale forays with occasionally as few as ten of us. Usually these were foot patrols, but on occasion we incorporated vehicles. At one New Year, the King of Winter, a big spiky blue puppet, and the Queen of Summer, a golden smiley sun puppet (each mounted on converted aluminium American army rocket trailers we bought from a local scrap dealer), did Brueghelian battle with firecrackers in disintegrating clouds of papier mâché.

The character of Lancelot Quail re-emerged in off-beat processions, usually led by a percussion band. Invariably, maybe like Welfare State itself, he was a wilful dreamer, searching for unattainable birds of paradise, digging holes to find ice

giants, making spaceship runways with lines of fire, desperately trying to take off from the decaying mills of Lancashire in a home-made craft. And always carrying a telescope to peruse the heavens.

In Barrowford in 1973 a mill town in Lancashire, we created a two-day event over New Year. On the last evening of the old year, we constructed a mysterious black mountain on a trailer pulled by our Land Rover. The mountain on the trailer was constructed with stretched black tarpaulins which also covered the Land Rover. In the middle, a burning brazier of coke and wood was mounted on a raised metal platform. Four musicians, a bodhran player, a bagpiper and Lol Coxhill[2] sat inside on the floor under the tarps, where we played wailing harmonies in a minor key.

With this primitive image of an elemental mountain emitting volcanic sparks and Valkyrian excess, we drove very slowly round the labyrinth of small terraced streets. We couldn't see our audience from inside our mountain. We had to concentrate on the brazier for fear of random sparks and, of course, as it was freezing everyone but the driver, we needed to sup whisky and green ginger. I remember the smell of coke burning and the spitting of sleet on the rim of the brazier. Looking through a tear in the tarpaulin and seeing smoke curl up round orange sodium lights was memorable for us, but I suspect spectators presumed it was just roadmenders unlucky to be working a late shift on a bank holiday.

Many of those early experiments around townships in North East Lancashire became rather inward. In Barrowford, at 7 a.m. on the New Year's morning after the Black Volcano a beautiful image was seen by very few people. Two slightly raggedy adults, a man leading a white horse and a woman playing a flute, passed like ghosts through the same streets, quiet after the raucous drinking of the previous night. On the horse's back, Daniel Fox, aged five, wore a pair of big, real goose wings strapped on his back. Maybe a few early morning risers glimpsed this angelic apparition through frosty panes and are still wondering if it was a mirage. There is a case for infiltrating an unexpected image on occasion. In this case, we made up for any indulgence by producing a playful carnival of games in the park in the afternoon, with side-shows, the comic burial of a time capsule (an unadorned scrap refrigerator), the planting of a cherry tree by the town mayor and loads of ambient sweet brass music.

Sometimes a procession was confrontational. In Bradford in 1973, we tried in vain to stop the wilful demolition by developers of the beautiful Victorian Kirkgate Market with its iron arches and tracery. Here, we dressed as black-faced tramp

Daniel Fox in Barrowford, 1973

mummers and as our band blew a strong lament, we paraded, carrying a massive tableau of flowers delicately fashioned from geometrically laced bamboo. Quail took a metre-long prop carving knife and cut it to pieces in a ritual slicing in front of six policemen who threatened arrest when he produced a firebrand.

We connected with existing traditions such as mumming. In Thorpe Thewles in Cleveland in 1978, we worked with Bill Hall, the local vicar, and farmers to cut the last sheath of corn in a new field re-created out of a derelict quarry. This was to be a true harvest festival where the bread to be broken in the communion service would be baked from that actual grain.

More often than not, the processions were comic. For example, a clown team of Keystone Cop-type firemen in big, old-fashioned helmets marched into pubs. Their ladder was sawn into sections and reassembled with thick elastic (so they could go round corners) and the script was a modernised charade based on traditional English mummers' plays. These processions were sustained by an inner logic. Sometimes they led to a concluding image, but often they were just what they were. They originated in folk art and memories (probably false) of rural mummers and the revivalist ritual dances (with the death and resurrection symbolism) of Morris men, plus animal horn dances, trade-union marches and Whit Sunday church parades. Northern traditions we remembered or found in books.

Earthy, comic and ironic as these processions were, they were also influenced by fine-art traditions. Much is left out of official art history. Rubens designed carnivals. In 1918, the Russian constructivists worked on revolutionary floats. So our processions were also conceived as mobile sculptures on carts. Framed with vertical slabs of colour, flags and windsocks mounted on backpacks or carts, they were designed to bounce visually off the red bricks, grey cobbles and squat Lancashire terraced houses. Whether we were toying with non-existent Utopias, self-conscious ecological awareness or forced seasonal jollity, we maintained a strong and unpredictable energy on the streets with many wild inventions. Small children in particular became as much fans of Welfare State as the Pied Piper. Now with their own families, I wonder if any tell tales about an evening when, for instance, a strange clown on his bike with an odd cardboard telescope revealed a crimson bird of paradise shivering in their garden.

Installations

Many of Welfare State International's artists spring from a fine-art background. Our modern (as opposed to Stone Age or medieval) performance predecessors were those artists who first jumped off the gallery wall. Constructivists in Russia. Futurists in Italy. Kurt Schwitters's performance poetry and Merz Barns. Picasso's assemblages, plays and cubist costumes. The surrealists. Cabaret Voltaire. The carnival architectural environments of Nikki de Saint Phalle and Tinguely in Sweden, France and Italy. Gaudí in Barcelona. The happenings instigators and provocateurs of the fifties and sixties, like Yves Klein in France or Fluxus and Joseph Beuys in Germany. Kaprow, Oldenberg and John Cage and others in the USA. Also, non-fine-art inventors like Heath Robinson in England. Many so-called 'Outsider Artists' who fill their own gardens with cement cornucopias, like Le Facteur Cheval near Lyons in France or Simon Rhodia with his Watts Towers in Los Angeles. These are our inspiration.[3]

With such energetic icons at the back of our minds, we tend to construct visual shows from a given site, literally building out from the found environment in a series of linked physical collages or assemblages. Often the work is sculptural, a disparate exhibition or installation, usually figurative, which the audience walk round. Words, songs and full scenarios are used but frequently come late in the process as linking lassos rather than backbones of the work.

The installation method can grow into a repeatable show and be more time-based, with a beginning, middle and end where the audience are led psychologically (or literally, in promenade) from one space to another or one light to another (say, real dusk to dawn, or sometimes with artificial theatre lighting where appropriate). Even in these shows, though, objects, or built environments, or sculptural expressionist costumes often play a visual role far greater than that of props or scenery. Music or sound is also crucial in our work. All events have an original score (nowadays sometimes sounds are triggered electronically by the audience touching pressure pads) or live music, often with songs, or pointed silence to counterpoint and give atmosphere to the imagery.

Our multi-media method of creating plastically (and improvising collectively) is still relatively unusual in England. In 2002, performance art has its own regular festivals and a few companies like Complicité and DV8 and many dance and some circus companies such as Bim Mason's Circomedia in Bristol do maintain a dynamic physical language with their actors or dancers. But generally the mainstream tradition of English theatre still follows the writer, the book and the

Beauty and the Beast, Burnley, 1973

director.[4] *Beauty and the Beast*, in 1973, was our most elaborate early installation. Built on the reclaimed rubbish tip of our base site in Burnley, it took us three months to create from junk timber and scrap metal. Stretching over hundreds of metres, it rambled round our living trailers and incorporated a crashed aircraft, a pilgrimage trail of fifty cinema seats, our circus tent, a hut on a hillside and an octagonal arena with raised wooden seating. Resembling an animated allotment, it was an extreme example of a living art work. The story, for instance, started with Quail recounting mythological incidents from his life which were beautifully painted on his own caravan.[5] The whole installation was another allegory of England, where unspeakable monstrosities were depicted by the company (everybody) performing in side-show huts in a crazy labyrinth. Freakish showmen, demon barbers and film-star zombies (Judy Garland) bombarded the promenading audience of two hundred with close (but safe) performance tableaux. We acquired an 'illusion box'. By means of diagonal mirrors, you could fake a disembodied head. Five-year-old Daniel Fox stuck his head through a hole in the back so that when the door was opened he became the roaring spider in his web.

Quail variously escaped as usual, first to a Shangri-La in the tent (which inadvertently resembled a desert island with ukuleles playing to promote Bounty bars), then to a wooden bullring where he headbutted incarnating demons of Mammon and finally to a honeymoon hotel – a wooden shack on a mudslide. More and more wild Burnley youth came each night, so we incorporated story-telling to catch their eye and forestall their random forays backstage. Each night, the story changed. I guess the show didn't do much in the long run for Art or Society, although it must have been the biggest live-in sculpture in England. But we learned how to construct and perform in environments of our own making. This was seminal to many of our later performances, in particular a completely reworked theatre version which we took to Holland.[6]

This work was full of energy, naive risk and expressionist imagery inspired by among others Gilray, Rowlandson, Edward Lear and Goya. As soon as the day started, we worked collectively and intensively, seven days a week for twelve weeks to create a performance that lasted for three weeks. This intense devotion was possible because we were living twenty metres away from the work. How many art centres ever have their own accommodation? Artistic creation accelerates organically with rushes of adrenalin and it's hard to gain that if you are clock-watching or travelling to work every day.

In *Beauty and the Beast*, with all the timber and narrow alleys and wanton vandals with matches, there was a considerable fire risk. Despite the apparent anarchy, we always took health and safety very seriously, and asked advice from the local fire brigade. We had built up a good relationship with them, so when I dreamed up a final image of the whole labyrinth turning to ice (in a fit of dire climate change brought about by industrial pollution), they lent us a fire engine to pump in hundreds of gallons of white foam. With careful lighting from follow spots with wide-angled lenses and steel blue gels and hundreds of tiny bits of paper fanned high in the night sky plus a howling wind (heavily amplified), the set became an arctic glacier in a blizzard with a glistening ship locked in pack ice. I think we paid the fire service two hundred pounds. But what price a fantastic image?[7]

We were originally invited to construct the installation at the Serpentine Gallery in London instead of on our doorstep. Despite the valiant efforts of Sue Grayson, its dynamic director, those in charge of Royal Parks don't (or didn't) permit circus tents on their lawns. Without our Shangri-La Paradise, which needed the tent, this would have only been a doom-and-gloom show - too much Grosz and not enough Miro. So we declined in a big telegram (which we came to use as a poster for the show) and Burnley received the world première. Our absence from the Serpentine needed to be acknowledged – so we papered their gallery in a dull, minimalist black-and-white chequerboard of Roger Perry's photographs of the show. We also tried to train a mynah bird to sit on a coat stand in the entrance to the Serpentine, mimicking 'Fuck off, bureaucrats. Come to Burnley.' But it is unforgivable to teach the ignorant to swear, so it died and I am sorry.

I love fairgrounds. Sue Gill and I had our first date at Hull Fair. Burning oil, frying onions, wisps of candy floss, thundering hydraulics, puddles of rain, colanders of stars all spark a cocktail, tangible as sweaty palms. Living in caravans with our children for ten years took us closer to the life-style of real showmen. We weren't playing at it. We had to top up the generator in the mud at midnight. After challenging the then exclusivity of the Showmen's Guild, we acquired a caravan site exemption certificate and bought a thirty-foot trailer with four wheels, air brakes, cut-glass windows and a walnut interior. A glass of sherry in here was a good way to convince the local police inspector that we weren't really long-haired weirdoes even if that was what we looked like. But of course we had access to art subsidies and could return to teaching if it all went wrong.

In 1977 we bought a ghost train, two Noddy engines, rails and a wooden booth about the size of a tiny cricket pavilion. We soon separated out the trains from the architecture. After laying tracks on the floor of a disused Methodist chapel in Burnley, we constructed an installation with extreme vistas, shocking surprises in corners, dangling wet things and *trompe-l'œil* close-ups of trains falling off viaducts. Largely based on the discovery that Burnley was constructed on a geological fault and if there was an earthquake the town would be flooded from the canal viaduct, we constructed a chilling installation which was a huge success. At the time, I wrote this scenario for the event:

A JOURNEY ON THE BURNLEY GHOST TRAIN

After the Burnley earthquake the Old Engine Driver greets you in the waiting room. The town has broken asunder. The streets have cracked. The banks of the canal have fallen, the railway viaduct is smashed, ghosts haunt the empty houses and sewer rats emerge. As the legend says, whenever a local disaster occurs the phantom Hell Hound (the Striker) rises from Burnley Churchyard. Peg O'Well, the water spirit of the burn, draws victims to a drowning death. We drown in an underground tunnel while lives and deaths float by. In an upside down kaleidoscope, historical figures rub shoulders with ancient ghosts. The hermit and the holy man, the white stag miners and priests raise their monstrous bellies to the pointed moon. In the Aquarium in the Sky, Lancashire coal once again burns bright, looms weave a wayward tapestry and in one misshapen lunch hour we see the promised planet. In your lunch hour, have your photograph taken in the waiting room (with a Polaroid camera). This will be an unforgettable souvenir and undeniable proof of existence.

Hundreds of customers queued round the block for a three-minute ride in our trains. Ten pence a go. Even the grumpy bonhomie of Diz Willis, performance artist and archetypal night guard, at the entrance platform, with frying pan, blood pudding and paraffin lamp, drew them in. A perfect format. The audience had a great ride through Dr Caligari tableaux. Art met the masses because no one called it 'Art'. We also learned how hard it is to service any exhibition with parts that are continually moving. Night and day we had to fix the trains and their engines. Dynamo brushes burned out. Bearings jammed. Wheels derailed. Corners were too steep. Even the rails themselves jumped off the floor. Machines have a life of their own. Real fairground operators have to be thorough professionals.

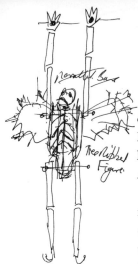

Much of the invention and three-dimensional images looming off the walls were due to the painterly skill of Bob Frith,[8] who was about to found his company, Horse and Bamboo. We had found another prototype which was to resurface much later, in 1993, in our fine-art fairground in Tramway, Glasgow (see Lanternhouse). And the booth itself gave us a way to tell stories.

Look at fairs carefully before they disappear. These juggernauts of dreams, truly mobile villages which materialise overnight with ingenious engineering, whirling cornucopias of brash lettering and a total family life-style are still a vernacular wonder of temporary architecture. Beware our litigious society, overwhelming health and safety regulations and the prejudice of local councils which could destroy fairs as it does other unpredictable street gatherings of nomadic entertainment.

Story-tellings

Although most political theatre has now gone, Welfare State International did lash out with propaganda in carnival guise as in *The Titanic* (LIFT, 1983) or *The Golden Submarine* (Barrow-in-Furness, 1990) and we have aligned ourselves to specific causes, such as supporting the miners against the Tory campaigns in 1972.[9] This Time/Next Time or, in 1984, The Tolpuddle Martyrs in Darlington, for example. But usually we prefer to make our politics more oblique and implicit. Audiences don't like being preached at and unless the approach is as well crafted as Brecht, Dürrenmatt or John Arden and Margaretta d'Arcy, it doesn't work either artistically or politically.

Effective and imaginative political theatre is now located with the interventions and myth-making of anti-airport or motorway tunnellers and tree dwellers or Friends of the Earth (e.g. their *Lifeboat against Global Warming* in Bonn, summer 2001) or anti-globalisation protests.[10] The campaigns pioneered by the women of Greenham Common or Greenpeace, for example, not only offer hope and solidarity (once provided by religion), but, like music concerts and sports meetings, they provide opportunities for large gatherings and effective non-commercial (and necessary) carnivals. Campaigns have always used theatrical and dramatic techniques, but in their unpredictable one-off excitements and their real risk, they are increasingly more engaging than many representations on the art-centre theatre circuit.

One objective of our big-scale community events is for participants to gain some control over their lives by accessing their creative potential and by taking to their streets together. Welfare State International, however, has a cyclical pattern of work. Expansion to an epic, very public horizon, with many participatory workshops, is often followed by contraction to much smaller, more self-contained performances, where we link poetic stories in a fairly traditional theatre format without any obvious political motivation.

In presenting stories in more intimate and focused settings, often away from mainstream locations, we recognise that story-telling theatre still has the important role of bringing individuals together. Sound systems, television and even film offer mainly solo experiences, with one-way communication. In an age dominated by skilfully made entertainment products, some of them extraordinary, there is also a need to demonstrate accessible beauty and stillness directly at close quarters; to take audiences on journeys away from frenetic hype to slow them down, to reveal home-made surprises at first hand.

Well-crafted sensual journeys, resonating with archetypal imagery, open up our consciousness, stimulate and liberate the imagination so that audiences can dream their own dreams and make their own journeys and feel better. We were and are full of questions, such as: where do archetypal images originate? Are we artists good enough to discover and articulate original and necessary truths, or are we distracted from more essential issues? Can we sidestep expectations of 'good-time' spectacle and cliché and sentiment and still hold an audience? How do we reveal hard truths without generating despair or preaching to the converted?

Here are some examples of our experiments. Many of them were developed with Boris Howarth.[11]

In *Stories for a Winter's Night*, 1976–7, we used the wooden ghost-train booth (minus trains) to make a candle-lit café where our audience were treated as special guests:

> Outside in the frosty night festoons of coloured bulbs sparkle round the low entrance. Inside an iron kettle and pots of tea steam on an ancient stove stoked with split cherry logs. Carpets patterned in burnt sienna and ochre cover the floor. Round the walls cosy spaces are constructed with wooden partitions (interlocking plywood) framing small tables. Audience groups of ten or so sit in these sub booths where table cloths glow magenta under hanging lampshades. In the centre is a pit one foot deep by twelve square made by removing a floor section, scattered with sawdust and lit with gentle pink spotlights. Here is a frame to conjure intimate pantomime ghosts.

As conversation settled to a quiet, you could hear the crackling logs and the hissing kettle, as Sue Gill as Patronne, in a green suede suit fringed with ermine, sang Adrian Mitchell's 'The Moon has Packed her Bags':

The moon has packed her bags
she's caught the evening train,
the moon has bought a ticket
she's gone with the evening train.
I'm standing on the pavement kisses falling down like rain.

Standing on the pavement
kisses falling down like rain,
cold wet concrete pavement
kisses falling down like rain
lay my head on the railway, wait to catch the midnight train.

Heaven's raining kisses
drops of love all over the earth
Heaven's raining kisses on the
smiling faces of the earth
I'm going to my bed to dream about my birth.
Had a dream about some words
carved on a marble stone
dreamed about some golden words
carved on a block of marble stone
here lies all the loving that once upon a time you called your own.

Then half a dozen stories unfolded in a Christmas stocking of my poetry often set to music by Boris Howarth:

Tales of old live long they say
All on a winter's day.
When the ice melts a seed will grow.
When the moon wanes a wind will blow;
The prince is gone. The princess too.
The wolf is turned to ice.
All on a winter's day.

The Island of the Lost World, which we performed between 1974 and 1976, was another travelling performance, this time designed specifically for summer. Here, rather than the wooden hut with its fairground associations, we erected a high, more minimalist white-canvas courtyard specially fabricated and open to the sky. As musicians played outside, gently tapping piano frames and exotic drums and invisibly observing the audience and players through a covering gauze, the audience of only thirty at a time were led to formal seating in an inner courtyard for a half-hour performance which we repeated every hour.

The principle was the same as for the wooden winter space, to take people through a decompression chamber to a New World where all their senses were heightened. Here, we drew from the Japanese Noh and Bunraku traditions. Thanks to one of Boris's obsessions, we even had a *hanamichi*, a blue gravel surround along which we processed (rather clumsily in my case), in self-conscious slow-motion entrances and exits to and from a central, earth-coloured carpet.

In *The Island of the Lost World*, we articulated poetic myths with little musical plays that brought to life ancient and magical demons and spirits of nature and technology. Simple mystical tales which drew inspiration from folk art, childhood fears and contemporary news stories giving vignettes of humanity and warning fables. Some of the stories were bleak, some comic and others warming, offering our guests something 'playful and strange, rich and humane' (*Plays and Players*). Plots were taken from found texts and others we made up.

In *The House that Flew Away*, a masked woman, her dress laden with fat swinging bags of seed, placed a small iron house on stilts over a man's head. He nearly suffocated but together they transformed the metal slabs into a sailing boat with which they danced, following it out of the canvas arena in an act of reconciliation. *Iron Man* was the story of a blacksmith who, as the last survivor on the planet, turns himself into a metal man to survive a nuclear holocaust. He sang:

Iron, iron, iron, iron man
Survive on white-hot fire
Iron, iron, iron, iron, man
Your bones will never tire.

Suck the juice of atom bombs
Suck the fetid juice.
Suck the bark of treeless limbs
suck the blackened fruit.

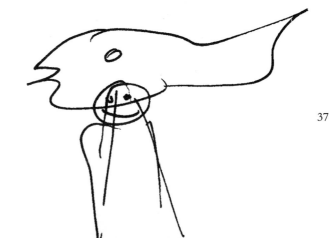

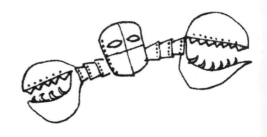

Suck the juice of sea birds' eggs,
Suck the penguin's eye,
Suck the oil-black wheeled machine,
Suck the cogs or die.

The story ended with tiny, oriental-looking children, as Hiroshima ghosts, their faces coated in white ash, dressed in kimonos, carrying yellow paper kites round the space while the desperate blacksmith (Pierre Schwartz)[12] built a friend, a huge, vicious-looking non-human, welded dragonfly, which he whirled round the delicate canvas space on the end of a well-judged rope.

In the *Three Blind Men*, straight from Brueghel, borrowed and retranslated from the Belgian playwright Ghelderhode, three sightless beggars, after ignoring the warnings of the One-Eyed King of the Ditches, fell into a swamp. Finally, in *The Astronaut – a Creation Myth*, a contemporary astronaut in firefighter's helmet and knotted rope kilt danced his own cosmos with sticks, mud balls, car mirrors and toy cars. He was nearly lured to another galaxy by a grotesque forest giant (with lumpy beard of tree fungus) tempting him with a black ziggurat embedded with diamonds.

These tales usually worked well and after understandable initial trepidation, audiences were prepared to be taken on an unpredictable voyage. We had a problem in Easterhouse, Glasgow. Trapped in a triangle next to high tenements, a railway line and a busy main road, Zen stillness was hard to achieve and *hanamichis* were unusual. Also, as we were overlooked, our every move was monitored by gangs of small children aged eight to ten. When they weren't drinking whisky, they were in the backs of our living vans removing anything, especially bicycles. Also, the open-air canvas box was perfect for lobbing in bottles. We did parades and made friends, but we were too much a sitting target. Not for the first time, we beat a hasty retreat, timing it secretly for the early morning so that after our fastest de-rig ever, we were up and away in minutes in our convoy of yellow trucks and trailers.

Before we left, the CID had visited. Two huge plain-clothes policemen knocked at my trailer door. 'We urgently need you for questioning,' they huffed fiercely in Glaswegian. It turned out they required specialist advice. One of them pushed deep into an inside pocket of his gabardine to pull out Wullie. Wullie was a tiny squirrel. A glove puppet used in their road safety campaign in primary schools.

'When Wullie is run over (by a drunk fox on a zebra), his tail falls off,' said the more senior detective.

'But when the tail comes off, how do we stick it on again, sir.'

'Try Velcro,' I suggested.

They left well pleased.

Then, we were earning about ten pounds a day, much less than a policeman, and many of our actor friends were out of work. But I thought it best not to mention Equity.

Earthworks

The stuff of the ground, digging holes, mud between our toes, trees, plants, fountains, ponds, the shape of landscape, allotments, soil and sustainability has always been fundamental to our work. Boris and Maggie Howarth were the experts. Long before self-sufficiency was fashionable, they had poultry and a cow, a smallholding, a tree nursery, an earth closet and their own Eden on top of a hill. Even Lancelot Quail was once a pig farmer. Maggie is now a world expert in designing and constructing architectural pebble mosaics and Boris, among many other talents, is a letter-cutter in stone.

In the seventies and early eighties, before ecology became the new Catholicism, and maybe then as an escape from the harsh realities of the Toxteth Riots (1981) and long dole queues, there was also a general interest in 'ancient sacred spaces' which included burial mounds, prehistoric earthworks, menhirs and henges as astronomical calendars, early settlements like Maes How in Orkney, Celtic archaeology, mythology and, of course, ley lines and their connection with the pre-Christian geometry and orientation of churches and cathedrals. People were starting to look for pre-industrial ancestral links and alternative congregational and spiritual ways outside Christianity and civilisation. Lubricated by the occasional malt whisky, we often joked round camp-fires about the fake primitive ruralism of it all. But any Boy Scout or Duke of Edinburgh Award recruit triggered by the Milky Way, woodsmoke, alcohol, tobacco and a late night is as romanced.

Whatever their source, these legacies and their later parallel developments by David Nash, Andy Goldsworthy and Richard Long, have been absorbed, so that in 2002 we are designing and growing a 50-metre-diameter performance earth amphitheatre near to our warehouse with willow seating for 'seasonal mythological tales' and the grounds of Lanternhouse itself are a continually developing installation with a stream, pathways, plants, barbecue points, sheds and a performance platform in the centre of a pond. The pattern of working in the open air, attending to astronomical, tidal, diurnal, nocturnal and seasonal rhythms, and the weather, provides us with a useful geophysical and ecological perspective, a stimulus for imagery and mythology.

Promoters are sometimes surprised when we advertise the start of an event as being 'at dusk', which of course can change considerably over a month, or that an event continues all night, or for a hundred days. But when our lives are timetabled to a microsecond at work or slotted into time bites by the leisure industry, and when our night skies are so light polluted, it is worth trying to reconnect with 'planetary' time and space. Hence our installations and processional entrances are often laid out according to compass positions, the sound and directional flow of water, prevailing winds, the size and position of the moon. Equinox dates are important to consider, too, because then storms and strong winds are common.

Such thinking is of course second nature to farmers, gardeners, climbers, fishermen, sailors and some sports people (and to many non-Western cultures in general), but it is unusual for most city dwellers, who rarely have moon phases or tide times in their desk diaries. So often the weather is our best ally and offers moments of unpredictable beauty. Just the simple act of taking people outside can be a strong experience. Although we have worked in all weathers from 30 degrees below and in desert sun to heavy rain, we have only cancelled three or four shows because of inclement conditions. We go with the weather. In Canada, we made a cinema structured from snow pillars, fiery poles and ice lanterns, but it was so cold the keys on my saxophone froze and fell off. In an outdoor island performance of *The Tempest* (see chapter 5 in *Engineers of the Imagination*), in thunder and lightning, three hundred spectators huddled under shiny grey umbrellas to become a living painting by Manet. In Tanzania, we made shadow puppets from thin goatskin (there was no cardboard) to silhouette against the late-afternoon sun. In Australia, in hot, dried-up riverbeds, we made sculptures from different coloured sand and rocks and 'performed' long vigils in the cool moonlight.

The critical time for 'rain insurance' in the north of England is over tea-time. If it rains then, people won't go out, but once they are out, dressed for the occasion, with performers daft enough to brave the conditions, audiences will fulfil their unspoken contract and stay to the bitter, or rainy, end.

Memorial to the First Astronaut was designed by Boris Howarth in 1974 at the instigation of the Mid-Pennine Arts Association. It was a large 'science fiction' installation, an object for meditation. Located in a forest walkway leading from the Elizabethan Gawthorpe Hall in north-east Lancashire, it was about 15 metres across and constructed within a perimeter circular stockade of thirty sawn-down telegraph poles partially covered in tar.

These resembled a frozen explosion from a subterranean crater. In the middle, on a bed of white lime punctuated by small troughs of nasturtiums, a life-size figure lay in a cruciform position. Shaped from chicken wire and moss it seeded itself with grasses, eventually mellowing and turning back to earth. Above, swaying on wires hung from tall trees, a wooden skeletal pagoda swayed in the wind. Tiny bells tinkled and a few rags fluttered in the breeze. It lasted a year or two and was never vandalised. Until the council refuse collectors were instructed by Heritage North West to remove it at two days' notice because of an impending visit by Princess Margaret.

Each December between 1974 and 1976, we made a seasonal installation on a piece of disused land in Wath on Dearne, a town on the outskirts of Rotherham inhabited, then, by shift workers from the coal-mining and steel industries. Each year, we made a variation on a theme using a mix of earthworks, coloured sand, fire, ice, performance, music and procession. Over an area about the size of four tennis courts in a square, we shaped the soil with a mechanical digger and shovels, making mounds and a small amphitheatre, framing it with empty bean cans of paraffin fire, braziers, simple flags, tin lanterns, scarecrows and an array of candles in glass jars. Occasionally we enhanced our 'sculptural winter tapestry' with small-scale fireworks, mainly crimson Catherine wheels, white flittering rain and a silver waterfall from high black trees.

In these temporary shifting garden spaces, on three or four evenings each year before Christmas, we created simple process performances. One year we made a henge of big ice blocks, elevating them, drilled and hung from chains, above long metal troughs of red-hot coke. Another time Maggie Howarth made a half-ton *Ice Giant* in a big glass fibre mould, eight feet long.

By experimenting, we found the right way to fill the mould with broken ice and the right amount of hot water to release it. With difficulty, we raised the giant a yard high on stone supports. We placed fire cans under it and chandeliers of candles round it so that it glowed orange and silky in the moonlight, slowly melting in the wind until, by morning, it was like an anorexic Henry Moore, a strange but beautiful and unexpected discovery. We gathered our audience, which varied from thirty to a hundred, each evening by processing daily in the town with our small brass band. They stood round the big square behind a rope held on metal stakes.

In each corner of the performance arena we repeated 'performance tableaux' in an emblematic Bread and Puppet style, once even taking on the journey of Jesus and Mary and representing it as a story of contemporary refugees accompanied by voices and flutes playing traditional Christmas carols. This series was an odd kaleidoscope, but public and promoter liked us well enough to invite us back three times, until the affair of the Municipal Donkey.

Normally, having carried many children in summer play schemes, he, the only council donkey in England, anticipated rest and recuperation at Christmas and resented us borrowing him, even to carry the pregnant Mary. He had to go back to his compound. Once out of the van, having seen 'alternative theatre freaks', he refused to move at all. Indeed, he remained rigid for three hours. Thinking he might respond to a child on his back, we put Dan, now six years old, up there but the donkey threw him off. Boris, our smallholder, with experience of chickens and a cow, recommended a shotgun. Eventually, eight of us held hands under its belly (the donkey's, that is) and as its legs stiffened we lifted him an inch off the ground. Then, quite gently, Jamie tweaked its balls and it did move. Very fast, up the road and away.

A six-hour saga followed. Ropes and carrots and more lifting, drums, a siren and the whiff of a tweak got him inside the van, which he then tried to kick his way out of. By now, it was 2 a.m, too late to return him to the council. We backed the van up against the outside wall of a public toilet, but the thunderous kicking and the braying got worse. Our technician, who liked animals, volunteered to stay with him inside the van until 8 a.m., when the Donkey Depot opened. Unfortunately, the high-rise blocks all around our square were full of miners trying to sleep. They had tolerated and even enjoyed our strange art forms, but this time we had pushed our luck too far.

Fire Shows

Once upon a time, theatre punters believed – and sometimes still do – that all Welfare State International ever did was find new ways to build huge images, then set them on fire. Even in 2002, many people still come on our summer schools to learn the arts of fire technology. The stated theme might be 'rites of passage' or 'ecology' or even 'ceremonial food', but they still expect our Engineers of the Imagination to teach them the secrets of fire. It is understandable. Fire was indeed our trademark and we have certainly developed simple techniques which are easy to copy, and which are indeed copied all round the planet. We have also passed on

Ice Giant at Wath on Dearne, 1974

many tricks through our courses. Fire will always appeal. It's elemental, primeval, dangerous and beautiful. Given the time we spend inside our offices and homes, replete with central heating, microwaves, war movies and apparent security, the more exotic it becomes to see and smell real, unpredictable smoke and flames.

Like prehistoric earthworks and Celtic spirals, it is embedded in the psyche of us Northern Hemisphere island dwellers. We know about fire festivals through The Wicker Man, 5 November, Up Hellya and other tar barrelling. Many dream of a Viking burial. We all love fire and, however much we at Welfare State International now say that most fire shows have become mindless and even macho spectacles, with gratuitous carbon emissions, fire will still appeal. Our two specific inventions were the fire can and the fire drawing.

To my knowledge, Dave Whatley, a wild blacksmith and part-time farmer and friend who lives in Diss in Norfolk, was the first person to fill a small, 8 ounce tin with paraffin, put in a wick of hessian, weight it down inside with a few stones and set fire to it. With multiple cans, you can draw big shapes in landscape in pinpoints of fire. Circles and spirals, with giant fish in them, look particularly good on beaches when seen from cliff tops. Dave Whatley invented the system in Leeds in February 1974, when he also invented the burning pyramid constructed from four hollow metal telegraph poles, each wrapped with paraffin-soaked hessian sacks tied with wire. This was a dynamic if primitive forerunner of the fire drawing. Both these devices were used in a Leeds cemetery in a most Gothic event, when we constructed a burning runway for a horse-drawn glass hearse filled with saxophonists.

I invented the fire drawing in Adelaide in 1978. I had seen many classic firework display endings when the organisers wrote *'Goodnight and Thank you'*, or *'God Bless Our Queen'* in blue, green or red lances (small tubes of coloured fire linked with fuse) but I needed something cheaper, more fiery and repeatable and easily transportable for a tour we were planning along the Indian Pacific Railway. I wished to depict the havoc created by animals imported into Australia from Europe and contrast this with more mysterious and lyrical visions of the so-called Inland Sea.

Eventually we had a rabbit and a goat in dancing fire played against a goanna and a wombat in ethereal blue light. Out in the desert, at an indeterminate distance, these images placed high in the air on metal frames were so awesome that the children and Aboriginals in our audience ran away into the black night of the Nullabor Desert.

To make the goat, I drew it in chalk on the backstage concrete floor of the Adelaide Playhouse. After bending the image in quarter-inch steel rod, it was then welded on to a frame by a theatre technician. Finally we wired on asbestos (!) rope and just before the show (because of the fast-drying desert wind) sprayed on kerosene from a garden spray.

Back in England, the technique was improved by the discovery of paper rope, used originally for lagging pipes, and lay-flat plastic tubing. The inventor of this was probably the late Miklos Menos.[13] You first soak the paper rope in a drum of paraffin, then push the tubes of paper into the plastic tubes. If the ends of the plastic are tied, the paraffin will not evaporate, so great lengths of it may be prepared in advance and then simply wired to elevated sheets of weld mesh to make big, impressive drawings. The dancing winged flying house on the front cover of this book was made in a similar way. In this case, it was used as part of a community Lantern Festival Finale in Ulverston, although the image is one of our recurring symbols.

Instead of paper rope, you can use hessian or rags but you have to be particularly careful with cloth (as you still have to be with paper rope, too) because fragments can blow on the wind and cause fires, particularly in resinous forests, dry bracken and thatched or wooden roofs. Man-made fibres are toxic and drip with boiling melted plastic. All firework business is dangerous, even if you know what you are doing, and the necessary insurances are expensive for big-scale work.

Engineers of the Imagination gives detailed instructions about these tricks, but take care and employ experts, preferably licensed professionals. Pyrotechnics can be amazing and with due precautions and due scale should be available to everyone, not just the big operators. But all of us, including the big firms, have had near misses.

November the 5th is Britain's last remaining fire festival. It was once a political carnival but it equally recalls the sun's heat in a dank autumn. Toffee apples, burning saltpetre and jumping crackers in dustbins and pockets. It remains the stuff of childhood legend. Our sculptural fires originally developed as a refinement of the standard communal 5 November bonfire, typically organised by sports or Rotary clubs. Instead of the usual hasty and random piling-up of old furniture, dead mattresses and the remains of yesterday's shed, Boris and Maggie Howarth's idea was to take sculptural practice and put it into traditional neighbourhood celebrations. At the time, the idea was radical and visionary. From then on, we started shaping the material and building it into three-dimensional constructions. We often incorporated the rubbish whole, but framed it in a skin variously made from wooden pallets or discarded plywood, often recycled from old theatre and television scenery. These giant figurative sculptures, for that is what they became, were sometimes held together with carpets or discarded felts from paper mills. A paint job and lighting brought to life umpteen castles and carousels, galleons and whales, simple visual anchors to which we added any amount of music, live or recorded, plus performance and pyrotechnics. The only restrictions were our imaginations and the size of the field, plus, of course, resources such as labour, time and budget. It is easy to forget the cost of transporting otherwise free timber.

Guys are another matter. I was once taken to task by a local paper for suggesting that children don't know how to make guys any more and they need arts workers to tell them! Unfortunately, they don't know, and we are now asked to give child beggars pound coins for trousers stuffed with plastic bags. As for the communal bonfire steered by accountants, dentists and solicitors and occasionally some community artists, they can be so brainwashed and scared of political correctness and their funding masters and sponsors in the bureaucracies of councils and arts associations that they don't burn a guy at all.

As bigotry against papal Catholicism has declined, Guy Fawkes himself is on the decline, but then it always was an example of dodgy government-inspired propaganda for Catholic-bashing. Maybe we should include contemporary villains? What about symbolically burning sports shoes made in Asian sweat shops, or Star Wars missile systems, or nuclear waste transporters, or symbols to represent the hypocrisies and incompetence of Railtrack or Equitable Life, or the briefcases of arms dealers? Maybe objects should be burnt rather than effigies of people, but why not protest through a cathartic burning? Yes, it can end up with echoes of a Nuremberg rally, but complacency and failure to tell the truth can equally suck us into a swamp of inertia.

Under Boris Howarth's direction between 1973 and 1981 we made five *Parliaments in Flames*. Ever bigger and even more fantastical constructions modelled on the Houses of Parliament became our trademark. We made them in Burnley, Ackworth, Tamworth and Milton Keynes, with the audience doubling in size each time. They would take two to three weeks to build, then in a show similar to a self-destructing *son et lumière*, we would set fire to them with extensive performance, soundtrack and pyrotechnics. The last one in Catford for an audience of 15,000, with a 15 metre high Big Ben and a 20 metre skeleton Guy, was an extraordinary summation of the others. Despite the efforts of our best inventors (their drawings are in *Engineers of the Imagination*), a fierce heavily amplified soundtrack lifted from the Rolling Stones and the Sex Pistols, 'Sympathy for the Devil' and 'Anarchy in the UK', an excellent wheel-about effigy of Margaret Thatcher, who wasn't in fact burned, and a most lyrical image of a giant stork (built on a car by Tim Hunkin and Andy Plant)[14] laying a fresh egg on the steps of the House of Commons, it didn't make any difference to the years of rampant Thatcherism which were just beginning.[15]

Our image was one of generalised provocative and comic anarchy taking the Guy Fawkes incident to its original intended conclusion in a theatrical spectacle of denouement. In 1978 we had to bulldoze a whole build because hours before firing a retired gas board plumber pointed out that we had been encouraged to build our sculpture over a major gas main. So it was we invented a new genre of processional demolition theatre. Maybe as a reward for our flexibility the promoters at the Milton Keynes Bowl talked about a colossal second show in the Bowl – an arena capable of holding an audience of 50,000. The spectacle was getting too big: it was time to call a halt.

Scarecrow Zoo including *The Tower of Babel* in 1982 was a good example of a symphonic site-specific event with a fireshow and was another attempt to turn our audience into a congregation. Another significant fire show which has to be seen in a wider context.

The fire was constructed at South Hill Park, a thriving Art Centre on the edge of Bracknell. Made in October and November 1982, it was our first and only sculptural fire that was intended to move. It was again designed by Andy Plant, Tim Hunkin and Greville White.[16] The structure, higher than a terraced house, was built in the form of a Tower of Babel (after Brueghel) with a big world balanced on its summit. Bolted on to a metal frame and mounted on car axles, it could roll on the car wheels when pulled by a hefty winch. Clad in a wooden skin and filled inside with sawn-up wooden palettes it was covered in scores of flashing nightclub signs which we kept illuminated as it was burnt. The edifice and its signs remained blinking for a surprisingly long time even when we blew it up with the rockets and Roman Candles lodged inside.

The Bracknell background was typically complex. The town was prosperous, partly because some of its inhabitants were making military components for Ferranti and other armaments companies. A few miles down the road at Greenham, women, 50,000 of them on occasion, were protesting against Cruise missiles at an American air base.

Eventually we amalgamated Hallowe'en and November 5th in a big build, a one-off fire (*The Tower of Babel*) with ancillary and repeated performances of *King Lear* (for which we built a seated arena on scaffolding), plus a participatory *Scarecrow* competition and a climactic celebratory Barn Dance in a big marquee.

Over a hundred people worked on the event; it took six months to plan and hundreds paid to see all or part of it. Three weeks before the main team arrived, an advance team, with a mobile store, marquee and caravans, was in residence. They conducted concentrated workshops, small-scale entertainments and 'barter' parties with the community until the main team arrived; then there were three weeks only to assemble the whole show.

We modernised the Hallowe'en demons by seeing the scarecrows as externalisations of inner fears, alter egos or even personal totems to warn off demonic black crows, including Cruise missiles. The money prizes, up to £100, attracted some wild inventions, mainly technological science fiction, but in the main we received sub television Wurzel Gummidges. All of them were stacked on the waiting fire.

The Babel tower, resembling a giant fruit machine, a multi Las Vegas icon, was pulled slowly from the back of the field, towards the large audience. Planet Earth was represented by a painted round septic tank balancing on top. This was eventually rescued by Donald Quixotty, a naive angel (Andy Burton)[17] who appeared to climb courageously up a tall ladder under gunfire surrounded by a circling Mad Max pack of Hell's Angels from Bracknell Chopper Club, headlights blazing, rockets up their exhausts and Molls on their pillions. Meanwhile in the foreground, thirty metres from the audience, three politicians (Thatcher, Foot and Jenkins) sat behind a massive table indulging in an excessive banquet. Behind them their backdrop was the Falklands War with Thatcher and Galtieri puppets chasing each other in armoured cars. As an after-dinner cabaret two other giant puppets, a seedy American eagle (which looked more like a Turkey made with scabby dishcloths) and a pompous English Bulldog Toby Jug (each carried on platforms by eight stagehands) intermittently fucked each other. Finally the National Cake (and jelly) exploded in their faces, triggering a holocaust until everything, including the war cabinet, caught fire. Except for Thatcher, who wouldn't burn despite extra rations of paraffin.

In the end a motorised whale, a fire engine draped in white with its top hose ejecting a stream of water, and a wooden Trojan horse full of lanterns flanked by children, drove away the maelstrom and extinguished the fires. A long parade of

Poster for *Scarecrow Zoo*, 1982

war wounded led by the Fall Out Marching Band and the Bagshot Brass and Reed Military Band playing 'The Dam Busters' pushed hospital screens. When I explained to the Military Band our anti-war motivation, they humbled me by saying, 'We are there to make the peace too, you know.'

At a final *Scarecrow Barn Dance Ball*, while the shadows of huge black crows were projected on to the outside of the canvas roof, we gave the participants small, date-stamped, dried cherry leaves for them to wish away bad memories. And people did. Scores of them. Carefully Andy Burton took the cardboard canister (a miniature Tower of Babel) full of bad memory leaves and placed it on a small sculptural cone constructed by Tim Hunkin from chunks of railway sleepers. In a small ceremony we set it on fire. There was an audible release of breath as the congregation felt their bad memories disappear. A big theatrical event had turned into a small useful ritual. Maybe, within the whole complex tapestry, it is that simple, but singular, burning of leaves that people will remember most.

Seasonal Celebrations

Welfare State International has always placed its celebrations at seasonal crossovers. These started in the seventies, with our mumming plays at Christmas time, and have continued in Lanternhouse with a themed installation with echoes of a winter grotto. Other pageants and parades are consistently planned to fit in high points of spring, summer and autumn. Underlying this programme are the traditional church and farming calendars which themselves overlaid pagan and Celtic festivals, all of which still mirror our climactic pattern in Britain. So a child of new hope (originally born in a Middle-Eastern stable) is now born into our dark forest, symbolising a return of the sun in the bleakest days of winter. We booze and fall over for twelve days until just after the party at New Year. Not much happens on the first day of spring (21 March) but on May Day, at least in some places like Padstow, the sap still rises up a garlanded maypole and a 'dragon hoss' tries to trap young women under its heavy tarry skirt. By midsummer, we go into the round of gymkhanas, country shows, factory shutdowns, town carnivals and sunshine escapes. After harvest, we mark Hallowe'en, reflect a little maybe on the souls of the dead, then set fire to dead wood on 5 November and though the end of the year can be misty and miserable we are distracted in every sense by Christmas. The Great Shopping Festival assails us, led by Santa, the patron saint of merchandising and eating, so we are duffed and trussed and marinated for the stressful return of The Family.

The underlying framework is a useful if sentimental reminder of the roots of our past and despite revivalism and fake ethnicity we can all get pleasure from imagined release after Lent and a few carols sung with friends to raise funds for the hospice.

In 1978, we spent Christmas and New Year in Nimbin, Australia, where European cultural mores can override seasonal imperatives. Christmas falls in Australia's midsummer, yet on 25 December, in scorching heat, old (English) immigrants still rally round turkeys, Santa, Christmas trees and the Queen's Speech. The Fox family, consisting of Sue Gill, me, Daniel (ten) and Hannah (eight) were engaged as consultants for the Australian Youth Performing Arts Association for the International Year of the Child, spending six months on an interstate tour. After all the resources and skilled artists of Welfare State International, it was both daunting and a liberation to discover how much we could achieve from four backpacks, two of them very small, with a few tools and musical instruments. We spent one month in Nimbin in New South Wales, not far from the Queensland border.

Nimbin was then a thriving 'alternative' community, almost a capital of Counter Culture, and in 1978 it was well on the way to becoming an inspirational oasis, demonstrating that a vision of a creative community wasn't just a pipe dream. There were undoubtedly many pipes smoking with delusions in Nimbin, but we felt there was every possibility for an embryonic Utopia, although by the 1990s it had deteriorated into a stopover for drug addicts.

Following a successful Aquarius Music Festival organised by Graeme Dunstan, numbers of 'hippies' (or new-age settlers, as they called themselves) stayed behind in Nimbin and raised families. Some had had reasonable jobs and could afford to buy the cheap, fertile, almost subtropical land and beautiful wooden farmsteads that had become available through the demise of the dairy industry started by the original settlers. Although there were misunderstandings between the old traditional farmers and the new immigrants, we did find a sense of prosperity and community energy, with a clear, if romantic, belief in a post-industrial economy. This thinking was far more advanced than anything we had seen in England, where land is expensive and change is difficult in the face of prejudice and age-old planning regulations. In Nimbin, we found an anarchic and alternative co-operative owning 2000 acres, with fifty dwellings and 120 residents. Breaking the convention of the nuclear family, new patterns of communal living were emerging, with extended households sharing facilities like kitchens and washing-machines. Smallholders were nearly self-sufficient; local produce was served in two new cafés (brightly painted with rainbows by a local shamanic character called Benny Zable); there were three healing centres, one for women, converted from a closed hospital; numerous alternative therapy classes; a craft gallery; a community school with sixty children; a Homebuilders' Association; home birthing groups; a weekly newsletter; a local radio station; community transport; a bush co-operative selling bulk food; solar-powered electricity; and, significantly for us, an interest in community celebrations and new forms of ritual.

Obviously, art, like rites of passage rituals, is informed by the intrinsic values of its wider culture.[18] In Nimbin, a few hundred young people had, then, a shared, optimistic belief in change. They had rejected the dominant large-scale market economy with its stressful excesses, its war footing, its stimulation of false needs, its pollution, exploitation, work-ethic neurosis and so on. Although many people in Nimbin were dependent on welfare, there was an acceptance of a different life-style, with more sharing, more voluntary material simplicity, an awareness of using limited energy and simplified technology and a definite attempt to connect with the earth, the landscape and the history and mythology of the indigenous Aboriginals who had been mostly killed or driven away.

The energy came from the land, which was surrounded by stark volcanic plugs which rose viciously above verdant forest like suppurating teeth. It was so fertile that if you dropped some muesli at breakfast you'd have a forest by lunch-time. It teemed with wildlife. Wallabies leaped over the white fences of our camping ground, we found a duck-billed platypus in the creek and one day, under the bonnet of the truck, a carpet snake. In our original home territory of the Yorkshire moors, there was never such boundless fertility.

> Poetry and poetic imagery are the tip of an iceberg the rest of which is the political, economical, educational and institutional realities of the social context.
> In Nimbin we laid on some imagery and why it worked is that basically we were talking the same language. We were all in search of sacred values.

The *Nimbin News* headline was 'The Christmas Season Rite: a veritable orgy of buying and consuming – a monument to the spiritual bankruptcy of our society'.[19]

It was a good start. It confirmed my view that Christmas as a celebration was oversubscribed, and, in Australia, seasonally disjointed. So we decided that New Year's Eve (the death of the old) and New Year's Day (the birth of the new) would be more relevant and collect more unity. And so it did.

We spent four weeks in Nimbin. It took a week to suss the place and people out, after which I wrote a scenario of poems. Then, with the assistance of a wide range of local organisations, representing both old farmers and new settlers, we set up a workshop at the local show ground to produce our 'symphonic celebration in three acts performed over two days'. Twenty people from all over Australia camped to work on the production. We often started at 5 a.m. to avoid the midday heat. In a frenetic burst of activity later described as a 'working meditation', we produced all the props, puppets and costumes and rehearsed music, action and dance. In the end, we had a scratch theatre company and even a wild street band.

Act 1: The Passing of the Old

Scene 1. A horse and cart driven by 'an old hermit of the mountain' passed through the small township of Nimbin at sunset on New Year's Eve. Eight pall bearers followed, carrying a five-metre-long greasy grey giant, made from papier mâché. Every hundred metres or so, the hermit called for people to bring out their vile memories of the year – tax returns, old love letters, jaded theses – and then to stuff them into the belly of the giant. The street band played a funeral lament which ended at the Bowling Club, the centre of the old white settlers, who were more familiar with the conventions of 'Auld Lang Syne' than these new rites. Fortunately, they hung out of their windows to wave encouragement.

Scene 2. Twelve kilometres outside Nimbin lies Blue Knob Hall, a tiny wooden structure that had, over the previous two years, seen a mixture of old and new settlers sharing a knees-up with a live band of local musicians. The hall committee agreed to a change: 'Better than a booze-up,' they said, and persuaded their neighbours to drop a fence and open up their land. We asked people to make and bring 'kinship lanterns', emblems of their family, household, tribe or whatever. seven hundred people turned up, with only twenty lanterns, but we had made sufficient extra lanterns. These were the first lanterns we ever invented. They were crude but effective. Candle-lit paper cones held to the ground with wire tent stakes and even paper bags weighted inside with sand for the insertion of a night light. There were also some sculptural forms a metre across, constructed from fencing wire, covered in opaque white polythene and lit from inside with electric torches.

All the lanterns were used to mark an ellipse orientated towards the 'sacred' Mount Warning, which receives the first rays of sunlight in the whole of Australia. A local woodsman had prepared an oblong fire trench of glowing embers, much bigger than the giant. At 11 p.m., we carried the old grey beast into the ellipse. It was now very heavy with a mass of junk in its belly. A 'songman' called for the final vile memories, a sandman and a skeleton danced in the firelight, and, together

(I am still not sure how), we hurled the giant on to the fire. There was a powerful blaze of pre-set saltpetre and sulphur. We clapped and sang a chant which echoed from the face of Lillian Rock, towering above.

The energy shifted to an adjacent dam, where around the black water we lit fires in earthenware bowls (kerosene-soaked sawdust). Our dancing skeleton lit a small straw figure which was slowly towed to the centre of the lake, accompanied by two songs. One was a lament for the burned old year sung by a man and the other Alan Price's 'Changes', sung by Sue Gill:

All the world is going through changes,
No one knows what's going on.
Here today and gone tomorrow.
But the world still carries on.

A gong struck twelve. (It was actually 12.30, but this was Nimbin time.) 'Auld Lang Syne' came and went again.

Act 2. The Birth of the New

Scene 1. A naming ceremony. As we had created these for the newborn in our own community of theatre workers, we were encouraged to discover there had been three in Nimbin. It was a homecoming. At 3.45 p.m. on New Year's Day (the next day!), in a lush meadow bounded by a creek and groves of trees, people brought kinship parasols, in parallel with the kinship lanterns of the night before. A circle was marked with bowls of flowers and small flags. As they arrived, people were greeted and gathered on the edge of the circle. We expected to name three infants but twenty-five went through the ceremony because many people decided to join in on the spur of the moment. Three cultures, Christian, Buddhist and Aboriginal, met in the meadow, represented by a solicitor, a monk and two Bundjalung Aboriginal elders.

There was a local legend, probably a recycled urban myth, that 'there would be no prospering in this land until either the white race is reborn trusting and innocent as little children or they take on the spirits of the dead Aboriginals'. A myth maybe, but powerful, and the presence of the two elder tribespeople gave it a very special significance. John Lynes, a much-respected lawyer, first spoke of this legend and how it was in the nature of Aboriginal culture to adapt, to learn and to live in the moment with the earth and the framework of their ancestral rules which worked for the good of the whole. He described the two tribes of old and new settlers as being the warp and woof of the changing Nimbin community and, finally quoting Kahlil Gibran, said: 'Life and death are one — even as the river and the sea.' Beth Freeman sang 'Wild Mountain Thyme', unaccompanied. It had last been sung here the previous November at the funeral of a two-year-old and, we understood, the grieving was still unresolved.

Then, quite informally, the naming began. The ceremonial circle was about thirty metres across. Families used it in their own way. Most walked to the centre, held up their children and proclaimed the name of their child. Some told stories, some were on their own, but others brought friends as witnesses. Some asked for their infant to be blessed by one or all of the quartet of resident wise men. A few took additional Aboriginal names. The elders, Uncle Lyle and Albury, who were in their eighties, one in a suit, tie, hat and shoes (the only person who was), concluded with a shuffly dance to the rhythm of clap sticks – good for our health and a blessing for the infants.

Towards the end, a new sapling, a white gum tree, was planted in the stump of a tree that had been felled long ago by ring barking. Then we gave the wise men three big white weather balloons filled with helium. Together, in the centre, they held the strings. Unfortunately, before they were released, one burst, leaving us with a riddle. Then a clown bird man released pigeons which had been hurriedly collected, one for each child. We ate watermelon and fresh mangoes and chatted under the colourful parasols. The Aboriginals said they felt as if they were on the sacred path to the initiation sites of the valley and that next time they would bring babies from their own communities. Here was a new era opening up, not just a New Year.

Act 3. The Cow Jumped Over The Moon

The final act occurred during a late-afternoon cream-tea party on the same New Year's Day, the official opening of the 'Nomads' Theatre' in an old butter factory recently acquired by the Bush Co-op. Not since the school of arts had built a hall in the 1920s had a performance space been opened in Nimbin.

We described the reopening as 'an evocation of images depicting Nimbin people and their history', and after considerable research made some bone-simple mythic/reminiscence theatre with songs, stories, dances, shadow plays, a concert and a photographic exhibition.

Inside the converted factory was a square concrete warehouse space, polished but softened a little with drapes and a semicircle of candles. A very mixed audience

55

of about two hundred old and new settlers, with tens of children, were welcomed by 'Danny's tune', a Ghanaian riff which I played on a D tin whistle. Then an unaccompanied female voice sang 'Donna', as an overture, 'for those who treasure freedom like the swallow have learned to fly'. Dan Fox (now just ten) sang his first song in public, 'When I first came to this land'.

The main narrative, accompanied by a rich, 'folky' score from local musicians, depicted the rise of Nimbin's prosperity in the early days of the butter factory, from the clearing of the forest to the building of the factory, followed by its later decline and fall through centralised big business and subsequent recession. At one point, I persuaded four current community stalwarts to set sail in a hobby-hoss ark, with one oar. We used images of chance and unpredictable violence to tell the story. A milkmaid meets a dark stranger; a small girl's rainbow bird is killed by a honey man, who in turn dies. A longstanding family feud is nearly resolved by a Romeo and Juliet-style liaison, but the newlyweds die in a fire on their wedding night. The metaphors we used were ironic, especially since the four were quarrelling for real because every anarchist wants to be the leader.

At the end, we all processed to a bridge outside, following a corny angel on stilts who released another helium balloon. It made up for the one that burst, and as it disappeared and candles flickered on the water, the Song Man, from the previous night's Mountain Burning of the Giant, sang his own song about 'time the people got together'. It was a typical and fitting end to our sojourn in Nimbin. The whole residency was inspiring and unrepeatable. The community — well, many of them — were happy with the seeds we had sown. They would have probably discovered them anyway, but we did seem to arrive at the right time.

We learned that there could be a healing role for theatre. It could 'make whole' and join together the many talents of a disparate group, giving them a shared imagery and specific roles within the context of a lumbering seasonal celebration. On this occasion, many of this small community had been connected on the fragile bridge between a wilfully remembered past and a problematic future.

At the time, Graeme Dunstan asked me why I put so much energy into community celebrations and I replied with an off-the-cuff manifesto:

Problem: To redirect surplus to sacred roots.

Old Theatre: Sit in the dark with naturalistic re-cycling, so escaping from the reality of boring work. Leisure is negative work. Such is the illusion of capitalism.

New Theatre: Celebrate existence with sensual style (when necessary). Transcend rational didacticism; ceremony grows from and enhances living values

Moral : The meat of a poisoned beast rots the bones of man; fly with the land between your toes and dream of joy.

Why? Because Nimbin is the greatest place on Earth. Fake unbelievable art now!

★

A few months after Nimbin, while we were still in Australia, we felt that the whole Australia journey had been so fulfilling that we wanted to emigrate. On 22 February 1979, I wrote to our board to explain that after running some workshops in Northern Tasmania with Bill Mollinson (one of the founders of the Permaculture movement), we had found our spot. We had also been provisionally offered a job as cultural development consultants and had put a deposit down on a house. It may be that after a six-month interstate tour we just needed to stop and anywhere would have done. Perhaps we were seduced by the beauty of the historic town of Stanley on the north coast of Tasmania where the air was unpolluted and the ocean ultramarine. I guess we should never have made a decision under a full moon, but we did. The Mollinsons talked of simply farming in tune with the environment rather than the modern approach of destroying nature with more chemicals and ever more invasive techniques. We felt that there was a parallel with our way of making theatre, which we preferred to grow naturally from the ground.

The Stanley community seemed to be following similar values to Nimbin. Groups of people who worked with their hands (gardeners, farmers, fishermen), were actively creating a holistic culture. We dreaded returning to England. We felt in Australia we could breathe and grow with like-minded people. Also, there was a surplus of cheap land, an amazing landscape, a totally different sense of time (especially in the desert) and it was a great place to bring up our kids. We planned to return to England for a few months, then emigrate to Australia for good. I was fantasising already about an international network of Welfare State artists and that we would somehow purchase a trawler. They were on sale in Hull for about £15,000. I foresaw a 'Trawler of Fools' that would sail around the planet with its wayward cargo. Stanley had an appropriate deep-sea port.

It didn't work out. At least not in the way we anticipated. Maybe we should have just stayed and not come back at all. Perhaps on that night of the full moon the gods had the dice upside-down. Or were we were scared by the stories of Tasmanian tiger snakes living in the burrows of mutton birds on The Nut, the headland above Stanley? Mutton-bird chicks preserved in barrels of oil are (for some) a gourmet delicacy. You catch them by putting your hand into a burrow where they have been abandoned. If it feels warm, then the mutton bird is still alive and maturing. If it is cold, then it has been eaten by a deadly tiger snake which is certainly still there. As it turned out, when we returned to England, my father was ill with a heart condition and we had to stay. He died at the end of 1979, but by then we had realised that our children needed to be settled in one place and I had abandoned my fantasies of piloting a small plane from Stanley's vast beach to be the Flying Showman-Shaman of Oz. But I had not abandoned my notions of building a cultural village. The question was where.

We couldn't return to the caravan site in Burnley. Before we left for Australia, there had been a big, traumatic split in the company, when more than half of our artists left to form I.O.U.[20] Boris and I struggled on with a smaller team, expanded with artists from the Idaho company in Holland. This was one reason why we performed in our small canvas courtyard rather than the big circus tent. Our offices had also moved to Howard Steel's house in Liverpool. There was no reason to return to Burnley. So we signed our toilet block and two big scout huts over to Burnley Youth Theatre (who are still in existence in 2002) for a peppercorn annual rent of one shilling and we never went back.

The Foxes' personal Living Wagon (our fairy-tale cut-glass and walnut showman's trailer) was parked up in Welwyn Garden City, beached after the last show there. Each weekend, we trucked north from there with our Volkswagen camper van, hunting for a house. After scouring the north-east and north-west coasts of England, we eventually ended up (by another coincidence) in Ulverston in Cumbria. Round the corner was Stanley Street and on the hill above the town stood the Hoad Monument, a replica lighthouse with no light. Eddystone Lighthouses were always part of our imagery, so here was an omen. We had arrived late on the afternoon after Ulverston's annual carnival. Curiously, with the evening's energy spinning with nowhere to go, it felt as if there was a job to do. Maybe we were coming home after all.[21]

2

On Tour

In the 1960s and 70s, it was all touring. There was often a site-specific element to the theatre we made, but some products were repeated around the country. Each time you opened the trailer door, there were new vistas. At first, we toured with little outside shows like *Superman and the Fleas*, *The Humpback Jester* and even *Punch and Judy* (1969). These were performed on car parks, park lawns and beaches, where we made a three-quarter-circle of small, decorated oil drums, played rough music on drums and saxophones, drew a crowd and bottled hard for money. Usually there was a back to the circle, formed by a van and some scenery. When we could afford it, we bought a circus tent, which later became a geodesic plastic bubble and, later still, a wooden ghost-train structure and a white canvas courtyard so that we could draw a paying crowd into a more controlled space.

Sometimes we built little theatres with marquees and benches. The most elaborate of these was for the entertaining and dreamlike *Uppen Down Mooney* (1978), directed by Boris Howarth and written by Adrian Mitchell. In that show, mythologised country folk and strange animals living in rural madness played out a poetic phantasmagoria to an audience seated under tent awnings, while the performers and musicians worked, in all weathers, in a central open courtyard.

But we often stuck to the oil drums and in shows like *Blood Pudding*, *Eye of the Peacock* or *Tales for England,* created very elaborate outdoor theatre. We mixed dance, puppetry and story-telling, with quite complex theatrical trickery. Shows lasted an hour and drew big crowds of up to five hundred, as many as a good rep theatre might attract. At the back of the horseshoe 'stage', there was usually a canvas booth or even a garden shed on a towed chassis, or a dust cart which turned into a Wurlitzer organ, all ideal to hide or chase behind to reveal puppets, flags and props of every scale from a foot to ten feet high. We learned many tricks of entertainment: conjuring, coloured smokes, bangers, big flags, windsocks, rapid transformations (for which Japanese Kabuki was a good source) and interventions of live music were handy devices to stop an audience feeling cold or just walking away. By the eighties, as we left our mobile village behind to become more building-based, our pattern changed and we started to parachute into other people's spaces and even connect with established circuits for touring theatre.

We were constantly researching ways of making old forms of celebration in progressive ways. One of these was the Barn Dance (1980–1).[1] Under the direction of Greg Stephens and Taffy Thomas, we developed our band and a caller to play tunes for social dancing. Most of the music was traditional: reels, gigs, polkas, waltzes, circle dances and so on. Over three years in the early eighties, we transformed dull village halls into unrecognisable dream palaces with specially designed lanterns, illuminated paintings on canvas and strings of bunting. The evening usually lasted four hours or more. In between dances, we slipped in themed theatrical episodes using songs, story-telling and street-performance techniques. In this context, we performed to many people who would not normally have been interested in theatre. Indeed, when someone told us of a strange theatre company they had once encountered in the village, we didn't admit it was us. In between the evening's dances, they were enjoying theatre just as strange. Extended barn-dance and street-theatre styles were incorporated into many of the long epic shows.

The Tempest on Snake Island

In this show, which we staged in Canada in May 1981, we worked in partnership with an excellent and exceptional host community on Ward's Island in Toronto harbour, and included a participatory circle dance, with the 300-plus audience joining in. The mythic theme of Shakespeare's original *Tempest*, in which a disillusioned Prospero engages in a power struggle with the indigenous folk of a magical island kingdom, was the perfect vehicle. Island people were in reality fighting a mainland bureaucracy determined to take over their precious self-built wooden homes.

In the context of the Toronto Festival of Theatre, we involved forty of the islanders, along with the company, in organising, making, animating and performing the show. Two weeks were spent creating the environment and building the

64

structures. Five performances, each lasting four hours, were made on five successive evenings. We ferried our audience of 300 to a remote part of the island (and some gatecrashers arrived in canoes). Then, in a complex promenade performance, we paraded round six sites in a series of intensive stops, using large-scale puppet tableaux, a shadow play, the communal dance and much more.

In his long descriptive article about this work in *Beginnings in Ritual Studies,* Ron Grimes wrote:

> *Tempest on Snake Island* worked. It galvanised a group of islanders and mainlanders, entertained and enlightened spectators, salvaged a lot of junk, taught numerous skills, generated several thousand dollars of income, facilitated important contacts, initiated ritual processes with on-going possibilities. Welfare State had not provided an answer to the socio-political problem but had transposed it to a more sensual medium, that of a nursery rhyme celebration rite in which people are more free to imagine alternatives.[2]

It is the unexpected details that can catch you out when you are planning a site-specific work on paper which is to be realised thousands of miles away. Despite two essential site visits, we nearly got it wrong. The *Tempest* scenario written by Boris and myself called for a certain amount of the show to take place in daylight, a certain amount at dusk and much in darkness. The time had to be written into tickets and programmes distributed months before our arrival. In Toronto, the time of the sunset was crucial. We had to bring people on a twenty-minute ferry ride, in varying winds, in order to reach a certain jetty on the island just as darkness was falling.

Although we had it worked out to the last second, five weeks before we were due to depart, we realised the calendar we had been working from contained a misprint. British Summer Time had arrived a week earlier that year and the calendar was out of sync. We had to change all the plans by telex very rapidly, so that everyone would be in the right place at the right time.

The Wasteland and the Wagtail

When, at the height of the Renaissance, Michelangelo painted his Sistine Chapel ceiling, he entered into a deal with the Vatican. 'You give me a good advert for God and you can paint your musclebound chums,' said the pope. So the sponsor called the tune but the piper still played his own version and we inherited the vulgar Cinemascope cartoon everyone queues to view today. It has always been

65

thus, whether the sponsor is the Church, the State or the Banker. In the early eighties, Margaret Thatcher wanted to impress the Japanese with a zappy image of a youthful Britain and we were chosen as the appropriate cultural diplomats or Special Arts Service. We were invited to perform at the Toga Theatre Festival in July 1982. The festival obviously fulfilled the government's political and economic objectives because the Japanese firm Nissan duly extended their car factory near Sunderland shortly afterwards. How bizarre that capital dripped from diplomatic bags freshly squeezed by Maggie and me.

Content hardly came into it. We were at first asked to deliver a touring version of our anarchic *Parliament in Flames*. We were deluding ourselves if we thought that we were being hired for our style rather than anything to do with content. Eventually we persuaded the British Council to risk something else (which they boldly did), although they still wrote intrusively asking us to create a piece 'related to our attempt to present a fresh image of contemporary Britain through the arts this year – tradition and diversity, technology with ecology, fantasy with precision, that sort of thing. At the risk of usurping his [John Fox's] right to create a title, might I suggest something on the lines of "The Magic Island", suggested both by the image of Britain as the Western Japan (dubious though this may be!) and by the outside stage at Toga. It hardly matters provided it does not restrict Welfare State International's creativity in any way.' There was to be big publicity, with live TV.

As well as having diplomatic and PR objectives, the British Council were already steering us in the direction of the main stage. They sent us photographs of the festival site, an extraordinary theatre village which had been designed by the theatre director–impresario Tadashi Suzuki. Working at everything in a personal style between Grotowski and Hannibal, Suzuki had reassembled a collection of beautiful antique Japanese farmhouses in a landscape of lush forest three hundred kilometres north of Tokyo. In the centre of these, in order to reinvent Greek tragedy in a Japanese format, he had designed a ten-by-twenty-metre concrete and stone amphitheatre which projected over an artificial lake where they had initially expected us to present *Parliament in Flames* on this stage. Apart from the fact that it was too small, it was clear that they didn't understand our way of making our art. They expected us to dovetail our production with other shows, as if we had a lightweight movable theatre set rather than a very heavy sculptural installation which was built on the ground. All we could do before visiting the site in person was to stall on the ultimate location, continue to research ideas and maintain a dialogue with Tokyo.

The dialogue was very productive and ideas started to emerge from striking cultural parallels. Family structures in both countries were changing. Both nations are islands – each had followed isolated feudal paths under kings or emperors and suffered hierarchical authority and cataclysmic war. Each had a long history of economic expansionism and a unique theatrical tradition. Japan was more high tech and from a distance more mysterious. But mystery is about the unknown and I guess all those Japanese tourists trekking round our cathedrals and Wordsworth's Dove Cottage are equally awestruck.

Japan has official Buddhism, Zen Buddhism and Shintoism. Maybe angling is England's equivalent of Zen. I read that Shinto temples are built to be taken apart, to be cleansed and exorcised by rebuilding when necessary. Their interlocking joints resemble our fairground architecture and the symbolic knots of plaited bamboo-leaf rope are coiled in the way we once coiled ropes round poles in our circus tent.

I found an 'anthropological' photo of old Japanese men, probably village elders, standing high up on a wooden platform with a large mulberry tree growing out of it. They were symbolically defending their territory from climbing hordes of muscular young men with uniform headbands and big drums. In another picture, twenty snow igloos lit with candles looked like lanterns glowing in a row under an ultramarine sky. I looked again at Kurasawa's horse and banner movies which are much more appealing than our Trooping the Colour. His *King Lear* on video (*Ran*) was inspirational for theme, scale and landscape.

King Lear seemed to be a good beginning. Here was power, family, isolation, and Boris Howarth had already written an excellent mummers play for another tour. Then, by magic, a handy Ainu creation myth dropped in from a book of folk tales which began 'In the beginning, the world was slush'.

The Ainu are the native aboriginal people of Japan. Subjugated by the Japanese in AD 812 and forced to retreat to the northern islands, the 16,000 remaining Ainu are hunters and fishermen. For them, the primordial earth was slushy and unformed until a wagtail formed dry places by beating the mud. The story continued;

> He fluttered the water with his wings and splashed it here and there. He ran up and down in the slush with his feet and tried to trample it into firmness. He beat on it with his tail, beating it down. After a long time of this treading and tail wagging a few dry places began to appear in the big ocean which now surrounds them – the islands of the Ainu.

I could imagine this pesky wagtail impatient with God, stomping about in a bobbing tailcoat. Dario Fo would have been good in the part. I could also imagine a monstrous King Lear in the form of a wheeled Tower of Babel. I had a Clown and a King. The British Council was asking urgently for me to send a statement. In March, and in haste, I wrote the following (edited) and plucked a title out of the air.

THE WASTELAND AND THE WAGTAIL
An evocation of change for the first Japanese International Theatre Festival
"Tis the times plague when madmen lead the blind"
Gloucester, *King Lear*, Act 4, sc. 1

In common with a number of western nations, Britain is moving, albeit unwillingly, into a post industrial phase. We know that creativity has been and is deliberately repressed by political, military and commercial vulgarity. Such materialistic consumption is common in the Northern Hemisphere and, like lilies on a rubbish tip, we grow innocently to project a microcosm of new primitivism. We do this by working directly, cheaply, simply, roughly, humorously, relevantly and collectively.

We demystify high art by demonstrating the 'home-made' creative process in action within a community. Our theatre is celebratory; we liberate the imagination. This task is joyous, essential and sacred and not given to psychedelic Elastoplast. Once upon a time the shaman steered the tribe into magical flight. Now jet-set jesters are invited to magnetise the circuits of the global village.

WE HAVE NO CULTURAL PRODUCT FOR SALE.

We seek to discover for our 'audience' and ourselves and if the truth we find is as black as night then the poetry we create is black as tar. If the vulture is bald we polish its skull till we see our face. Explanation and rationalism are the rats on a sinking ship. If grain silos are disguised missile garages who will bake the bread? If life expectancy in Britain and Japan is more than 70 and in West Africa a mere 40, can we dance round the abyss for 30 years?
"The weight of this sad time we must obey;
Speak what we feel, not what we ought to say."
Edgar, *King Lear*, Act 5, sc. 3

Like *Tempest on Snake Island*, *The Wasteland and the Wagtail* was designed to connect with local rhythms. To an outsider, these are always unpredictable. Hence the frantic telegrams. 'When does the sun set on 25th July in Northern Japan? How long does it take for the sun to set in your part of the world and, most importantly, when do the midges bite?' But there is a limit to how much research is possible from a distance. There is no substitute for a visit to the location.

The Japanese newspaper I picked up on the plane in April 1982 contained my horoscope (suspiciously syndicated from the *Los Angeles Times*):

SAGITTARIUS (NOV 22 – DEC 22)
Do not let a preoccupation with details cloud the picture. Double-check facts and figures. A mistake could send the whole budget down the drain.

The first rule of reconnaissance is to check out the site exactly a year ahead to mirror the same climate, light conditions and precise timing of the event itself. You can hazard guesses through astronomical charts and tide timetables. But there is always an extra street lamp or a prevailing wind, the smell from a chicken factory, the noise of a hooter, or an unexpected reflection from the sun or the moon, or even a regular carnival parade on your site, that no one thought to mention.

It was too late to visit Japan a full year ahead. Our event at Toga was to take place in summer in subtropical heat. But in April, when I landed, the land was six feet deep in snow. The houses were made of paper. Peeking through a minute tear in an interior wall, I discovered my supper laid out in what looked like a candle-lit cave decorated with many tiny porcelain bowls, each reflected in the dark varnish of a low table. Every dish of black local fungi or emerald vegetables, framed by chopsticks, was a delicate offering from some strange kingdom of the trolls. Legs were wrapped in blankets, and I sat on straw matting which smelled of hay time. My jet-lagged senses were on overdrive. How could the snow be so dry? How could tons of crystals be piled so high against this fragile house and yet I wasn't freezing? Above all, could I find a site in the allotted two and a half days and establish the bones of a performance event for July? Could it ever be as rounded and welcoming as this feast? And could we make our images work for the people of this exquisite rural, peasant mountain culture and the visitors from Tokyo too?

The official theatre stage was everything I had feared from the photographs. It was built for tightly focused epic performance. One evening, Suzuki's company played *The Trojan Women* outdoors in a monsoon jabbed with lightning. Big puddles formed on the concrete stage. The red ochre and burnt umber costumes turned to sodden rags, but the reflections alone were like those in a slaughterhouse. Even 'flower arrangers' turned out to be beefy men who used chainsaws like chopsticks to slice through forest, creating kilometre-long vistas topped by thirty-metre bamboos and tangential fountains. Elemental, but still not suitable for us. Conducting a reconnaissance for a site-specific show is a very odd skill. It is like water divining. In between the inevitable and necessary politicking and socialising with management, you rush around with tuned antennae, waiting and hoping for the right poetic judder. Some managements understand and leave you on your own, but not always. Here, they were very courteous and it was possible to dream on the ground away from the throng. The main difficulty, though, was finding a site at all! Apart from the official stage, which I had already discounted (public relations were the hardest bit here), every location was too steep, too wooded, too remote, too exposed or too near the main road. I spent hours plodding along a dried-up riverbed, thinking I had nearly got it, but could find no enclosed, comforting area. The scale and grey of the boulders were always too dominant and there was always the worry of a flash flood.

The only place left was a long slope up a mountain next to a commercial ski run. This was over a mile long and every time I trudged up (even when I hitched a lift on the ski-lift chairs), I didn't want to believe that this was the only possibility. Anything on this mountain had to be big, not quite as big as *Parliament in Flames*, perhaps, but still big. We upped our team number from nine to twelve, but after their arrival we would still have only fourteen days and limited resources to achieve a big event.

On that bleak mountain, staring through blizzards to the river far below, I had no idea how to achieve the expected epic with the available team, time and budget. That is, until the mountain came up with an answer. The summit, as far as I could tell with the snow, was barren, steep and inhospitable. Apart from a small plateau with a tiny thorn tree, it was an awesome wasteland. Descending from the north to the valley, boulders turned to rubble as the slope fell away. Halfway down, near the highest stanchion of the ski lift, the way narrowed to a convenient plateau sufficient for many people to sit in a circle. Below this, the ground rolled away again, although there were flatter pauses. At the bottom, a few hundred metres from the main road, there were three useful locations, a grove of fir-trees on a small hillock next to a meadow, a big tarmac square and the ski-lodge hotel with car park.

The landscape gave me the structure. Physically, it mirrored the life of a person. Merging ideas from *King Lear* and the story of the Wagtail, the rising slope could represent the journey of the life of a man, from his turbulent youth (the rising river), mounting to a remote and barren summit. Depending on your perspective, it could also symbolise a final return journey from lonely heights to a mellow resettling (or recycling?) at the bottom. A number of inspirational theatre directors such as Peter Brook (in Iran), Murray Schaffer (in Canada) and Robert Wilson (in America) had created scenarios round mountains and we ourselves had considerable experience of taking an audience on journeys in the landscape.

I calculated that a Japanese audience would probably respond to an idea of pilgrimage and, even if they were quite old, I reckoned it was safe enough for two or three hundred participants to walk up and down with good guides. I scribbled a sketch. I guessed that at the very top, after the most difficult climb, we could rest for a gentle meditation (or vigil) on the themes of old age and mortality. On the return path, the central plateau offered a spot to gather and sit (on carpets or cushions) under the dominating rocky wasteland before descending at a more leisurely pace to the two or three obvious locations at the bottom.

This was more or less how it worked out, except for one ludicrous mistake. By summer, the little snow-covered plateau at the top to the east, which I had assigned to the vigil, was inaccessible and heavily overgrown with subtropical forest. Only an audience with machetes could have got through, so we abandoned the top third of the slope.

Back at the digs, I scrawled in my diary:

> A theatrical journey from mountain to valley in which monstrous kings become their own victims and mischievous wagtails re-create a new destiny. As the sun sets high on the mountain we contemplate what lies below. Together we journey into the abyss, skirting the ultimate decadence of the Royal Palace, experiencing the Wasteland and witnessing the explosions in the Royal Bunker. Journeying down more gentle slopes, we rest, then dance together . . . theatrical pundits and village dwellers, Japanese and foreigners together for a joyous instant in a remote mountain hideaway in North Japan.

After a public dress rehearsal, the three-hour show was performed three times on three concurrent evenings at the end of July. Its form was symphonic, with musical and visual ritual cameos depicting themes of King Lear and the Wagtail repeated in different styles and different locations for our congregation of three hundred trusting pilgrims walking up and down the mountain.

First, towards sunset, we all gathered near the ski-lodge. Then, after being greeted and cajoled by our bizarre *Carry On* tour-guide usherettes (with basic sign boards and even more basic Japanese and electric torches), everyone howled with laughter

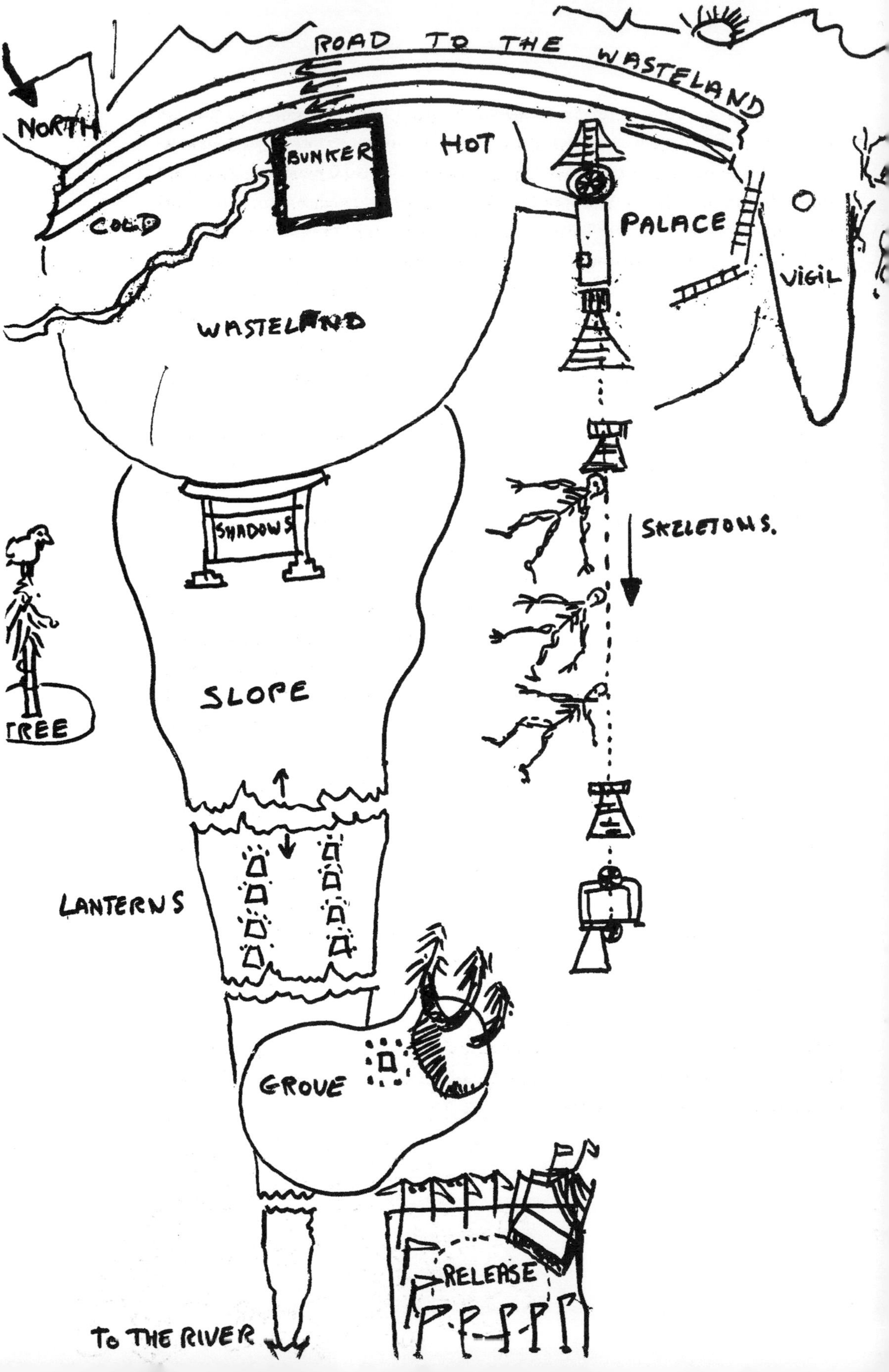

ROAD TO THE WASTELAND
NORTH
BUNKER
HOT
COLD
PALACE
VIGIL
WASTELAND
SHADOWS
SKELETONS.
SLOPE
TREE
LANTERNS
GROVE
RELEASE
TO THE RIVER

and happily zigzagged upwards. Ten-year-old Hannah, sitting Pan-like as the Wagtail on a central rock, wooed them from afar with her tin whistle. Crisscrossing between sculptural signposts, cairns and small pennants, our audience eventually arrived to sit round the circular plateau, midway up, where we served Japanese tea. Musicians with percussion and Northumbrian pipes played an overture to bring on the night. As darkness was falling, the mummers paraded around the arena with rough cut-and-thrust comic style. They acted out repeated cycles of violent death and rebirth interspersed with songs, lyric poetry and blasts from snare drum and bombarde. Our audience, close and excited (and warmed up with the hot barley tea), was soon in hysterics as we buffooned in broad English accents with the occasional interjection in dire Japanese.

As the mountain grew dark, the mood changed. The audience swung round to look up the stark hillside above them. A grotesque dinner party emerged from the blackness. Accompanied by a recording of a string orchestra playing a distorted My Way, an oblong fifteen-metre table covered in white linen and silverware materialised in fluorescent blue. Seven rich rulers (kings, businessmen and women, emperors and their consorts) consumed a decadent feast. It ended in a drunken orgy as they tried to outdo each other, wallowing in a huge tub of noodles and fisticuffs.

Lit by distant maroon and white flares (fired electrically), the violence and destruction accelerated rapidly until the whole mountain wasteland mirrored a war-zone in Beirut or Berlin or even Hiroshima. The soundtrack Pete Moser had created in England was a carefully selected collage of partially recognisable extracts from wars, war speeches and concentration camps, played very loud.

The most terrible image was a hideous King ten metres high, who, unannounced, came rumbling down from his mountain bunker, jolting over the broken scree. An immense gargoyle had broken from a decaying fortress and he hurled blazing missiles towards the audience. Our skilled pyrotechnician David Clough[3] had carefully measured fallout distances, but nevertheless, isolated as we suddenly felt at night in this barren place, the sudden impact was frightening. It worsened as the King blew up in a fireball of rage. Even those of us working the effect were stunned. Echoes and flashes refracted and reflected on adjacent peaks until it seemed we might trigger a real earthquake beyond this theatrical fragment of World War III. Finally, above us, a dozen giant skeletons gyrated grotesquely.[4] Rigged on the chairs of the out-of-season ski lift, they clanked slowly past, dancing high against the stars and disappearing to the river far below.

Gradually, silence returned until an exquisite melancholic reprise of the mummers' lament on solo violin played by Andy Burton, was heard and a hair-raising wailing rose up. A man was crying for his lost mother. It was a real recording made by the Allies at the liberation of Belsen. As the weeping continued, a white-faced Clown dug through the wreckage to find the body of a burned child dressed as the Wagtail. The dead child came to life and with a torch of fire led us all down the mountain to the next station.

The blackened body of the King, now on a horizontal stretcher, followed behind.[5] We all became the funeral cortège. Accompanied by a muffled drum, a large section of our audience helped us carry the considerable weight of the dead warmonger over the uneven ground.

In the distance, glimmering below, was a cloth shadow screen. The audience gathered in a semicircle to witness our fusion of the tale of the King and the Wagtail. In Shakespeare's version, Lear is the only character who changes. In our Japanese version, the soul's transmigration permitted a more optimistic finale. Played out with cardboard puppets lit by flambeaux and accompanied by live music on gongs and accordion, it ended comically, with the King's soul reborn as a stroppy, stomping Wagtail. During this distraction, the Puppet King was whisked past to be set up on an elevated operating table in the meadow next to the grove of fir trees. As the audience left the shadow screen, the mood became more gentle. Borders of paper lanterns lit the way.

In the meadow, the scene was set for a Grand Guignol operation. Clown surgeons with a wild anaesthetist, accompanied by appropriate screechings and honkings from bagpipes and overblown reeds, operated on the King's cadaver. After some belly-slicing and removal of fake offal (fat, pink metre-long polythene sausages), a twitching was observed in the King's stomach. Slowly, a small bird emerged. It was the Wagtail again, Hannah pushed up from below, from inside the scaffolding bier, by two strong men. An arch of silver rain sparkled in the dark trees. We were back full circle to the child sitting on the rock and playing her tin whistle in the overture of two hours ago. Time to celebrate our slightly dangerous communal journey and mark the ultimate return of the Wagtail as lyrical but unpredictable hope in the midst of darkness and noxious slurry. We had decorated the asphalt square with big, round cloth lanterns and festoons of coloured bulbs. Immediately after the Wagtail had played her gentle flute, the lights came up some fifty metres away, drawing us all to an open-air ballroom and joyous barn dance. It was one of the craziest dances. For more than an hour, we leaped and spiralled in lines and circles, swinging our partners to wild northern English tunes. Waltzes, polkas and Cumberland Square Eights played by us all alongside ska and reggae rhythms. The dance steps were called by two callers, one slightly ahead of time, then immediately translated into Japanese. All the audience were rapidly up and dancing. We had forgotten that they (or their parents) had learned square dancing after 1945 from their American conquerors.

By the end of the evening, the three hundred of us, plus a number of villagers who turned up just for the free dance, were bonded. The mix of pantomime, carnival, rough ritual, strong archetypes and fierce poetry, music and dancing had, as usual, bypassed reserve and cultural difference. By the time the coaches came to take our customers back to their hostels, and we had held hands in a last circle dance and Boris and Andy played 'Auld Lang Syne' on bagpipes (the tune is curiously as big in Japan as in Glasgow), there was not a dry eye on the buses. As our whole company stood bowing at fleets of coaches, scores of faces pressed on to the steamy windows. Handkerchiefs were waved and, tired as we were (with a considerable de-rig ahead of us), we knew we had delivered.[6]

We took our own lanterns to Japan and hung them in our outdoor ballroom. There were four big round lumpy ones built around hoops of black plastic water pipe and painted by me (with astronauts stealing the moon, and pink roses growing from the skulls of dead cattle in a desert). We also had ten elegant cloth tubes painted by Maggie Howarth with contrasting stripes of singing colour. Ironically, we had pinched the idea of lanterns from an old Japanese tourist guidebook, so the idea was recycled and taken back to source. Rough and obviously hand-made, their style was much appreciated by our Japanese contemporaries.

The main surprise and the prime catalyst for all the lantern festivals we and others have created in our home town of Ulverston, Europe, Canada and Australia was the Lantern Sea Ceremony we saw on a brief holiday before we returned to England. By chance, we found ourselves at dusk in a seaside town in north Japan. High above us in a temple on the edge of a forested volcano, immense drums were being beaten. What looked like thirty tall stained-glass windows, each maybe four or five metres tall, processed slowly down a vertical track and swayed perilously through the trees. As they emerged, we saw that each float was carried by a turbulent wave of thirty muscular sweating men in white loincloths, accompanied by the drummers.

The lanterns themselves were made of shallow cloth or paper boxes, with candle-light, framed in carved mahogany and emblazoned with lurid painted demonic caricatures of gods and warriors. They were constructed as the sails of ancient ships rocking on the timbers below. It was a blessing for the fishing fleet and each giant lantern was surmounted with a small boy of no more than ten years old. He was strapped in as if on the yardarm or crow's nest of a galleon, which swayed terrifyingly. Each boat was placed on the sea and floated round the harbour until, in the distance, they became tiny as glow-worms. As the primal drumming ceased, we heard plaintive bells rung by the small boys on a leaden sea.

It was an unforgettable rite of passage and thanks to Tadashi Suzuki, the Toga festival and the British Council, thousands of people round the world now make their own marvellous tissue paper and willow lanterns as a result of *The Wasteland and the Wagtail* and the perfect chance vision that followed.

The Wasteland and the Wagtail was the most product-based of all our international forays. Language, time, distance and cultural habits did not permit any extensive participation from the local community, although by journeying up a mountain to parallel the life of King Lear, perhaps we enabled our audience to become participants in a kind of pilgrimage. We certainly wished to break down the pattern you get at such international festivals where everyone is just passively consuming art products. By involving them in a processional 'pilgrimage' and social dancing, we gave them a tangible physical and mental experience, which maybe drew them together with some sense of belonging to a temporary community at least.

Raising the Titanic

Part theatre, part encampment, part community gathering, market, social dance, pageant and regatta, *Raising the Titanic* was an allegorical political and mythological extravaganza.[7] It was a ritualised rejection of Western capitalism, workshopped, devised and acted out within a six-week residency. Commissioned by the London International Festival of Theatre (LIFT), it was performed in July and August 1983, on Regent's Canal Dock Basin in Limehouse, and played to 325 spectators on each of twelve evenings.

Before the bathyscaphe and video technology arrived to locate and scavenge the real sunken *Titanic* and before Hollywood's hyper hydraulics reared up to levitate Kate Winslet to the biggest box-office love affair ever, we humble alternative theatre practitioners assembled on a decaying dock in a decaying part of London with toolkits, caravans and barges. The idea was to use the story of the original disaster (a perfect mythic pattern) to reflect the ironies and contradictions of Thatcher's Britain and to point out that not too much had changed since 1912 in the Britain of 1983.

In the original *Titanic* disaster, 1513 people died through a mixture of arrogance, vanity, incompetence and greed. Much of the same symptoms were in evidence in the redevelopment of the docklands during the Thatcher era. Access to the dock water, filthy as it was, was about to be denied to the local population by the encroachment of an exclusive marina. In full view of our performance site, people lived in damp conditions and many houses were boarded up. We managed to get one old lady moved by showing photographs of her flat in the foyer of our show. Wealthy people were converting warehouses into penthouse flats. Dr David Owen drove over to peer at us on his way to his riverside home.

Some of the conditions that informed the shows were that air pollution from traffic was extreme, as was the noise from trucks, burglar alarms and police sirens. Unemployment was high. Meanwhile, in the Falklands (in 1982), young British and Argentinian men were killed. Some of them had gone into the Navy because they couldn't get work ashore. Some were killed on the *Sheffield* because our ship-building bosses didn't know or didn't care that Exocet missiles burn up aluminium, and some were killed on the *Belgrano* as it was in retreat.

There were many ironies and contradictions about the show. Welfare State International's professional team of performers, makers, technicians, engineers, designers, stage and publicity managers, cooks and community co-ordinators, on the ground in ancient white Army bell-tents and sundry caravans, numbered about sixty. About 150 other non-professionals were involved. Thirty-eight young adults and sixty children via the 'A' Team, a multimedia community arts company based on the Isle of Dogs, run by Elizabeth Lynch and others. Many local people were recruited via a community video and photography project and through the Chisenhale Dance project, based in Butlers Wharf. There were more local artists than local artisans.

Our technical research, on the hoof, into raising a big ship from the dock was hair-raising. As a basic sculptural armature, we had planned to use an iron barge filled with water and then to pump in air, driving out the water so that the ship would suddenly and miraculously bob up out of the blackness. It did work, but not twice nightly. The phenomenal pressure broke the back of the barge. I have always believed that you should start from ideas and images and that, however impossible they seem, a way will be found to realise them. Sooner or later. But this was Mayday drama. With a week to go to opening night, it was back to the drawing board. Reluctantly, we had to fall back on the old familiar sky hook and twenty tons of scaffolding.

Andy Plant, Tim Hunkin, Les Sharpe and Baz Kershaw (one of the authors of *Engineers of the Imagination*, who has a degree in engineering too) had to design, and build with their own hands a seventy-foot open framework simulating the stern of the ship that would sink below the water. They were an extraordinary team. No one else could have done it. By up-ending it, hanging from a massive mobile crane, we gave the illusion of a huge ship coming out of the deep.

Before it rose, two clowns in a rowing boat (Tony Lewery and Les Sharpe) first found a funnel just under the surface.[8] The rising funnel was the cue for the audience, who had been wandering round the first 'act' (a dockside market with itinerant players and our brass overture band the Titanic Syncopators), to move back to the raked stand of theatre seats. It was also the signal for a crane to drive in, to be hooked on to the sunken model of the ship.

The show was highly technical and timed to the split second. We had umpteen 'tech and dress' rehearsals. As the containers with their rigged sets were whisked in (with the precision of our fork-lift drivers becoming the star turn of the show), they had to be landed exactly for the lighting to penetrate. Meanwhile, David Clough, our intrepid firework wizard, was out in the dock, rigging the raw material for a fireball in an oil drum on a small raft; hidden behind the containers, a crew was clambering on to the greasy wet scaffolding to wire on paraffin-soaked paper rope so that the ship could burn as it sank; meanwhile, another crew were sliding a half-ton ice giant out of a refrigerator truck to mount it on a wheeled sledge ready for an iceberg procession. And so on.

As well as the feats of clever, last-minute engineering and ingenious sculptural water-borne pyrotechnics and lanterns, the show was held together with cameo scenes, an elaborate musical score, played with a big processional band directed by Luk Mishalle,[9] and many songs written or workshopped by Adrian Mitchell. Baz Kershaw wrote: 'It began in the early evening with a real open-air market with local community produce on sale, continued beyond dusk with a two-hour spectacular variety-style show and ended often after midnight with a high energy dance for the audience.'

The scenes give some idea of the elaborate structure: The Dockside Market, The Raising of the *Titanic*, The Container Tableaux (Dinner Party, Fancy Dress Ball, Stokers, Slaughter of the Albatross and Ice Procession, with Sea Wolves, etc.),

The Sweeping Away of the Containers, The Sinking of the Ship, The Trial of the Instigators on the Dock Edge, The Rise of the High-Rise Monsters from the Dock, The Ghost Ship of Small Lanterns. Nature as shadow play and iceberg as silver rain. Social dance for a participating audience. Finally, a launch of twelve sculptural lanterns mounted on boats was rowed by local participants in a quiet circuit in the darkness.

Overall, it was very well received, especially by the paying public. Criticisms were predictable. Theatre critics would only write about the wordy, scripted middle bit, when they could concentrate in their recognisable red theatre seats, and they hated or refused to understand the pairing of performance and participation. Real shark steaks were barbecued in the dockside market during the overture but our critics couldn't see what eating shark steaks or social dancing had to do with drama. Had they ever experienced events in a temple, say, in Bali, where the market, the priests, the shadow plays, the mythical representations and the social music are all fused together, or imagined the way things were in our own medieval cathedrals?

Local Marxist community-art lecturers hated the mythology and 'hippie' baroque extravagance, and sensual good-night-outers and some 'hippies' hated the blunt political didacticism. There were many other difficulties intrinsic to the event. With a total team of well over 200 people on the ground or on the water, I had to lead it remotely and hierarchically. (Not unlike Napoleon or the captain of the *Titanic!*). The exposed location in the inner city forced us to spend almost as much on security guards and fences as on the show itself. Based on their presentation of a rates bill, we offered cheap tickets to local residents, but not only were they outnumbered by middle-class LIFT customers, we also kept them and their children awake with the late-night fireworks. In another irony, the cargo containers which we piled on top of each other to build up the doll's-house-like set represented the very reason the economic life of the dock had come to an end. As far as I know, we didn't stop the marina being built, David Owen didn't come to see the show and we went way over budget.

But who could ever forget, among other images, the inimitable Marcel Steiner with his Smallest Theatre in the World (built on to a motorbike and sidecar) converted into a miniature version of the *Titanic?* The rear of the sidecar up-ended hydraulically (and therefore appeared to sink). Marcel, as the Captain of the Ship, checked you out. If you had big teeth, you were put into third class to experience a mildly rough ride. It was hilarious, rough, vintage street theatre in the best traditions of English music-hall. We all loved Marcel. He played King Lear in our community film version in Barrow in 1983. We asked him to take the role because, as an ex-worker in a rifle factory, he had more than enough street credibility to explain in the macho bars of Barrow why he had given up the arms trade to become a successful entertainer.

He died in July 1999. I last saw him by chance in Ulverston, at a street comedy festival that had become rather separate from us. With his tiny three-seater theatre, he was playing a wild, outrageous version of *The Hunchback of Notre Dame*. Banging an empty Calor-gas-cylinder bell and courageously and deliberately flaunting PC agendas, he was an hilarious over-the-top Quasimodo genuinely loved by all his audiences, whatever their own physical abilities. A lesson observed and celebrated by much Guinness and chocolate that night (which by this time was all he was able to eat).

False Creek – A Visual Symphony

This was a complex and ambitious site-specific performance and event. Maybe, apart from the building of Lanternhouse at the end of the next decade, it was our most complex collage of events, history, people, mythology and occasion. Commissioned as one of hundreds of events on the downtown waterfront round False Creek in Vancouver, the site allocated to Canada's EXPO in 1986, it was a composition in five acts performed in five locations between 9.30 p.m. and 1.30 a.m. and repeated eleven times between 9 and 20 July.

The process began early in 1985 and included my making two site visits, one in the summer and the other in the late winter of 1986. After writing an initial scenario and a detailed script (most of which was jettisoned), thirteen of our company and sixteen selected musicians, performers and stage crew from Vancouver met up on site on 10 June. Then everything (performances, mechanical sculpture, costumes, props, songs and music) was put together in a month.

We were going to invent *The Night the Racoons ate Dogmeat*, a vaudeville parody and parable with anthropomorphic creek creatures. Eventually, by a very long process, we ended up with *Mirrorman*, an hour-long musical variant on *Pinocchio*, sung and acted out within the envelope of numerous animated tableaux located in different parts of the site which were linked by participatory processions, mythology and occasion. The very glossy early publicity stated:

> The whole world is heading to Vancouver, British Columbia, Canada for EXPO 86
> – a World Exposition in the grand tradition! Eighty nations, provinces, territories,

states and corporations will gather on 70 waterfront hectares in the heart of Canada's largest West Coast city. You are going to love the way the world unfolds at EXPO 86. By day it's a kaleidoscope of international pavilions, fabulous entertainment, spine-tingling rides, and food from around the world! By night it's fireworks and lasers, fine dining, sensational cabarets and the unparalleled Royal Bank/EXPO 86 World Festival of the performing arts. If you yearn for adventure, the world has never been more fascinating, more fun or more accessible!

In the course of our research we discovered that much of the history of the people who lived around False Creek had not been documented. In particular, there were immense gaps when it came to the native (Indian) people, and hundreds of squatters who lived in shacks, until many were burned out by the authorities in the 1950s.

There was however, over the last century, one clear pattern – a wave movement, which continually rose and fell from boom to depression and back, where amazing occansional affluence and invention were replaced by frequent decline and stagnation. Always a minority suffered, be they native Indians, Chinese, Japanese, poor and elderly whites and women. This pattern was maintained to 1986, when three suicides were attributed to the eviction of tenants from downtown hotels, to make way for EXPO tourists. The creek was the microcosm of capitalism. It was also a shop window of the values and lifestyle of the affluent (including Welfare State International).

The hidden agenda was real estate, increasing the value of the waterfront and ultimately establishing a free trade zone to attract investment mainly from Asia to North West Canada. Some individuals were going to make a lot of money, and it could be argued that the cultural jamboree was an elaborate smokescreen as it is of course in so many of these other world jamborees, wether it is an EXPO, the Olympic Games or football. This is nothing new of course; the arts patronage of the Medici in Florence were equally hand in hand with energetic commercial dealing as it does with Saatchi and Saatchi. Most artists in most systems have to work out how they deal with the dominant culture.

On the first reconnaissance in the first local newspaper I picked up was a photograph and a story about an old man who had killed himself by jumping out of a high-rise hotel. The carefully composed photograph – a small white tent covering the body and a group of policemen and medics standing or kneeling to gaze in horror pity at the dead man – was a contemporary *pietà*. After making a set of drawings I discovered there were parallel and bigger white tents erected

81

<u>programme</u>

we are not rich because of what we
take from others but through what we give
to others. "

man can only interfere with the whole of
the Mystery through action. "

Now Fireworks at 10.30
Site open until 12

after the cataclysmic fire which consumed Vancouver in 1886. I then took my sketch to the City Museum Anthropology to see an extraordinary historical collection of artefacts from local native people. As well as magnificent Kwakiutl transformation masks (where the wooden jaw of a sea monster would open up to reveal the mask of another demon inside), there was also information about a truly different system; the Polatch.

> When one's heart is glad, he gives away gifts. It was given to us by our Creator to
> be our way of doing things, to be our way of rejoicing, we who are Indian. The
> Polatch was given to us to be our way of expressing joy.[10]

The word 'potlatch' means 'to give' and came to designate a ceremony common to peoples on the north-west coast. At the ceremonies of naming children, marriage, transferring rights and privileges and mourning the dead, guests witnessing the event are given gifts. The more gifts distributed, the higher the status achieved by the giver. I pondered whether, if we had a generous gift exchange between world nations with equal reciprocity rather than hierarchical relationships, then maybe there would be no need for excessive splurges like EXPO which seem only to ensure that the rich get richer.

It was not surprising that missionaries and government agents imprisoned the locals (and stole their artefacts) whenever they practised a potlatch. Such a daring and primitive method of sharing and distributing surplus was too revolutionary for the alliance of Capitalism and Christianity.

The history of Vancouver and False Creek in particular revealed just how many times groups on the fringes of different waves of capitalist expansionism had become alienated or dispossessed. Indians, Chinese, squatters, loggers, prostitutes and now old people in cheap lets were moved out, as their land was claimed by the developers of real estate. I wrote a song which summed up the process of capitalist boom and bust in Vancouver.

In 1872
You built a wooden bridge
over river water and flood.
You built a timber mill
Poisoned the Creek with acid mud.

In 1886
You built a railway bridge
over salmon fishing traps.

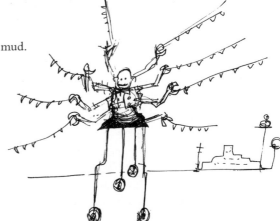

You brought the coasts together
But the fishing could not last.

In 1932
You built a concrete bridge
Over Squamish apple blossom
The natives lost their orchards
Their trees were all forgotten.

In 1954
You built a grander bridge
Over squatters floating homes.
Tourists brought their yachts
Then their glitter domes.

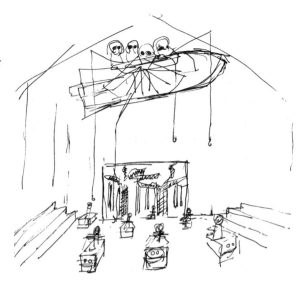

The biggest glitter dome was a giant geodesic golf ball at one end of False Creek. In front of it, the dock opened up to make a small harbour and I decided after days of anxious pacing round the huge building site that this area and that of the adjacent miniature Folk Life park, with the only lawn in the concrete vista, were the best locations for our work.

One of the joys of dropping in on other cultures is discovering amazing stories which may be commonplace locally but which are jewels to new eyes. The raven is a mystical bird in many cultures and in Europe we tend to stress its sinister side. For north-west-coast Indians, it is the amoral trickster and creator. In Haida legend, Raven steals the light, brings the sun, moon and stars to the earth and finds the first humans in a clam shell. Raven is a liminal being, prowling the areas between boundaries and categories. Raven can step into chaos and tap the raw power for creation. At the end of our show, it was Raven who led the audience out into the night after they had been inside the fake longhouse.

I wrote a song called 'On a Clear Day' which derived from Pauline Johnson's story 'Deer Lake' in which she describes how, until the day of his death, the first Capilano fisherman searched for the unknown river up which the great seal travelled from False Creek to Deer Lake.

We made a two-headed metal bird which flew on wires in the roof of the longhouse. It was a contemporary equivalent of a Salish Indian myth about such a two-headed bird which causes paralysis and a three-masted ship based on the first view the native people had of Europeans. 'A floating island of trees . . . a winged canoe manned by the white-faced dead.' A plague reference came from the

Tugboat with smoke, Vancouver EXPO, 1986

smallpox scare of 1892, when loads of the sick, frequently women from the red-light district who had been visited by sailors from the 'Empresses', were taken by boat to Dead Man's Island. After my trips to Canada and before I started to write scenarios, there was a considerable exchange of letters, books, tapes, ideas and photographs channelled through the researches of Howard Broomfield.

We had planned to work with local professional artists so we workshopped with a score of mainly local theatre workers, who were gathered through an imperfect mix of chance, publicity, lectures and contacts of contacts. Kathleen Doody, for example, came over from Shadowlands in Toronto, a company she had developed fully from our 1981 *Tempest on Snake Island*.

Special Delivery Dance Music Theatre, who toured internationally, were already resident on the EXPO site with a large-scale, tightly choreographed obscure 'ritual' dance piece called *Samarambi: Pounding of the Heart*. Their extravagant Katakhali-style sculptural costumes were wonderful. Snake-in-the-Grass Moving Theatre were well known for accessible transcultural clowning; their wild Japanese front garden in North American suburbia was also a joyous refuge. Pamela Harris was already performing a stunning leaping bird transformation on very high stilts and Themba Tana (originally from South Africa) and Ross Barrett, a Vancouver-based rock'n'roll jazz composer, together played an unbelievable number of instruments.

The spread of talent was enormous, but I think I vowed afterwards never to work again with so many nice but demanding artists unless I had had at least a year of close contact with them. It was a nightmare trying to make an integral show that accommodated everyone's different expectations, styles and energies in the time available. Everyone was very professional. We didn't quarrel, or I have forgotten if we did. But there was a constant inevitable negotiation of a shared language, rewriting and rehearsal tryouts. At the Welfare State International end, we had a very strong team too, all equally talented, egocentric and voracious. They also took a bit of lassoing, but at least most of us had worked together for a decade or so and had built up considerable trust and pleasurable creative rapport.

As usual, a few wild cards popped up. If they arrive with their own funding, they can provide unexpected additional richness. In this case, Mike Hares from Over the Top puppet company, on a research sabbatical from England, took on the role of Gassy Jack, a legendary saloon-keeper from 1867. We asked him to make new marionettes for a stretching solo appearance in which he demonstrated all the spectres dredged up from the bed of the creek. In the show, Gassy Jack's wife spoke for dispossessed women from all ages of the creek.

Then Bob Bossin arrived with his Medicine Man show in which he sold remedies for nuclear war. There was a place for him, too, in the wandering busking overture. After all, it was estimated in 1986 that approximately fifty nuclear-armed or nuclear-powered warships would visit Vancouver, notwithstanding a local by-law proclaiming the city a nuclear-free zone. Almost a hundred years before, to the day, a fire holocaust had destroyed wooden Vancouver.

The biggest wild card was the site itself. How were we to gather a crowd, then hold a consistent audience for sufficient time to develop our theme symphonically? Traditionally we create our shows outside, yet here was a random audience that had already paid a high price for a walkabout ticket and there were always intruding sounds, dominant plastic imagery, massive light pollution, tribes of obese people on electric wheelchairs devouring chips and mayonnaise (more surreal than anything we could devise), security guards whose radios never stopped chattering, and then every night there was an obligatory forty-five minutes of fireworks and lasers. Dusk had been obliterated and planetary rhythm buried under the clatter of commerce where even concrete could be turned to gold in the glare of never-ending sodium lights.

During the day, it was appropriate, with the proper health and safety barriers, to have our engineers build their fantastical machines on site (under a noisy and dusty motorway bridge) and daily they drew a good crowd because it is rare to see artists at work. That was a bonus. Parts of the show had to be designed round flocks of close-up role-playing musicians and busking performers who could dart into the crowd. (Mike Hares did a subversive Charles-and-Di wedding in a walking booth.) Parts of it were in self-contained parameters which could hold a crowd of any size. The central section required tickets, which were free but had to be sought; the interval was timed to coincide with the firework display; and the final coda was played out very late on a deserted site which was strange and atmospheric.

We were not looking to produce strict dramatisations of historical information, but rather, abstract performances with documentary inferences. We were looking for a series of resonating images which would present a mythic pattern of aspects of life in and around False Creek. There was a sense of science fiction, as if the images were seen from a different time in the future – and had become a legend of what went wrong . . . 'We tell a story for and of our age. A poetic legend re-constituted with fragments dredged from the swamp of history's brackish creek.'

At 9.20 p.m., by the edge of the East Dock Basin, our buskers gathered a crowd by any trick in their book. At 9.30, from over the greasy water, a creaky old fishing boat steamed in with foul black smoke spidering from its funnel, silhouetted against the sunset. The crowd spotted it half a mile away. In a marina of celebrity yachts and cruisers, our ugly duckling was a compelling and vulgar sight. Patriotic mayors with garbled speeches, a ringmaster in a top hat and a raggedy brass band overacted in a rough street style which increased the vulgarity. The fanfare was completed as ten rotten herrings were detonated in a ten-herring salute.

The boat had trawled up a strange canister from the black creek. Lying starkly on the upper deck, the shiny shark design recalled the severed tail fins of an ancient Cadillac cut from a multiple pile-up. With due ceremony, the canister was craned over the dock parapet and lowered on to the back of the Limping Horse of History. While we were all looking out to sea, the Horse, a staggering and honking steamrolling self-propelled type of machine, had ratcheted itself in very slowly from its pitstop under the motorway to the north side of the quay.

Cunningly invented by Andy Plant and Greville White, who had done deals in every aluminium scrapyard in downtown Vancouver, its battered but gleaming body contained a hydraulic ram ready for the end of Act One. The beast, complete with its new canister, was led off in carnival style by a percussion band. As the whole contraption was propelled a few hundred metres to end up on the lawn in the folk-life area, many curious spectators followed in procession. Shark surgeons and engineers materialised and with many a blue flash and arcs of sparks from a grinder, plus pyrotechnic strobes, they operated to cut open the mysterious container. There was an eruption and some very loud bangs until suddenly an organic form started to rise from the split cylinder. A mirrored skull the size of a Mini car covered in metal plates shuddered and rose on the ram to the height of a house. It was now relatively dark and as the skull shimmered in reflective green neon light, red smoke poured from its teeth. We claimed the apparition as the birth of the spirit of Mirrorman.

This provided a good opportunity to talk to the big crowd and offer tickets for Act Two, soon to be performed in the fake longhouse. In the meantime, they could watch the fireworks and then return at 11 p.m. for the hour-long fairy-tale in which they would learn of the past life of Mirrorman.

In a series of flashbacks, dreams, nightmares, songs and dances, Act Two told the story of how Mirrorman, an entrepreneurial financier who told lies and whose nose grew enormously, was ultimately eaten by a shark. Following a disastrous quarrel between loggers over the last cedar tree by the creek (presented as a shadow puppet play), he was born from the tree as a wooden puppet. During his journey

misery
ghosts of Loggers are tortured to
Reveal the secrets of the Lost River
of Gold

Donkey Treadmill

to locate his missing heart, Mirrorman became real. His conscience (in the form of a swamp roach and a raven) warned him of dangers while a mysterious Bag Lady with an ancient shopping trolley looked on. On his journey, he was continually waylaid by two villains (Mars and Mammon), disguised as a fox and a cat. They took him to Gassy Jack's Museum of Creek Ghosts, where he almost became a showbiz star, but he escaped to the Field of Miracles and climbed the Money Fat Tree (at EXPO).

Tortured by nightmares and caught between the temptations of greed (for instance, he was strapped to an eight-foot whirling roulette wheel) and the ghosts who offer premonitions of death or salvation, he was nearly rescued by a spectral bride who seduced him from the Kingdom of Greed and Death. But under the pressures of Fox and Cat, he succumbed to vanity and avarice, manipulating all before him until he turned into a self-consuming shark. Terry Hunter from Special Delivery, who played the part, gave a stunning performance, mixing mime and dance, effortlessly transforming from a collapsed wooden marionette into a spiky vaudeville madman. Finally, he climbed into the roof of the theatre and grabbed a magenta neon heart – and electrocuted himself in a geyser of smoke. There was extensive neon on the EXPO Site. The neon factory was owned by the president of EXPO, who had built up his fortune by selling second-hand cars.

In the last *pietà*, recalling the suicide photograph from the newspaper, his creator, his father carpenter (played by Sue Gill), held him across her knee while the whole tableau was enclosed and frozen inside the jaws of a giant shark/Cadillac. This had driven in from the back of the space and, in a wonderful theatrical coup, unexpectedly split open to reveal the *pietà*. Thanks to that Kwakiutl whale mask in the Museum of Anthropology.[11]

The next act was outside again on the deserted folk-life lawn. A salmon barbecue stayed open, serving beer, and the evening developed into a participatory carnival dance celebrating tentative new growth. The Welfare State International Golfball Terminal orchestra played jigs, reels, waltzes, polkas, salsa and rock'n'roll and Sue called the dances. At the end of the dancing, the new wooden puppet effigy was gently placed in a simple rope cradle, surrounded by tiny hand-made paper lanterns and paraded back to the East Dock from where the canister had arrived. Now that everyone except for our audience and a few desultory security guards had abandoned the bustling site, the dock became still and strangely beautiful. As the boats had left, there was space left in the black water for the big golf-ball geodesic structure to be delicately reflected. Slowly we rowed the cradle out to the

centre of this reflection. Here, Tony Lewery had constructed a raft, a monumental geodesic bamboo boat. With the cradle inside, it revolved, spiralling pinpoints of clear fire into the dominant reflections of the glitter dome's electric light. As Luk Mishalle, our musical director, played a lilting soprano sax which bounced and echoed from the creek, a Canada goose flew overhead, every night. It wasn't a real Canada goose, but another wondrous Tony Lewery invention. A big Canada goose made with discarded plastic Venetian blinds found in a skip flapping underneath the carriage of one of the aerial cable cars. It shat, too. A big gob of white emulsion paint dropping on target towards the floating cradle. Just before the obvious lyricism degenerated into too much schmaltz. A good goodnight.

We needed something lyrical and earthy to hang on to because the whole project was framed by death. On Monday, 3 June, six members of Welfare State International, myself included, were nearly killed over Iceland in our Boeing 747, which passed within fifty feet of another aircraft. We only found out when we landed and read about it in the paper.

Then, on 5 July, the day before our dress rehearsal, Howard Broomfield, our researcher, killed himself. Theatre and ritual suddenly became indistinguishable. On the first and last nights, we explained the situation to the audience. His death was totally unexpected. On the evening of 4 July, he had returned to our workshop to remind me that we had forgotten another bridge which needed to be added to our history song. All had seemed normal.

We told ourselves that the little tree planted in Mirrorman's burned heart cavity was a tree for Howard. Koko (the Japanese performer with Snake-in-the-Grass Moving Theatre) nurtured it, took it home every night and carefully watered it.

After our last show, we stayed up all night and at dawn took our tree on a little procession and, with Howard's family and his faithful dog, carefully planted it in an appropriate garden of remembrance. It was in a wild inner-city spot, near a motorway. Probably the same motorway under which we had constructed the Limping Horse of History.

On the Perimeter

From 1984 onwards, we also all made some touring shows designed to fit into given spaces such as village halls, community centres, domestic front rooms and, on occasion, studio and other sweaty black-box theatre spaces. The economics of touring theatre forced us to work with very small casts of usually two people. Initially, we had the luxury of a support crew of two or three more people plus

Sue Gill in *On the Perimeter*, 1988

a big van, but we managed to reduce it to two people with an estate car. This was historic. The first touring show of this type was a two-hander about the revolutionary mutineer Percy Toplis (which was later made for TV by Alan Bleasdale). Written by New Zealander Ian Wedde, Boris and I performed it in a vaudeville style round northern venues in 1984.

In 1985, Sue Gill and I created an enjoyable two-hander, *On the Perimeter*, which we toured over three seasons, first with Sue and me as performers, then with Tim Fleming and his partner, Elaine Whitewood. The script allowed for audience contact and for the story to be carried on image and music. The big delight was how much stuff we could generate from two big suitcases. Even the lighting was just one anglepoise lamp operated by a front-row member of the audience and one table lamp balanced on a painter's big easel which doubled up as a table and repository for conjurers' silks.

The story goes that Sybil, a slightly paranoid housewife, imagines she had a man who has left. The audience is never quite sure if this is true. In a series of communications to a space tramp, she confesses her fears and dreams and her longing for a seaside kiosk. Tom, the postman, collects her letters and postcards and, to make her happy, lands on the doormat as her Space Tramp. In a delicate courtship, they fence with existential questions involving the nature of the universe, the bombing of Dresden on St Valentine's Day (the biggest single deliberate destruction of civilians ever) and the origins of an extraordinary blue lobster.

Tom has learned conjuring by mail order, rather badly, and in a series of Tommy Cooper-inspired gaffes, creates snowflakes and burning children from torn paper and even a one-clawed lobster modelled in blue balloons. He invents an extensive universe and a big bang. Under their chins, audience volunteers hold metre-wide black felt rolls which unfold, revealing painted silver skeletal forms, transforming them into 'galactic monsters'. Then he tosses a giant white weather balloon into the auditorium, gives people tiny lighted candles on the ends of thin willow sticks and plays a wavering tune on a tin whistle. The balloon bounces slowly on outstretched hands while time winds down, until five or more minutes later some or all of the candles come together under the balloon, which eventually bursts, scattering 500 fragments of silver star foil.

In the inevitable denouement, Sybil rapidly sees through Tom's clumsy disguise but admits she always knew her dreams were fake. His crime is to undermine her conscious day dreaming. Sybil pretends to forgive him and they open a kiosk together, pretending they will live happily for ever after.

In performance, the final scene was worthy of the best pantomime walk-downs. We stuck bamboo poles in tubes in the sides of the weighted suitcases and erected a kiosk in seconds. Draped with bunches of bright feather flowers, paper cuts, rubber chickens, masks, silk fishes and Japanese parasols hung with tin stars, we too believed we could transform any space anywhere. And we did. From village halls to pubs, we drew people back to live theatre. Once we enacted it as a mystery trip. We started off on a coach with air-hostess life jackets, escape instructions and individual yoghurt-pot breathing masks dropping down on strings. We left the bus to drive ahead, overtaking it at ninety miles per hour to welcome people into the top room of a small country pub. *On the Perimeter* succeeded everywhere, except in a few art centres. You need promoters who want you and pass the word through an active network which arts centres often don't tap into.

The Lantern Coach

We didn't develop this until the late eighties, but after strenuous tours into other people's inhospitable venues, it was a reactive attempt to establish our own portable environment. Through clever carpentry and welding by Greville White, we extended the back of a Leyland single-decker bus with a folding compartment, put trapdoors in the floor and roof and upholstered red velvet benches so that thirty people could sit inside the bus and watch a little proscenium stage at the back.

It worked well for three winters. We usually parked in a school or institution car park or in a city shopping precinct and switched on the generator to perform five or six thirty-minute shows each day. In *Jack and the Beanstalk*, we pulled a beanstalk up into the roof and a giant, or at least his massive boot, appeared through the ceiling. In *Aladdin*, jewels and hieroglyphic cave paintings materialised in ultraviolet gauzes and in *Robinson Crusoe in Space* we invented a computer parrot programmed with all the knowledge in the world. It broke down and could only recite half the Lord's Prayer intercut with a fraction of the recipe for Lemon Meringue Pie.

I loved *The Lantern Coach*. It took me back to my childhood, when the only theatre I saw was old-fashioned pantomime at the New Theatre in Hull – I was ten. I would return home to make puppets, paint scenery for a table-top theatre and perform it for half a crown cash at children's parties. I can still smell the newspapers for papier mâché boiling on the Aga. *The Lantern Coach* provided the opportunity once again to imagine, write, sing, make bits and pieces and play accordion music, even changing the lights, which the small cast operated themselves (via a domestic dimmer switch from Woolworths), hidden stage right.

These simple if not quaint transformations with sequinned scenery, mirrorball illusions, spray-on snow, rhyming couplets and live music were great fun and about as far from avant-garde art as Miss Muffet is from *Vogue*. With Tim Fleming playing Jack, I could even take on another first, as Widow Twanky. Tim himself became a regular pantomime dame, playing the role three years running in Wakefield Opera House's civic panto. On one desperate housing estate, one Christmas Eve in West Cumbria, where the typical gift at a children's party was an orange each, one child believed we were a travelling TV. They had never seen any live theatre.

I hope *The Lantern Coach* form is not already a relic. Without the habit of seeing live performance and with so many tight commercial productions dependent on electronics, I fear children are disappointed if a show is not as seamless as the video and as speedy as the fast-forward soundbite mutation.

Hollow Ring

In 1993, when we were just recovering from near bankruptcy, we risked this next two-hander touring experiment. Pete Moser and me in a Mercedes minibus, back seats removed for boxes of tricks and fifteen concrete discs (the bases of trees) each weighing a quarter of a hundredweight. Leaving behind all that boring Arts Council politicking and fundraising for one-night stands on the road again was invigorating, although loading half a ton of concrete into the van at midnight was no fun.

We took it out twice in 1993. The first run, in May, for the 'Deliciously Different' Festival of Performance Art in the north-west, was mistakenly described by us as a 'work in progress' tour. In England, if you want to set up a genuinely open theatrical experiment on a tiny budget with ongoing changes and appropriate feedback, keep away from the touring circuit and critics and assessors who demand finished, polished product.

The second run in the autumn was much more successful. As usual, we had to believe that *Hollow Ring* was breaking new ground (and to some extent it was). As always, our trajectory of dreaming fell short of our intention, but on reflection, aspects of this and also of *Wireman*, our next touring experiment with a younger generation (see *New Generations*), have all fed into our current (2002) Lanternhouse preoccupations. In our programme, we described *Hollow Ring* as:

> A secular prayer, moving from blackness via shadow to action and light, it offers a dramatic meditation on how to laugh facing the luxury of despair.

Hollow Ring was intended to develop as a catalyst within gatherings such as conferences dealing with violence and grow to a larger 'symphonic form' for a landscape arena with day-long performance, feasting and social dancing. Providing a set of emblematic icons for different meditations, the basic structure was bone simple.

In the overture, a stereotypical handyman in a brown warehouse coat sits at a DIY Workmate bench where he cuts out delicate white paper silhouettes of a stereotypical central European peasant family with a scalpel. The handyman and a troubadour play a melancholic waltz on accordion and flugelhorn.

Scene One represents a dark thicket of trees (the branches stuck into the concrete blocks). The white paper cuts stuck on to the trunks or hanging from black branches fluoresce a little in the dark. With one match, the caretaker sets fire to them, carefully collecting the ashes to place them in a big, round leather box.

In Scene Two, while a troubadour sings and tells the story of the concentration-camp guard who spared an inmate in Auschwitz (after recognising him as a fiddle-player from his old town), some trees are cleared and the ashes grow into leather shadow puppets.

In Scene Three, a big circle of hazel branches is picked up from the forest floor. A pure white canvas circle is gathered from the leather box and stretched and bound by hessian rope to the hazel. This circular screen is then suspended in the branches for a violent and cathartic shadow-play telling of 'The Juniper Tree' by the Brothers Grimm; a story of a stepmother's terrible jealousy and her come-uppance as Fate disguised as a paradise bird drops a millstone on her head.

Scene Four sees a strange expedition in which the small workbench becomes a pier over the unknown, and the pretend-paranoid handyman fends off an attack of red plastic clockwork crabs and an innocuous bullfighter.

We'll dance along the pier my friend
No looking down below.
If we laugh beneath the mirror ball
Then all our fears will go.
We can beat whatever comes
From underneath the pier.
So dance along the cracks my friend
and laugh away your fear.

Scene Five is a resolution in which the hazel circle becomes the horizontal frame of a carousel. As it spins on a central axis tree, the peasant family are transformed again, into colourful lanterns dangling at equal distance round the circle. As the lanterns spin, the two performers play soprano saxophone and flugelhorn in a soft, lilting polka.

Once we had knocked it into shape, Pete Moser and I were pleased with *Hollow Ring* and pleased that we had taken the risk of parachuting once again into the world of small-scale touring, despite all its tribulations and contradictions. There were the usual questions about the relationship between acting and performing, communicating information and creating art, stereotypes and archetypes, and the moral imperatives of how far to go to move or manipulate an audience. Was it theatre? Was it really a vehicle for meditation? Some people hated it. Some were over the moon.

The Juniper Tree story, which is a thoroughly nasty tale about a stepmother's jealousy and her manipulation of sibling rivalry, went down surprisingly well with some women, who said it revealed the truth with an appropriate symbolism. Certainly, as in a medieval altarpiece, where an artist paints the blood of the Crucifixion in perfect carmine red, we had made the leather shadow puppets very well to counterpoint the energetic expressionist violence of the performance and the stories.

One critic said we were ripping off Jewish history and making gratuitous gain from the pain of people in concentration camps. Well, Pete is Jewish; his father came to England as a refugee from Berlin. But did the autobiographical connection make it more real or just more therapeutic for Pete? Great art is often based on personal experience. For instance, Grünewald's Isenheim Altarpiece was based on his experience of the Black Death.

In the finale, as the delicate lanterns swung slowly round our naive, home-made carousel and Pete and I sat on the leather box, playing good, simple music, in 90 per cent of our audiences there was a palpable joy and gratitude for the gift we had struggled to create. The questions, the doubts and the anxieties never stop, but at some point you have to stop worrying, construct the art with your hands and deliver the outcome as best you can. Our job is to react, absorb, objectify, make and present. It is never perfect and after digesting the process you go on to the next attempt, putting stuff out into the public domain again and again. As you learn, there are many critics and many jealousies and many contexts which can deliberately or unwittingly destroy your efforts.

★

Although *Hollow Ring* came eight years after *On the Perimeter*, the touring story was surprisingly similar. In rural communities we received rapturous receptions and sell-outs, but not infrequently in subsidised venues the middle-class audience, saturated with too much choice, viewed us as just another art commodity.

In the first decade of touring (1968–78), we learned our trade on the road. In the next decade (1978–88), we honed our skills and put the tricks together in complex event tapestries. In the extensive away residencies in Toronto (1981), Japan (1982), London (1983) and Vancouver (1986), we continued our attempts to find new audiences for theatre, or more often more precisely 'ritual performance', and new ways of establishing a community outside the black box; parachuting on to the street, into parks and on docksides, islands and exhibition sites. Making 'both topographical and mythical journeys of exploration and reclamation'.[12]

By using the modernist strategies of Dadaism, Futurism and Russian Constructivism of the 1920s cross-cut with popular traditions of English culture such as pageants, mumming plays, carnival and seasonal ceremonies, we developed our own glossary of strong images to reflect Western society in a contemporary way. In the eighties, as Britain was grinding through a shifting era of upheaval and crisis, we were increasingly seeking the full creative involvement of the audience and/or the community, both before and after the performance. But as we continued to intertwine our life and art work, we realised that it was crazy to try to do this on tour.

There will always be a role for the stranger or the nomadic clown, the wandering outsider, to drop into a fixed community. *Tempest on Snake Island* in Toronto was a perfect example of this. In the 'mediation of outsiders', people will tell you secrets, knowing that you will eventually leave. Sometimes they may rally round you because, sick of their own kind, they need an external focus. Even if you become a scapegoat – in which case, you have to have a good escape route – you can have a healing effect. This may work by lancing boils with cathartic satire or by using the classic fool's approach of persuading audiences to laugh at themselves by recognising their worst traits in you and your performance.

It is quite a different matter if you descend with a whole mobile village. It took us a while to learn this and to develop beyond our role as transient and world-hopping jesters; to understand that it might be better to have a solid root for an extended period in one major location, with our own fixed community.

Hollow Ring shadow play, 1993

The Barrow Years

In 1983, the northern barons of the Regional Arts Association in Newcastle-upon-Tyne were making little headway in Barrow-in-Furness. Virtually every other local authority in the northern region was paying a small levy from their rates to buy into the services of Northern Arts. Many Barrow city councillors were stubbornly proud of their non-compliance and the town did not have a policy for the arts.

Meanwhile, in 1978, Welfare State International had left its Burnley base for a temporary office in our administrator's house in Toxteth in Liverpool and in 1979 the Fox family moved to Ulverston, just nine miles from Barrow. As Baz Kershaw put it, 'in 1983 when most alternative theatre groups were running for ideological cover, Welfare State International began a seven-year residency in Barrow.'[1]

Propelled by experiences carried over from the Australian journey, increasingly dissatisfied with the transience of touring and still searching for some kind of Utopia, the jesters needed to settle in a community and develop more holistic work over a long period. The hunter-gatherer nomads were becoming pastoralists. Northern Arts needed a figurehead, a pathfinder for arts. So, a deal was struck. This stage of the quest continued until 1990. In seven years, together with the people of Barrow, we made a massive amount of art within the community.

Barrow-in-Furness is a friendly enough working-class town of 60,000 people, willing to accept strangers if you make the effort to connect. Despite their tourism office, which tries to attract cruise liners to this 'entrance to the Lake District', it tends to get an adverse press. Overnight, city journalists zap the place with patronising and melodramatic carve-ups and clear off fast for the cheque.

Invariably, they and well-meaning bishops photograph Barrow Island, with its cosy Glasgow-style period tenements festooned with washing, to prove that this is a poverty-stricken community. It isn't, financially, culturally or socially.

A variety of architecture reflects the taste and skills of the many immigrants (like Glasgow tenement dwellers) who, at the end of the last century, came to the docks, railways, shipbuilding, iron-ore and steel mills to make this place home. Once a tiny but vibrant 'Chicago' (unfortunately without any black immigrants), dominated by industries such as Vickers Shipbuilding and Engineering Ltd (VSEL), then Marconi, now BAE Systems, it now has the usual shopping mall, supermarkets, a rubber-stamped so-called 'Hollywood Park' with predictable chain stores and a cinema complex. It survives economically and is still dominated by the shipyard, which, since 1983 has reduced its work-force from 14,000 to 4,000, and it is still falling.

They regularly stage amateur dramas and musicals, plus well-made, energetic home-grown pantomimes, usually directed by David Marcus, who also played Raygel, one of Lear's daughters, in our community film *King Real*. Until the birth of the Barracudas Carnival Band, which developed out of Pete Moser's 1988 summer project, the annual summer carnival is normally based on trucks with minimal floats, dancing classes propelled by mothers and children and a few gangs of self-consciously sexy and jolly hoofers dancing in Shirley Temple, Disney and showbiz fancy dress.

In a vibrant music scene, first-rate singers and musicians play in pit orchestras, the high-standard Vickers/British Aerospace Silver Band (subsidised by the firm) and a trad jazz band, the Terry Turner Big Band. There is a male-voice choir and many younger pop and thrash bands who, in clubs and occasional festivals, belt out both covers and sometimes their own strong material. The Barracudas go from strength to strength and since 2001 Boom Dang, a young persons' novice drumming band, has grown well.

People work hard and play hard in Barrow. There is little tradition of original art or going to see plays, and the majority (particularly the young) prefer the five night-clubs on the 'Gaza Strip' or the many working-men's-style clubs. Much of the interest in the arts is generated by Helen Wall, a versatile and committed arts reporter on the daily *North West Evening Mail*. The *Mail* has the widest coverage of the arts in any local paper I have found, and was instrumental in the popularity of our shows, *Town Hall Tattoo* and *Shipyard Tales*. Socially, Barrow has always worked through an extended support network of families over generations. The way to Barrow is 'the longest cul-de-sac in the world', according to Mike Harding.

Barrow's like an orphan
a long way up the line
One way in and way out.
Forgotten every time
You've never heard of Barrow
I suppose you've heard of Blackpool, Southport, Morecambe too
But what of dear old Barrow
Barrow by the Irish sea.[2]

Barrow's isolation is its strength and weakness. They built liners there – 'like wedding cakes they sailed past my garden,' sings Lena in *What'll the Lads Do On Monday?* – but the main industry has always been arms dealing. I once attended a lecture by a Vickers marketing man who maintained that – 'We don't care what we sell as long as we have a contract.' The company started with the Vickers machine-gun; Trident nuclear submarines were built there until the late nineties; and now other submarines plus warships and Howitzers are on the books. In case of a nuclear emergency, should a submarine reactor go critical, local schools have stocks of iodine pills and the infamous, dangerous, narrow A590 from Lancaster, the one way in and out, can be sealed off with one road block. Equally, there is a sealed-off labour force for the one major employer at the shipyard, who have always leaned on the Labour council to discourage any major competition from any other firm.

Barrow has entertainment, very cheap housing, the Irish Sea, the Lake District, extended family networks, regular work routines and a fairly secure environment. In the eighties, despite its latent socialist tendencies, it was the perfect Thatcher town, rendered docile by threats of unemployment (with low wages), mortgages, credit-debits, family ties and the tyranny of distance. A couple of years after we bought our house in Ulverston, a neighbour gave me a ticket for a submarine launch. Today, submarines are lowered on a lift into a deep dock inside the huge macaroni-coloured hangers which dominate the Barrow skyline. But twenty years ago, the launch procedure was less secretive, more traditional and awe-inspiring. Angled on a slipway, pointing to the sea, lay a massive iron carcass. As long as a small football pitch and as fat as a distended whale, it towered above us. Higher still, on a scaffold platform, Navy brass, a bishop, a royal, an MP, councillors and a champagne bottle were poised.

On cue, the bottle was smashed, huge oak chocks were knocked away, piles of rusty dragchains, with links as big as Alsatians, unfolded and hundreds of tons of greasy black metal gathered momentum to slide thunderously into Walney Channel. The accuracy was phenomenal. One streamlined lump near the massive tail fin had, for instance, to penetrate a small cable loop set up vertically on the port side, seemingly hundreds of yards away. This connected critically with cables from tugs to restrain the beast from hurtling across the Channel.

The VSEL Works Band played 'Rule Britannia' and 'God Save the Queen' and many doffed their hats and cheered. The scale of the firepower and the showing off of the missile tubes was terrifying, but equally significant was the physical class division of the event. Our 'rulers' were perched loftily above spectators and the thousands of workers, below; slaves economically conscripted to a huge military industrial monster, even though a few apprentices defiantly wore CND badges. Here was the launch of a submersible metal planet, an incredible, self-contained and sealed ecosystem with its own climate designed to survive with 135 men under an ice cap for six months. What skill, what resources (a billion quid each, from our taxes) and what motivation! But where was the majority participation? And how on earth, above or below sea level, in this context could 'the Arts' have any relevance whatsoever?

King Real and the Hoodlums

In 1987, Robin Thornber described Barrow in the *Guardian* as a 'cultural desert'. It wasn't and isn't. But in 1983 it didn't have an arts policy or an arts officer. Barrow Borough Council's only gesture to the arts then was to hire an annual string quartet. But could a few artists stir the pot to prise out the dosh to pump-prime a cultural shift? In 1983, we began by upsetting the Powers That Be with the fifty-minute community film *King Real and the Hoodlums*. At first we had intended to produce it as a community play or musical but a community theatre was unheard of in Barrow and film is a more inviting route to stardom, so we opted for a community film instead. It was made with Sheffield Polytechnic Film school and Paul Hayward who co-directed it with me. More or less following Adrian Mitchell's script[3] (a lyrical pantomime tragedy with great songs and Pete Moser's music), we brutally recast King Lear as a geriatric monster living in a nuclear submarine.

Apart from Marcel Steiner who played King Real, all 200 performers were local. Three or four were skilled 'am drams', but most of them were children or adolescents bored with school holidays, pushed out on the street or bored with life. We offered a distraction and the glamour of a home-made movie. A lunatic team of artists worked extended hours a day in a freezing-cold derelict mill for twelve

Film production shot of the cast on King Real's
throne of pink cars, 1983

winter weeks, dressed up as Mad Max warriors, put fireworks up the exhaust pipes of motorbikes, built Sphinx-like juke-boxes from car bumpers, fashioned a king's throne with a crane and a pile of twenty pink cars, cavorted as penguins on a crazy floating island of discarded fridges (the residence of one of Lear's cold daughters), and so on. Once a fortnight, we gathered everyone for a cabaret music and folk night, with guests, in the upstairs of the Strawberry pub.

When asked for permission to use a Ministry of Defence dock (explaining that the film was a fable about the abuse of power), the kindly harbour master maintained with gentle irony that he and his clients valued Shakespeare too. We processed into town with anarchic hoodlums and a jazz band. King Marcel, his feet up in the conning tower of a car submarine converted by an ex-welder from the shipyard, disdainfully read *The Sporting Life* and on occasion banged a six-inch nail up his nose. In 1983, Barrovians had never seen any street theatre except for members of CND protesting against nuclear war. To facilitate our (filmed) procession of King Real, we had stewards with big round 'stop' signs to control the traffic. Some local people still think that in our charity-shop fur-coat costumes we were real punks or CND marching to stop war. A greater discomfort for us came from the biting fleas in the coats which forced us to fumigate our workshop. At the première in the local cinema, we presented home-made Oscars to everyone. All our stars entered the foyer via a red carpet and, as it was just two metres square, it took an hour.

With *King Real and the Hoodlums*, we chucked a stone into a very uncertain pond and the ripples still reverberate twenty years later. The film has only been shown a couple of times in Barrow, but maybe the whole process was more significant than the product. It was a confrontational interpretation of Art and War and a different method of creativity and participation for the community. We were valued for keeping kids off the streets, for engaging a few disorientated or angry young men, for drawing excellent performances out of a few committed amateur drama performers, and we produced a long, energetic, if rough, film, with some hard-hitting poetry. Nevertheless, it took four years to ingratiate ourselves again, because our street style and Mad Max costumes were too arty and too confrontational and the film's message was too outspoken and critical for a town dependent on building nuclear submarines. The longest and most tedious, but necessary, part of community art is the political and financial negotiation with councillors and local-authority commissars who have their own agendas. In this case, it often had to take place over endless cheap beers in clouds of smoke late at night in a Labour club with a self-styled Khmer Rouge of the Arts, or in Victorian council chambers with some amazing, supportive working-class people, mainly women, who knew their own history well, as well as the value and place of the Arts. After countless workshops and performances in music making, writing with Deborah Levy and Adrian Mitchell, fabric printing, model making, flag and umbrella processions, with many groups varying from senior citizens and children to those with special needs, we re-established base camp. It was called the DIY theatre and from it developed a home-grown community arts team called the Electric Arc.

Our two secret weapons were Mike White,[4] our tenacious and articulate new development director, and Pete Moser, a most energetic, talented, charismatic and at that time youngest musician in residence. Both lived in terraced houses in the town. This was a crucial demonstration of putting our mouth where our money was. Pete is a trumpeter, keyboard player, accordionist and composer. In his three-year residency, he was in every band in the town. He started the centenary choir, which took part in virtually all our subsequent events and which continued for three years after we left in 1990. It was primarily Pete's address book that was the origin of everything we achieved in Barrow. That and the energy of tens of our artists, coupled with hundreds of local participants.

The Town Hall Tattoo

The next climax was *The Town Hall Tattoo* in 1987, a major opportunity for celebration. The centennial of the building which opened in Queen Victoria's jubilee year in 1887 was a perfect opportunity to regain the runway as civic magicians. Although built the wrong way round, the town hall was magnificent, if outdated. Here was innocuous, safe, neutral ground on which to build a 'Town Hall Bonanza', a celebration of the community in a six-hour extravaganza on a Sunday afternoon for 15,000 spectators.

As Queen Victoria had not made it the first time round, and knowing that with the magic of theatre you can do anything, we resurrected her on her elephant gun carriage. She and a larger-than-life cartoon mayor chased each other all afternoon and up the town hall tower too, with him, rather phallically, riding on a giant bee on an arrow (the B and the arrow of Barrow's Victorian coat of arms).

The build-up involved six months of interactive art work with many groups. There was an extensive press campaign with a Queen Victoria lookalike photographic competition (middle-aged men often strangely resemble her), street bands and the choir to be trained (with Pete's specially written oratorio), costumes to be made and full-size street hoardings to be silk-screen-printed by John Angus and Ali Jones.[5] One of the best posters, depicting a man dancing with a submarine above his head, was erected opposite the shipyard. Our artists led intensive schools' work and local-authority architects helped children to design their own town hall and a papier-mâché banquet for the Queen herself. My three favourite installations, from a wild and colourful collection, were the Typing Pool, with secretaries in snorkels and bikinis, an Engineer made with wooden yellow spanners (a perfect Constructivist sculpture) and the Treasurer, a fat man (after Grosz) with a cash register as a belly. How I envy the free imagination of young children and often wonder where it goes.

The big day, Sunday, 13 July, finally arrived. Fortunately, after six stressful months, it all came together; thanks again to an exceptional Welfare State International crew, which grew over the weeks from twenty to one hundred.

The audience size was greater than we had hoped for. They were warmed up by market traders, food stalls, Morris dancers and clown officials, accompanied by a small Welfare State International brass band carrying a small carnival float of the building, an unreal mayor and Queen Victoria (our actors) and real officials in a little ceremony knocking on the doors of the real town hall. Two council leisure officers transformed themselves overnight into an extraordinary street-vaudeville act of cartoon bureaucrats.

The real mayor introduced Pete Moser's Oratorio of Popular Song, featuring the VSEL Band, the 150-strong Centenary Choir, Sue Gill as the town-hall cook, plus singing dustmen and music-hall artistes who entertained the crowds for forty-five minutes with a combination of traditional and original material. I wrote a song, entitled 'Three Cheers for Anything', which recommended 'Three Cheers for Barrow Town Hall' and even 'Three Cheers for Curry and Chips' (a local speciality).

Suddenly the local climbing club, dressed as bureaucrats in pinstriped suits and bowler hats, abseiled from the top windows. Clutching their briefcases, they were waved in by the council ratcatcher (Les Sharpe), who was far below, leading the Mayor on the Bee. Keen but slightly trigger-happy naval cadets hauled up blue flags from bins evenly placed around the building. As these scooted speedily up the façade on high pulleys, the bureaucrats descended, and there was nearly a collision. Taffy Thomas, the famous story-teller, our commentator, glossed over this incident and drew attention to the three-tiered, thirty-foot-high birthday cake which was about to explode with a hundredweight of Chinese bangers. He was warning people about loud noises, but it was hard to hear him because of the loud noises and their long echoes. The carnival cavalcade led by police outriders came sweeping round the corner under the balcony, from which, in theory, I was cueing the gig via a two-way radio (though it was impossible to hear anything). I was shaking as I realised it was happening at last. I was brought down to earth by Alf Horne, a local Labour councillor, holding my arm. He couldn't believe it either. 'This is the first time', he said, 'that Barrow has become a total community.' It wasn't true, but it was good to hear.

Fire engines followed the Queen and the Mayor. More large bees sprang from their elevated ladders. A Bee-your-own Politician, with rosettes that changed colour according to the political persuasion of the audience, whizzed past on a motorbike and sidecar. Ten decorated garbage trucks (we offered a 'mammon dangler', a £100 cash prize, for the best one) were led in by a percussion band, followed by ten vintage cars and carnival dancers sporting flags springing from glass-fibre rods mounted on backpacks.

Around the top gutters of the town hall, firecrackers exploded to release four miles of pink and white streamers which at first hurtled down the sandstone walls and then billowed out in big bunches. Cables were strung between the two gable ends and the central clock tower so that the giants' bunting could be slowly pulled up in a triangle like a battleship dressed for the inspection of the fleet.

A large finger four metres long (Queen Victoria's), made with cloth and wadding, poked over the balcony and beckoned us all. Then her head appeared in the clock tower as she waved a giant lace handkerchief and our puppet Mayor waved back. This was the cue for simultaneous controlled mayhem. Massive daylight mortars exploded in the sky with puffs of crisp white smoke. Sam Samkin[6] and David Clough were our fireworks experts again. 'It was like the Blitz,' people said later. I thought it was like a Turner painting.

Pouring from serried pots carefully placed on a hundred little platforms along the roof ridge, billowing red and blue smoke plumes (the town's colours) engulfed the whole architecture. An arc of linked kites made by two Japanese kitemakers in residence with us (we had to stop them persuading children to trace Disney cartoons) made a rainbow a hundred metres long over the clock tower. Scores of church bells rang as planned. Ships' hooters blasted as planned. Shipyard alarms went off (not planned). Finally, as the rock band and every singer on hand sang a heavily amplified version of Stevie Wonder's 'Happy Birthday to Ya', the town-hall clock went berserk, with the hands spinning round quite hysterically (there was a man inside). Then, majestically, in a McGill postcard climax, the Queen's

Siege Tower, *Golden Submarine*

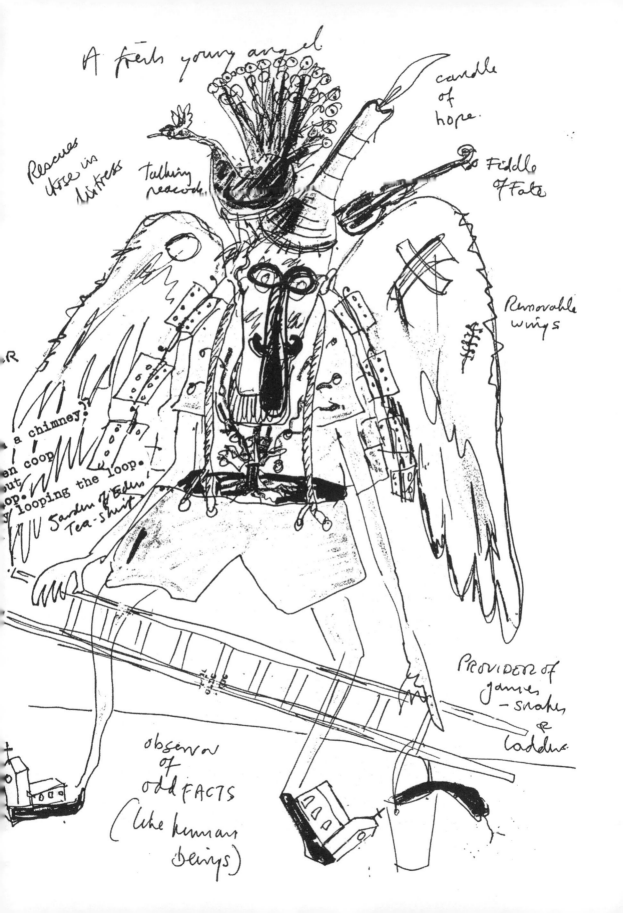

bloomers rose up the flag pole, filling out with a sharp wind from the Irish Sea. One hundred and sixty feet up, they looked quite small, but on the ground they were as big as a tennis court and had taken us three days of sewing. We nearly lost them (and four artists) as we carried them through a gusty gale. As they finally unfurled, there was a big gasp from the attentive crowd. From the guffaw, I knew we had got away with it and I also knew that no one could ever look at Barrow Town Hall or the Queen in quite the same way ever again. Finally, 25,000 ticker-tape copies of our 'Anthem' printed on fragments of pink paper were exploded from bags in the clock tower.

Anthem

I sing to the stars.
I sing to the sea.
Sing to my neighbour's heart.
May the loving and the living REJOICE.
May the loving and the living REJOICE.
For the stranger is given a welcome
And hunger can't find the door.
May the winds of July blow warmer
and the children outlaw war.

My words and Pete Moser's music, specially written for the occasion, a gift for Barrow that now crops up in various choirs around Britain. Afterwards, I wrote in my diary:

> We are developing a concept of vernacular art whereby we respond continually to local demand, producing plays, bands, dances, songs, ornaments and oratorios to order, so generating a social poetry of a high order within a very specific community context. Previously we were obliged to start from Art rather than from Living, to generate more product rather than process and work to rapid (and to an extent commercial) deadlines in strange lands. We could not allow ourselves to develop pieces organically over years, or respond to or follow up the longer term needs and rhythms of the host community, because essentially we were not part of any community.

After the considerable success of the *Town Hall Tattoo*, we became respectable.[7] The council invited us to a celebratory dinner in the town hall, presented us with an engraved goblet and partially renewed our funding for three years. So we embarked on a 'Tapestry of Celebration' with many strands which eventually came to a spectacular conclusion in *Shipyard Tales*, a two-week festival in the summer of 1990.

In the meantime, we nearly wrecked the whole residency in October 1988 with *Wildfire*, a misjudged fire show. It was a very cold evening. The sports field was windy and bleak. We started late, choosing to wait for traffic held up by an accident on a nearby bridge. The audience of a few thousand became impatient. Our main image was well made but too blunt. Forty foot high, it was a model of the end of the submarine sheds crossed with a one-arm-bandit fruit machine. We took too long to set fire to it, the ground-based imagery was too small and longwinded and couldn't be seen from a distance.

We weren't quite back to square one, but we had to begin the slow process of ingratiating ourselves with public and politicians again. *Robinson Crusoe Castaway*, written by Boris Howarth with music by Tim Fleming, a full-scale community pantomime with over sixty participants, was performed in the awful Civic Theatre of Forum 28 on fourteen evenings, seven too many. This was an original, daring and often lyrical piece directed by Tony Liddington[8] made on a shoestring and featuring Robbie Crusoe as a local lad setting sail from Barrow.

It went down well enough with most of the public. It had sufficient recognisable panto tricks, including a UV underwater scene and David Marcus as a pantomime dame, and an extensive walkdown in feather boas, some excellent transformations and wild costumes to reinforce expectations, but it still provoked an outrageous outburst in the foyer. A nervous leisure officer (who subsequently became a great supporter), with the mayor pressurising him, panicked because it was too much of a musical opera and not enough of a panto and the dialogue was too political . . . the correspondence went on for ages.

We regained full credibility through good luck and patient tactics. We workshopped four strong and sometimes disturbing pieces, all created and written by children. For example, *The Squids* involved tearaway six- to nine-year-olds gathered from the square adjacent to our increasingly vulnerable workshop. Pete Moser persuaded them to write a dozen haiku songs about their homes. These were shaped into a variety show with a simple set made from fridge boxes depicting bright terraced houses with coloured numbers. Some of the stories were very revealing – 'all my parents care about is Bingo and Betting and Beer' – and we had to be careful about the material, particularly if it dealt with domestic violence. Others took off into joyous fantasy, like the little girl who believed she kept a pet alligator in the bath. *The Shadow Factory* was a remarkable evocation of a child's inner fears. For over a

117

week, Meg Gleave, the courageous head of Walney Junior School, the school on the island which is immediately opposite the Trident shipyard sheds, handed over her whole school to our company of itinerant artists. (This is still possible, despite the National Curriculum – but you have to be enlightened and imaginative.) Tim Fleming and Elaine Whitewood, our project directors, had attended a stimulating pathfinding course with the education department of the Royal Opera House, Covent Garden, who continued to monitor and give thorough professional back-up. This was probably the best lesson we ever acquired from mainstream theatre.

The Covent Garden idea was for the children to invent and mount a whole production – a miniature opera – from devising, composing and performing to lighting and sound technologies, plus front of house, programme design and publicity. These children rose to, and above, the occasion. The poetry of *The Shadow Factory* was simple but profound. A monstrous factory had stolen the shadows of children, taking them into an underworld where there was no light. One child's grandmother had to risk a hideous journey to recover their lost souls.

Seeing children, with no experience of such original theatre presenting their own story with great commitment was very moving. The children's own PR department, set up in the school office, rang up Buckingham Palace to persuade Charles and Di to come. They couldn't, but sent a nice letter of apology. The school secretary (and most of the teachers) were dumbfounded.

Shipyard Tales

By July 1990 it was time to bring together all the strands of the 'Tapestry'. The council had by now recruited a full-time arts officer, Sue Jenkins, and involved Welfare State International in the selection process. This was a major breakthrough. Since then, for a decade, Sue has tenaciously driven a Barrow arts programme, giving it a formidable corporate identity, recruiting additional staff and gaining considerable funding both from inside and outside the town. Our job was soon to be over.

The steps were arduous. We recruited our own production company, hired yet another cold, disused, greasy garage and appointed Jules Hammerton as co-ordinator. The budget was extremely limited, but we tried to provide the highest production values and to service the performance and writing skills of Barrovians in a cycle of linked 'plays' of varying styles. With hindsight, we should have negotiated to put these pieces into the neighbourhoods, in community centres or working men's clubs or even night-clubs; it would have been the right vernacular approach.

As it happened, Barrow Council had found end-of-the-financial-year cash to invest in an urgent and well-meaning, but superficial, revamp of the municipal proscenium theatre. Forum 28 was the usual inflexible, end-on shoebox with a high, remote stage, no storage, lousy sound, an ugly auditorium, an expanding set of uncomfortable plastic seats, side rooms with low ceilings, poor proportions, plus a predictable franchised bar and a sort of restaurant glued on. Resembling a fifties secondary-modern school or a Stalinist crematorium made of Meccano, it rocked and rattled with every latecomer.

It was just the place *not* to put embryonic performers. But we had to use it, pride and politics, cultural snobbery and cultural ignorance ruled and politicians were paying the piper. And to be fair, we took the easy option. After seven years, we were running out of confrontational, or any other kind of, energy. 1990, however, was the crossover point and we were determined to end our seven-year residency with a showcase of local talent, demonstrating once and for all our vision that here was enormous creative potential. We also intended a big-bang farewell.

Shipyard Tales came in the full wrapping of the Feast of Furness, a total festival which included band and choir concerts, story-tellings, poetry readings, cabarets, tea dances and street events, including turning on the civic Christmas lights and the now 200-strong Barracudas. We even produced *Rock the Boat*, a regular anarchic night-club on the 'Gaza Strip' with guests such as the fledgeling John Hegley mingling with our own Kevin Fegan and local poets from the writers' group we had established. However, the core climax of our three-year 'Tapestry of Celebration' was to be fourteen separate home-produced productions, including repeats of the children's work, all with local writers and performers serviced by Welfare State International, and all to be performed over two hot summer weeks in Forum 28.

Recalling our earlier experiments, we were hankering after a set of short, up-front performances, in the tradition of the English Mystery Plays, to distil a secular and sacred litany of contemporary popular concerns mixing issue, narrative, song, image and archetype. We had to hunt out, or solicit, the right mix of themes and also give credence and support to local voices, who might not share our motivation but had every right to the main stage. We intended to use celebratory art to draw out the imaginations and interior life of Barrovians. In this category of art work (unlike dreaming up your own poetry), the primary duty is to the participant and their public and part of the job is to facilitate work that will entertain or hold an audience.

★

Some argue that the primary purpose of community art is the therapy of release. It is certainly about giving people and communities a strong sense of their own identity and worth, particularly when people have been isolated, dispossessed, manipulated and under-resourced for a very long time. You have to start positively and give people confidence and not be too judgemental or demanding too soon. There are always dilemmas of cultural taste. There is also the risk of ending up with a patronising, sentimental product or surrogate social work disguised as art, which local authorities often prefer to fund rather than truthful, well-fashioned, original art, which might well rock their boat.

A problem endemic to community art is finding the right balance between leading and facilitating. 'Rightness' is sometimes achieved by a combination of instinct, consultation, objective aesthetic assessment, trust and chance.

Brecht would have smiled at *What'll the Lads Do On Monday?*, a complex, political, full-length musical documentary play, devised and directed through workshops by Rachel Ashton, Albert Hunt and myself, and performed with a multigenerational cast of eighteen. Drawing on reported facts, this was a mildly agitprop and ironically humorous attempt to come to terms with the end of the Cold War and the implication of the so-called 'Peace Dividend' in a town which had always been economically dependent on constructing and selling armaments. Based on the phrase of the town's then Conservative MP, 'If Labour gets in on Friday, what'll the lads do on Monday?', it included a wake and funeral procession for a submarine icon framed like a church altar, the wedding of Gorbachov and Bush and two contrasting social parties organised by women.

In Act I, we witnessed an hilarious Ann Summers knickers tea party, brazen with innuendo and raucous hilarity (we learned a lot in the workshop improvisations). In Act 2, this was balanced by the same women brainstorming alternative industries for the shipyard. Given the fact that VSEL had consistently ignored such research, whether offered by the TUC, a Labour MP or university peaceniks, this was provocative and timely counter-propaganda which attracted both a big audience and the defence correspondent of the *Independent*, giving Barrow more and more positive press coverage than it had ever received from the arts or tourism. It was hard to deal directly with the amorality and greed of the contemporary arms trade. Anyway, who were Welfare State International – poncy, arty, intellectual incomers with degrees, the gift of the gab and some subsidy – to point fingers at economically conscripted welders working overtime for a basic wage? Never mind their bosses or the government or MPs, whose careers were all dependent on maintaining full employment in a 'Wild West Town' (Kevin Fegan) with one big sheriff.

Lord Dynamite

Not surprisingly, no material dealing with the shipyard arms trade was forthcoming from the Barrow writers. So, after much soul-searching (rationalising that by now I was local, too), I decided to co-write a musical (with Kevin Fegan, who was also nearly local as he had been around for a year!) based on the mythologised life of Alfred Nobel. With a century's distance, it was possible to analyse all the guilt, hypocrisies and well-worn clichés of Nobel, who, before establishing the famous Peace Prize, made a fortune out of dynamite, misguidedly believing that 'The biggest bang there is will stop the war'.

Lord Dynamite, as it came to be called, was immaculately directed by Gilly Adams, with a tough but accessible singalong score by Tim Fleming. A latecomer in our cycle, it had a production budget of only £1,100. Invention is sometimes the offspring of necessity. In this case, a classical austerity of style, a large cast of thirty (mainly, but not all, women with big voices), a small orchestra, a few lamps, a load of white cloth, more cardboard boxes, a bed, a comic car and Jon Atkins, the only professional actor in the whole of *Shipyard Tales*, were sufficient to pull us through. Plus, there was great dedication from the cast, who seemed genuinely to believe in the peace message. A year later, as a touring 'landscape-opera', *Lord Dynamite* was reworked in a more emblematic and symbolist form (see The Flight from Spectacle).

The Golden Submarine

This was, as we had hoped, our final farewell, a glorious bang (and a half). With a 50 per cent contribution from our delayed Gulbenkian Prize for a site-specific work, we almost had the budget. Our original idea for this project, maybe eighteen months before, was for an imaginary submarine which had gone out of control, managed to drill through the dockside ending up a landlocked night-club in the park in Barrow. We held on to this image and our site, but our scenario changed. A cartoon stereotype, Lord Shellbent, irritated by the declining profits caused by the end of the Cold War and hating rumours of individual creativity, socialist collectives and life-enhancing green alternative industries, flipped into full Robert Maxwell mode. He planned to launch a golden submarine and in a single Armageddon eliminate all imaginative deviants and left-wing tendencies.

In pouring rain, a cast of 500 people took part in a fun, carnival, agitprop denouement in a natural grassed amphitheatre on the edge of town. Under a sea of umbrellas, 3,000 paying spectators and 2,000 gatecrashers gathered on the hillside. The site was adjacent to Furness Abbey. Looking at the ruins of that earlier dominant culture with its magnificent Cistercian monastery demolished by Henry VIII in the sixteenth century, I kept wondering whether in the twenty-fifth century any of our lineage of carnival fools would be cavorting in the ruins of the submarine sheds.

In the arena, we had built a thirty-foot-high, eighty-foot-long 'model' of these sheds. Constructed with thirteen tons of scaffolding and carefully stitched white canvas, they rested on accurately set aluminium rails 100 yards long. The tail fin of the Golden Submarine stuck out menacingly at one end. Meanwhile, mirroring Charlie Chaplin's *Modern Times*, the whole side of the shed was illuminated and animated with a shadow play of moving factory gantries and antlike workers goaded by a loud soundtrack belting out 'GOT-TO-DO-IT-GOT-TO-DO-IT-GOT-TO-DO-IT'.

Many things happened, rapidly and often simultaneously. The Barracudas Carnival Band beat a thunderous entry, nearly driving off the rain. A warm-up procession of twelve wild stock cars and crazy bicycles playfully engineered with moving windmills, gibbets and swinging puppets executed a circuit. Lord Shellbent, built round a hydraulic ram thirty foot high on the top of an old car, rose and fell and roared round the arena, led by grotesque Dogs of War. His knobbly grey hands could disengage from his sleeves and as blood red ribbons dangled (another good trick from the Katakhali), his disembodied hands attacked eager children in the front row of our audience.

A wooden but high-tech siege tower of similar height, filled with consumer goods and spare Cruise missiles, rose on another car chassis. On its top platform were the Pillars of Society, four of Julian Crouch's big, wobbly puppet caricatures of the Hooray Henrys of our culture balancing a colossal champagne bottle on a yardarm.[9] Evidently, in the age-old tradition, they intended to swing the bottle to launch the Golden Submarine. Clearly rat-arsed (and very wobbly), they missed. Their bottle hit the sheds, which, familiar with those old launch routines, immediately moved down the waiting slipway. In fact, the thirteen tons of scaffolding were being pulled along the rails by a hefty winch a hundred yards away.

As the sheds moved along, very slowly at first, there was a revelation. The Golden Submarine was in truth no more than a cardboard shell. Just the thrusting stern we had already seen. In place of the expected submarine hull lay a huge, ugly nest fashioned from electrical detritus and the rotting skeletons of engineers and lost apprentices. Inside the nest, a monstrous Cuckoo gyrated and regurgitated fire.

The Cuckoo 'as a ravenous exploiter of other people's work' linked back to 'Cuckoo', another Shipyard Tale by Robert Drake, a stone waller and poet. In one of the few street plays of the cycle, a group of mummers enacted a traditional story about villagers who build a high wall to prevent the cuckoo from flying away, in order to perpetuate summer. It was a useful allegorical symbol for VSEL, which fails to maintain full employment for its declining work-force and devours creative potential.

The end came quickly. Factory women with a very large Nuclear Vacuum Cleaner made by Ray Brooks, preceded by a fire sculpture emblem of the same, upturned Shellbent in an expected come-uppance with a flourish of a triumphal 'traditional' Cumbrian three-pin-plug dance. This pageant of visual and social transformation was led by Madonna (definitely not the singing money queen). The plugs were props the size of coffee tables.

A procession of children carrying oil lamps then took over the sheds while slides of alternative technologies (by Mandy Dyke) were projected on to the sheds. As the ten-piece band with the Centenary Choir led by Ali Rigg and Pete Moser performed a rock anthem and Spontaneous Combustion[10] fired half a ton of mortars into the rainy blackness, even the crumbling sandstone ruins of the dead abbey reflected gold. But I knew that our Barrow residency with its seven-year process of celebratory protest was over.[11]

The seeds of *Golden Submarine* and our residency from 1983 to 1990 did bear fruit and twelve years on, in 2002, cultural industries are being taken seriously in Barrow. They may not yet be offering 4,000 jobs, which are all that are left in the shipyard, but the sector is evidently in a dynamic phase of early growth.

As always in our society, it is the economy, or, more precisely, the pressure for jobs which is the driving force behind any real social change. It is a salutary lesson to the cynical to see that Furness Enterprise, a local agency designed to promote new businesses, is examining how the arts can provide paid employment. Ironically, their consultant is our former company accountant, who 'dropped out' after one of our comedy workshops, believing his true calling was to run a flea circus. In 1984, neither the shipyard bosses nor Barrow Council would listen to any voice suggesting any alternative forms of employment. With a vested interest in maintaining the Cold War status quo, they steadfastly ignored the Barrow Alternative Employment Committee, trade unions, academic reports, CND research and even their Labour MP. According to 'Building the Trident Network', they turned away new commercial inventions, varying from devices to save shipping

123

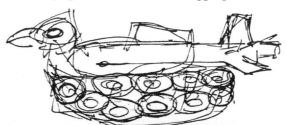

fuel to ocean mining systems and floating hotels, and successful export potential in soap, sewage and cement machinery.[12] They also failed to exploit their patents in marine industries and wave- and wind-energy technology. With their mind set on clearing the decks to build the four mammoth Tridents, they allowed the largest integrated shipbuilding and engineering site in Europe to succumb to the drive of the Ministry of Defence. This was successful in the mid-eighties: when other towns were suffering recession, Barrow was booming. In 1986, when VSEL was privatised, 80 per cent of the work-force bought shares. But, by 1990, hundreds of those who had bought shares had both spent their gains and lost their jobs.

During this period, we were sowing those art seeds. Our main effect was, as always, on individuals. Given the right circumstances, everyone is evidently creative. All we do is trigger what is waiting in the wings. In Barrow, we had a strong effect on perhaps 200 individuals. Now that we had abandoned our world nomadism, we had become embedded in the community net and discovered a different avant-garde on our own doorstep. What was new, though, was that original, creative people were now drawn to Barrow and young artists who went away came back.

Garry Bridgens, for instance, had been a spotty little hoodlum on the *King Real* movie and Buttons on the *Lantern Coach*. Then he toured with a professional pierrot troupe and was the artistic director of Barrow's recent annual street-theatre festival. Currently, he is planning a twentieth-anniversary celebration of *King Real* (for 2003) and supporting Furness's first Monster Raving Loony Party candidate, who is otherwise known as Catflea Massacre, shadow minister for procrastination. So, political theatre is not quite dead. Ali Rigg, a young blues singer on *The Golden Submarine*, now runs two choirs in south Cumbria for the Gateshead Music Centre and earns her living as a community musician. Amanda Quigley, a somewhat dispossessed teenager in our DIY theatre days, was headhunted to become a student at the Liverpool Institute of Performing Arts and is now an excellent alto sax player, a musical director and a stilt-walking percussionist, and teaches drama in primary schools. Les Clifton, the shipyard worker who played Gorbachov in *What'll the Lads Do On Monday?*, is an innovative restaurateur.

At a corporate level, under the umbrella of cultural regeneration, Sue Jenkins, Barrow Arts's commissar, has manœuvred millions of pounds' worth of investment via Northern Arts, European regional funds and the Arts Lottery into a public art programme. There is an extensive development of a dock museum with art gallery, a windy plaza and other building refurbishments, providing good rehearsal,

The Town Hall Tattoo, 1987

studio and storage facilities for the growing number of entrepreneurial artists' initiatives (such as Art Gene), which include Maddi Nicholson's Public Art and Banner Company, the Barracudas Carnival Band, Shoreline Films and Rachel Ashton's Contemporary Arts Theatre Company. Sixty Millennium Commission awards, varying from £2,500 to £6,000, are available for successful community regenerative arts projects, which vary from drama to music, sound technology to visual art and writing to new media.

All of these individuals and groups go from strength to strength and some have achieved a national profile. Maddi's painted haulage trucks drove from the Tate Gallery nationwide, to mark Visual Arts Year. The Barracudas, with their decorative and energetic work led by Jules Hammerton, are in 2002 making a big touring show *Spirit of Freedom* (with over 100 drumming and dancing participants) to celebrate the Commonwealth Games and the Queen's golden jubilee. Rachel Ashton's group, the only professional theatre company to have grown with local actors in Barrow, has been acclaimed in major city venues throughout Britain. Rachel was also commissioned by Barrow Borough Council to workshop the Barramundi cycle of plays for the Millennium and her Barrow Youth Theatre Group has produced original work on local themes with national musicians and designers.

Some of the radical edge in Barrow may have shifted into less art-based areas. It is not surprising in a town with considerable social problems – rising unemployment, allegedly increasing street violence, alcoholism, teenage pregnancies – that more resources become available for such schemes as Sure Start (an educational charity for children) or Community Action Furness. The latter, for instance, employs over fifty in a maze of co-operatives that offer funding for training and enterprise, and build houses, gardens and furniture, run a catering company, a print shop and a recycling project. Not quite up to those alternative industry visionaries of the early eighties. Barrow is not yet Utopia. There are not yet any Barrow-burgers made with local Cumbrian beef and Barrow is not the self-generating city state it could be, with, for example, its own orchestra and composers and its own musical-instrument factories drawing on many local engineering skills.

At a different level, it is a political act to give individuals access to and control over their own identity and creativity and the freedom to tell their stories. In 2000–1, Rachel Ashton directed *Once We Were Queens* by Peter Straughan, a play about the vulnerability of young male actors in Shakespeare's time. In its own way, this was groundbreaking in macho Barrow, where gay culture has not always been easily acknowledged. Rachel followed this with *Cold*, also by Peter Straughan. Some of the same team of now-professional performers act out violent patient/prisoners in a locked institution. The play questions the nature of madness and the relative madness of inmates and their disturbed but controlling psychiatrist.

In the shadow of the shipyard, given the madness of nuclear war and the failure of top-down management, this was timely. But it became even more pertinent when the four prisoners transformed themselves into a string quartet. With extraordinary energy and mime, and pretending they were virtuoso players (with no actual instruments), they emphasised the point that no one can stop anyone's creative will and imaginative fantasies transcending awful and awesome reality, with its powerful, controlling ultimate authority. It was a very different place, a very different string quartet from the one we and Barrow Borough Council had started with in 1984.

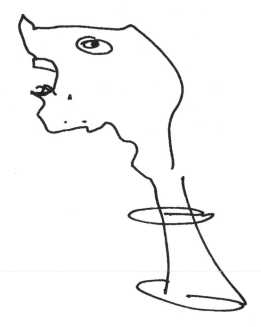

The Flight from Spectacle

The artistic and financial pressures of the early nineties were enormous. After seven years in Barrow-in-Furness, we were very tired, although we had achieved something to be proud of. Even reporters from the national press had come up north. Robert Hewison wrote in the *Sunday Times* in June 1990:

> Welfare State has transformed the town's self-confidence. They have opened up the questions. There is still resistance to what they are doing, but hopefully what's started now can't be stopped. *The Golden Submarine* is certain not to be a one-night wonder. It could even be the night the town wakes up to its uncertain future. Welfare State's options for change will need serious consideration.[1]

We learned that when you can't persuade theatre critics to write a review, then you should invite the crime, war or sports reporters. Chris Bellamy, the defence correspondent of the *Independent*, wrote:

> So, will the festival help redirect the energy and talent of Barrow? If conversion from armaments is to take place, it clearly cannot be left to VSEL and the Government. New, lighter industries are needed. Much will depend on individuals and small groups. Last Wednesday at the festival, nobody could doubt the talent of Barrovians or their energy. The show (*What'll the Lads Do On Monday?*) before a packed auditorium, was witty, intelligent and earthy, with some rollicking songs.

The creative skill needed to devise a submersible miniature planet is extraordinary, but it is not easy to switch a massive defence industry around and even for pathological optimists it is unthinkable to suggest that those huge resources could be immediately redeployed into producing art, even if entrenched attitudes to work and jobs and understandable fears of unemployment could be shifted. We had been inspired in Vancouver by the amazing culture of west-coast North American native people, who originally used their surplus of spare beaver, salmon and red wood to make things. All the time they saved (the surplus from which art has always stemmed) was put into carving transformation masks, painting, dancing and creating ceremonies; a rich artistic legacy.

If participatory art is to be perceived as integral to society or as part of life – as it still is in some Asian villages – then there is no reason, in theory, why the evident creativity of Barrovians should not be harnessed to a life-enhancing exploration. It could provide as much work and certainly more pleasure for most people than building weapons and might even have a small effect on stress-related depression and the considerable number of suicides among young men in Cumbria. It would save the NHS money. Although the amount spent on the arts in Barrow is now many thousands of pounds more than it was when we arrived, the total amount is certainly no more than the cost of one Cruise missile. If only perceptions and priorities were changed, then resources could be redeployed.

Glasgow All Lit Up

In 1991, at the same time as working in Barrow, we were also heavily committed to another major community event in Scotland. In 1990, Glasgow was selected by the European Community as the European City of Culture and here was an opportunity to demonstrate an alternative way of making art in a temporary shop window thanks to the vision of Bob Palmer and Neil Wallace. It was the centrepiece of the community programme. First, we recruited a Scottish team. Then, based in Govan, another ex-shipbuilding district and another area of urban deprivation, we worked for eighteen months with 250 educational and community groups throughout the region of Strathclyde to produce four big lantern processions to arrive from four cardinal points of the city. This 'symbolic community' of 10,000 people with 8,000 lanterns paraded through the city centre in the autumn for a carnival finale with fireworks and searchlights on Glasgow Green. The lanterns varied from the simple hand-held, candle-lit pyramids of tissue and willow to truck-sized sculptural floats illuminated by mobile generators.

Organisationally, it was a clear model of a successful community celebration (steered via the massive interlocking of innumerable self-motivated cells). Artistically, it revealed the high quality, range and accessibility of the lantern form. At the end of the parade, hundreds of lanterns were hung on five wooden towers. The towers were constructed of hexagonal wooden sections, strung together on cables, which were raised steadily by large cranes. As they grew in the air, the participants hung their lanterns on these rising pagodas so that before the final firework display they constructed several complex, celebratory sculptures to rival the wondrous Victorian engineering (and the bulbous lantern form) of the Greenhouse of the

Glasgow All Lit Up finale – tree, fireworks and fish, 1990

People's Palace on the Green. As Joyce MacMillan wrote in the *Guardian*:

> There were beautifully made lanterns and weak, battered messy ones. There were
> boats and space ships and churches and Mutant Hero Turtles, and lots of simple
> triangular lanterns with nothing but gorgeous, blobby abstract patterns on. In
> recognition of Glasgow's strange crest – the tree, the bird, the bell, the fish –
> there were hundreds of brightly coloured fish from huge sharks to tiny tiddlers;
> Lochgilphead primary school brought a whole shoal 30-strong.
>
> Later, down at Glasgow Green, the ground was very squelchy and things went on
> a bit too long, as these events do. There were gorgeous 40 ft. towers of lanterns,
> ice-cream vans, hot dog stalls, and a big firework display; and Welfare State
> produced a kind of visual fantasia on the tree, bird, bell and fish theme, which
> ended with the tree burning down, and a gleaming white bird rising – rather
> limp-wristedly, on account of the rain – from the ashes.
>
> 'Why's that tree burning and falling to bits, dad?' asked a tot in the crowd. 'Because
> it symbolises Glasgow, hen,' answered the dad, with feeling. But everyone laughed
> because we knew there would be a phoenix later.[2]

British Gas Scotland would not make their contribution to this event unless we
agreed not to use our name of Welfare State International! We included them on
the poster as 'BG' and we became 'WSI'. The City Chambers asked us to create a
big cathedral lantern to be carried in the parade by their eight civic footmen – later,
they sent us a bill for their overtime. A few hours before the event, Glasgow Green
was flooded. The blocked park drains were hardly our responsibility. Yet the cost
of hiring every sludge-gulper from Aberdeen to Carlisle fell to us.

It was also post-Hillsborough and every official feared the worst. A pre-planning
meeting proved to be the most unpleasant of my life, with thirty local-authority
suits and the police and fire service all on full male menopause, refusing to budge
on anything. During the parade, the police took over (via their helicopter and
radios) and, dangerously in my opinion, permitted traffic to flow towards the
processions, albeit on the other side of the road. Naturally, the street lights stayed
on. The council also sent us a bill for the extra standby ambulances the suits had
insisted upon. There were no accidents, although there was a danger of being
jumped on by teams of over-eager paramedics hidden up every back alley.

The funding of a community gig has to be budgeted very carefully. Barrow
Council had cut back on their original financial indications and in fulfilling our

ongoing obligations to the community, we lost £30,000. In Glasgow, we had naively agreed to a deal to provide free lantern materials and free bus transport for all the inner-city schools. Not only did the schools save on their annual arts-education budget, but we had to ferry children and materials on open-ended demand. Kay Greer, our indefatigable schools liaison officer, had a massive task. The more we offered, the more we had to provide. Originally, we had costed the total event at £360,000. We were finally offered £300,000 and as the event cost £330,000, we were down yet another £30,000!

Our decision to take on eighteen months' work in Glasgow at the same time as the Barrow work was insane. It took a long time to find the right team. Warehouses were expensive and all we could afford was a huge, cold workshop headquarters in a wasteland of rival drug dealers in Govan. It leaked remorselessly. We put down sand to absorb the puddles and the oil. We borrowed a cat to deter the rats and the sand became a giant litter tray. Our workshop, underneath a large paint depot, was fired by an arsonist, whilst we were inside. The local fire brigade extinguished it and rescued us just in time. A gang of kids stole our drums, but another gang stole them back for us.

Although we had other potential artistic directors lined up (including Graham Dunstan from Australia), they dropped out, due to money, love affairs, career moves, illness or fear, and I ended up directing this event, commuting regularly between Barrow and Glasgow. Despite some profound back-up in Scotland from a solid team, with old supporters like Ruari McNeill from Mid Pennine Arts Association days (which had given us that invaluable fellowship in 1977), and Hilary Hughes and Stuart Mitchell, the pressure was intolerable. It was hard to deliver the work in hand and impossible to think, to plan ahead, to make any policy changes and watch our backs (and bank balance) in the narrow and incestuous world of art politics.

Maybe tiredness also clouded my judgement when I allowed our ambitious new business manager (dreaming of the considerable fees that in theory were available on the European circuit) to persuade me to take out a touring version of *Lord Dynamite*, originally premièred as part of *Shipyard Tales*. After working as animateurs in the Barrow community for seven years, we needed to recharge our batteries and do something more for ourselves, but at a time of economic entrenchment it was foolish to try to set up an ensemble company with its massive start-up production costs and then tour with a relatively unknown product on those international festival circuits we had lost touch with.

Lord Dynamite Part Two

In the summer of 1991 we did open the touring landscape version of *Lord Dynamite* on the international festival circuit, beginning (again) at the London International Festival of Theatre (LIFT), with three performances at the end of June. It was a retrograde step.

We might have been returning to the *Titanic* model, except that in theory we now knew more about how to involve the community. Basically, don't do it on tour. This is exactly what we found we were doing and this one had to be adaptable to many sites. We opened in the underprivileged borough of Newham after rehearsing for ten days only (in another monsoon). The performances covered two football fields in a derelict sports arena with the distant audience of a thousand a night sitting on a raised grass bank.

Despite our doubts about community involvement on the hoof, the show successfully incorporated many dancers, carnival musicians and drummers from amongst the local people, plus a full professional electric band, three hydraulic cherrypickers carrying the main actors high in the sky and two large sculptural pyrotechnic mobiles. Now brilliantly re-directed by Tim Fleming, the show was adapted from our original version for a proscenium stage musical. As it was being performed outside, without such focused intimacy, the story had to be simplified, the dialogue minimised, songs emphasised and the cast reduced to five key performers with radio mikes. The style was large and physical with huge sculptural images and very courageous acrobatic and physical performances from Mark Hopkins playing Nobel and Liz Ingram as the Spirit of Niflheim, the Nordic god of war who infiltrates the mind of Alfred Nobel.

As the sun went down, the audience looked across a vista of real garden allotments. Nobel was born in a mobile garden shed. Soon, his mother died in an accidental explosion at a nitroglycerine factory and there was due lament and guilt. (This was a poetic transference, as in reality it was his brother who was killed.)

In the second act, the audience turned around on their grass slope to face the vast space of the full arena, where Nobel's Empire was depicted growing through large shadow puppets and a mobile giant factory made of tin sheets built on a car chassis. His mother's ghost and two other influential women rose like iconographic stained-glass windows in the sky. Explosions and fires marked distant wars.

By the third act, Nobel was isolated and repenting, but, confused and tormented, he continued to conjure up war machines and vicious inventions. Finally, faced with the terror of his own escalating deterrents and the countering wisdom of

Lord Dynamite, 1991

his ghost mother, his mistress and Berthe Kinsky, the leader of the European peace movement, Nobel rejected violence and sought to establish a peace prize. The final image was of Nobel flying away in the original garden shed. Now sprouting wings (and in reality hauled into the firmament on a hundred-foot crane), the shed disappeared in a panoply of fireworks. Nobel had returned to his childhood, to the original centre of all his (and our) creativity before we became corrupted by the commercial, political and military excesses of growing up.

> Peace is not the gap between
> the wars that men create.
> Peace is seeing clearly
> and giving up pretence.
> Peace is living better
> not sitting on a fence.

The message was obvious, but realising it was arduous and it looked as if we were going to lose money yet again. Britain in the early nineties was very different from the early eighties, and in the economic climate of 1991 our growing deficit was a potential disaster. Apart from that, I was tired of the responsibility and very real dangers of the big turn-on, especially trying to do it on minute resources. Our entire production budget was less than the cost of one stage cloth at the National Theatre and after minimal rehearsal we were exposed to London theatre critics. If you compare the costs and resources of mainstream and alternative theatre in England, the differences are colossal. At the end of an arduous run, we had to load the wagons and travel to Devon the same night. It was irresponsible to work under these pressures to create art, which should be a pleasurable and playful activity. When one of us nearly drove our truck into a ditch that night, I realised our luck was running out and it was time to stop and rethink.

The *Dynamite* tour was originally costed on the basis of a minimum of ten venues. In practice, we achieved three, and these with great difficulty. In Totnes, for example, because the town was celebrating the bicentennial of the inventor of the computer (and we desperately needed the income), we had to rewrite half the show to incorporate Charles Babbage, who wasn't even a contemporary of Nobel. Then, in Newcastle-upon-Tyne, the scheduled site was a war zone between local councillors. We had to rehearse in a warehouse, preparing to do one kamikaze version at a few days' notice in a riverside car park. In fact, successfully re-directed by Werner Van Wely, the founder of the Dutch Dogtroep, it was a hit.

In Belfast, a planned collaboration with the youth theatre would have to be anything but *Lord Dynamite*. Explosions were too close for comfort. So we had to create an entirely new show, *The Last Ferry*, based on the termination of the Liverpool–Belfast ferry service. Next, after a very detailed two-day reconnaissance, we had to cancel a show for the Dublin Festival when a bureaucrat insisted that the audience had to be 500 yards away from any worthwhile firework effect. The shortage of bookings brought on by the recession, the bureaucracy and insecurity of local government, the dominance of PR companies, the hugely increased costs of negotiating excessive insurances, nitpicking contracts, the fashion for litigation, the subsequent overcompensation for health and safety, the dull form-filling to prove, monitor and value every fart and any other output and the difficulty of raising commercial sponsorship for truly radical work were beginning to defeat us. Production and touring expenses, including basics like diesel, had increased out of all proportion and well above inflation. Maybe we were also overambitious and, having worked in the sticks for so long, we no longer had a 'glossy' reputation.

The chorus of factory workers in *Lord Dynamite* sang:

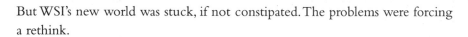

> A new world is emerging
> from the bowels of the earth.
> We want a place in the sun.
> Nobel brings us work he does
> he always looks ahead.
> Where there's muck there's money
> in the shadow of the dead-end shed.

But WSI's new world was stuck, if not constipated. The problems were forcing a rethink.

We were also rapidly heading for bankruptcy. By the end of 1991, our deficit was up to £100,000. In order to rescue our financial position, we took on *Light up the Bay*, a son et lumière for 25,000 people, in Cardiff Bay in 1991. Our promoters were a PR company who hyped the audience to 100,000, with the result that 75 per cent of the people went away disgruntled, unable to hear or see anything except a few aerial mortars. It also lost money. Another government quango, the Cardiff Bay Development Corporation, was determined to override the wishes of of local people. So, in the interests of economic progress, a marina barrage and the tides went. The mud of Tiger Bay was like the fissured face of an old black duchess. Now it is no longer visible – a touchstone of the extraordinary history of working-class people has been submerged and anaesthetised.

We found ourselves on the escalator of market forces. Only through the great skill and patience of our executive committee, the ultimate tolerance and generous advances of the Arts Council of England, the fact that we could double-mortgage our building, the Old National School in Ulverston which we bought through Richard Oyarzabel, our business manager, in 1987, and a grant from the Foundation for Sports and Arts, did we survive. Our executive committee instructed me to put our National School's playground on the market, which I did (although I took the estate agent's sign down when they weren't around). The land would have supported three houses (and was the subsequent site for the accommodation unit of Lanternhouse). We sold anything we could, including an expensive oboe, and I begged money for postage stamps from a businessman acquaintance. The bank kept pushing up the cost of our overdraft, as moneylenders always do when you appear to be a bad bet and they want to push you over the top.

Welfare who?

In the arts and in the world at large, the very name Welfare State International had become deeply unfashionable and very 'sixties'. In 1968, even Tory politicians believed in some notion of a caring society, but by the nineties, Thatcher had not only denied 'society' altogether but Britain had moved into an era of division, greed and gloat. Even I was having doubts about our name. I sent a letter to all our members, asking their opinion about changing it to 'Engineers of the Imagination'. We received fifty anagrams, ten appalling puns and a majority begging us not to change anything. The wittiest near-anagram was: 'Real tat went over itself'. Maybe it did, but we were broke and clinging on to the moral high ground was expensive. Many of our most inventive and younger artists were naturally growing away from base and were looking to develop their own companies. They were more interested in exploring the possibilities of multimedia, site-specific, transient spectacular fire shows than I was. The rather macho excitement of generators, elemental excess, physical sweat and dangerous pyrotechnics was wearing a bit thin for me. By 1991, I was over fifty and the search for novelty via dangerous and broad-brush sensations was no longer satisfying. Worse, I had a sneaking anxiety that however we struggled in the context of broad-based mass fire shows, most audiences and many local authorities and promoters couldn't tell the difference between heart-bashed poetry and Disney turn-on.[3]

★

At that time, we were mainly funded by the Arts Council Drama Department in London. We had a reputation for large-scale spectacles and there were expectations, if not demands (almost head-butting), amongst some arts administrators that we should continue along this track. When we talked of our growing interest in vernacular art and rites of passage, we were asked: 'What have funerals got to do with drama?' When we planned a (for us) new kind of small-scale touring with, for example, *Hollow Ring* (see On Tour) in May 1993, or large-scale, one-off ritual theatre such as *Trawlers at Peace* in Grimsby in October 1993 (see Rites of Passage), we were inundated by Arts Council assessors. I counted six in one show, all with their arms folded.

Another department of the Arts Council, however, gave me an unexpected opportunity to rethink. In 1991, they commissioned a paper for the National Arts and Media Strategy (NAMS). So, in between monsoon and rehearsals for *Lord Dynamite*, I scribbled away in my caravan at 'A Plea for Poetry' – a 'manifesto for looking forward and regaining confidence'.

I increasingly felt that *Lord Dynamite* was a backward step for us and that more spectator-sport spectacle, however radical the content and however well-fashioned the style, was just another manifestation of the problem. We were becoming state-licensed buffoons and professional lunatics, burning ourselves out to entertain the masses and provide a distraction from the awfulness of the daily grind when we should have been looking at the daily grind itself.

After decades of accelerating consumerism, the nation had moved into both economic and psychic recession. It wasn't just that the so-called alternative culture of the sixties had become worldly and cynical and commercial, but that Utopianism, generosity and caring seemed to have become unfashionable, communities fragmented and art merely a decorative mannerism; just another commodity manipulated by dealers and producers. The market economy was generating false needs and false choices which were shrinking rather than extending our being. I wanted art that would help us all to become dreamweavers, guardians of the unpredictable and shamen. The Royal Shakespeare Company were offering to sell me 'Perchance to Dream' pillowcases and Macbeth shaving mugs (big enough to puke in, I hoped) when I wanted Lorca's duende 'that compels Goya, master of grey, silver and pink to paint with his knees and with his fists horrible bitumen blacks. The duende which drags her wings of rusty knives along the ground.'

After the Gulf War, England was feeding off H. E. Bates's *Darling Buds of May* on the telly. Pre-industrial farming, apple blossom and cottage counterpanes were the nostalgic pretence, while a Tower of Babel was dominating the skyline in Canary Wharf. As D. H. Lawrence put it in 1936:

> Supposing a bomb was put under the whole scheme of things. What is the underlying impulse that will provide the motive power for a new state of things, when this democratic-industrial-lovey-dovey-darling-take-me-to-mamma state of things is bust? What's next? That's what interests me. What now? is no fun any more.[4]

I searched hard for the answers, but nothing satisfied my soul. Some (such as Myerscough) argued for the economic benefits of art – in terms of urban regeneration, jobs, tourism and exports. More jargon from the dominant culture of grocerism. Some, such as Wilding, wished to separate out centralist cultural leadership from its social aspects (which were deemed to be the responsibility of the local authorities), thus making no acknowledgement of the growing movement of community art. Then there were still the old Hush Puppies of excellence lurking in the cultural corridors of power; Bloomsbury, Keynes, Shaw, Hoggart, balancing uneasily on snobbery, taste, history, Oxbridge and the nauseating English class system.

I felt that the case for art ran much deeper and was better argued in terms of spiritual need and the realisation and extension of our humanity and our imaginative potential at all levels and within all styles, whether it was Elgar or Bob Marley.[5] Thinking back over all our work of the last decade, particularly that in Barrow and Glasgow (and Australia in 1979) and also of the personal rites-of-passage work we had stumbled across, I reckoned we had been on a consistent journey for two decades. I went in search of radical visionaries from other ages and cultures.

At a fanciful level, I felt more in tune with cave paintings than much contemporary art. Maybe it was all our elemental research with fire, ice and earth, but when I saw prehistoric cave art near Malaga in southern Spain, I could imagine those early hominids, in the same random galaxy as ourselves, creating rituals to mark the passing of their short lives. Their camp-fires must have burned similarly to ours.

Then I remembered visiting Grünewald's sixteenth-century triptych altarpiece in Isenheim years before. His immaculate painting of Christ transcending bubonic plague is as fresh as when he painted it. Here was truth-saying and celebration in dire adversity. This was the finest of fine art in context.

At the other end of the spectrum, I re-read Roger Coleman's book, *The Art of Work*.[6] As founders of Welfare State International, Roger and I had together pummelled around hundreds of ideas in 1968, when we were seeking that 'entertainment an alternative and a way of life'. Roger urged a fundamental reappraisal of the role of satisfying work to enhance the lives of the many rather than the few. If, as Roger puts it, 'the true function of Art is to shape, define, form and inform the ways in which we create our environment day by day', then we need to re-examine the way we perceive our normal reality, and if, when confronted by the insatiable linear-growth momentum of our materialist culture, we can begin to redefine real need, real satisfaction and the nature of celebration, then, maybe, art can take the centre stage once again.

Gradually, as I wrote 'A Plea for Poetry', the links between the fine-art end and the everyday became clearer. Jamake Highwater, a contemporary Native American, wrote:

> The greatest distance between people is not space but culture, and it is only through poetry in its most twentieth century manifestations that we have the slightest chance of making ourselves known to each other. In this way poetry is social change.

He helped me see that poetry gives us the capacity to create metaphors as bridges. Then, out of the blue, a paper on 'Vernacular Art' arrived from Clarke Mackay, a film-maker friend in Canada.[7] In researching the form, context and meaning of home-made art, he reaffirmed that as children we use such metaphors and make our own world reality through artistic play:

> The psychological consequences of robbing us of this possibility are considerable, both in terms of emotional and intellectual development and as adults for our psyches and the social order. But this is precisely what our commodity-orientated culture has done . . . The history of art and culture over the last few hundred years, when viewed in a global context, can be seen as a continuous erosion of home-made, local, participatory art, craft and ritual, and its replacement by standardised products fashioned by trained professionals for sale. Furthermore, these products are not ideologically neutral. They reflect the preoccupations and values or otherwise serve the interests of a relatively small group of people – the privileged within the industrialised Western world.

So, after consulting these visionaries, wise men and poets from the safety of my lonely caravan, I distilled my thoughts into a 'mission statement' which we still use:

> We are seeking a culture which may well be less materially based but where more people will actively participate and gain the power to celebrate moments that are wonderful and significant in our lives. Be this building our own houses, naming our children, burying our dead, announcing partnerships, marking anniversaries, creating new sacred spaces and producing whatever drama, stories, songs, rituals, ceremonies, pageants and jokes that are relevant to new values depicted with a new iconography.

I added the rider that to put this into effect we would need to change the fundamental premises on which we maintain our current society, its institutions, its economy; where people come before profit, and long-term interest before short-term gain.

Much to my surprise, 'A Plea for Poetry' was published in full in August.[8] Having got that off my chest, and partly to clear our minds further, Sue Gill and I went to Australia again on a sabbatical journey lasting from November 1991 to May 1992. In Australia, away from the domination of Europe, we found not only a refreshing optimism but some key stepping stones.

We had to earn our living through some teaching workshops which, of necessity, still dipped into our old tricks (such as a large, instant pageant in Bathurst on Australia Day to facilitate a carnival emu gaining wings after being attacked by a fly-past of crop-spraying kangaroos). But it was, as usual, the incidental journey which changed our perspective.

On 17 December 1991, I wrote in my diary in Lismore, New South Wales

> We create a ceremony for an Australian friend, Jyllie, who had been unable to attend her father's funeral in the UK. In her garden and house we decorate spaces with strings of white paper cutouts using salmon and moon imagery (her father had been an amateur fisherman). In a sheltered corner by a tree there is a place for meditation with a table of family snapshots. Sue makes a small elegant sculptural fire constructed with circles of chunky wood. I make a ceremonial lantern with white tissue paper and willow sticks. Inside this, which we construct as a miniature replica of her father's garden shed, Jyllie places the last photograph of herself with her father. In the evening, after reading from Rilke, Jyllie places the lantern on the fire. The solemnity is countered partially by her friend playing Glen Miller on a small electric keyboard in a far corner of the garden.

New ceremonies seemed a way forward. After taking part in Neil Cameron's Festival extravaganza, a typically New Age Australian confrontation between an Earth Mother and a Tower of Babel, at the Melany Folk Festival, we accepted there could also be a place in our work for such tribal gatherings. In late 1992 we stayed with Robert and Marianne Courtney in a beautiful self-built house constructed with local pine columns and a veranda to draw in air current (rather than air conditioning). It was an elegant and ecologically sound inspiration to feed our own desire to build an artists' centre. Robert and Marianne had been married in their own garden. Celebrants in Australia aren't tied to licensed premises as they are (for the time being) in England, so here was yet another reminder of how relevant ceremonies could be achieved. Two further strong experiences reinforced our feeling. In March we stayed in Alice Springs. More friends, the Schollys, a family of four were moving house after living for seven years on the same bit of land. It was a rare anthropological pleasure to observe the process of moving. They had trouble piling everything into a massive semi-trailer. Their dependence on stuff, like ours, was thrown into further relief when, with Peter Latz we camped in the desert and climbed up to see aboriginal markings – raggedy totems of emu and kangaroo and scarred circles made to signify a 'honey dreaming'. The experience opened our minds.

On my way back to England at the airport, I grabbed a copy of *Australia's Kakaduman* by Bill Neidjie:

> Our story is in the land . . .
> it is written in those sacred places.
> My children will look after those places
> that's the law.
>
> Dreaming place . . .
> you can't change it, no matter who you are.
> No matter you rich man, no matter you king.
> you can't change it.

In May 1992 we landed in England. After being in the desert, it was a huge culture shock, we invented our own community FLEAS (Front Line Education and Art Services) to continue servicing Welfare State International. We were inspired to stay and build our own Dreaming Place and used as our logo 'a Flea in search of the Universe'.

Ulverston

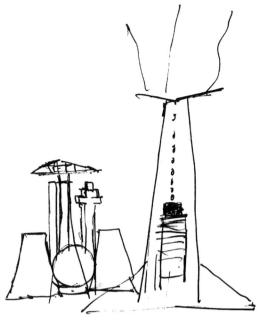

Following our first trip to Australia in 1979, we had landed in Ulverston, little knowing we would end up staying there for the next twenty and more years. The Southern hemisphere seemed to be a very long way away. In March 1980, a year after we had left Darwin, we wrote to all our friends in Australia, describing the town.

We live next to a big tarmacked car park which 150 years ago used to be a village green and a hiring fair for farm labourers. In the foreground of a photograph of our new house taken in about 1920 there are four Clydesdale cart horses on their last day of work.

We have ended up in Ulverston on the edge of the Lake District 40 miles from Windscale (a nuclear power station renamed Sellafield – as a propaganda exercise – after it caught fire in 1957) in a country where 60 per cent of industries probably depend (directly or indirectly) on the arms trade. The landscape is not unlike Tasmania except the shallow sea is brown and poisoned with nuclear waste, heavy metals and shit – contradictory but maybe ideal for us at the moment.

Our children need to be settled for a while. Bang goes the deposit on the house in Stanley, Tasmania.

We are creating Barn Dances that are very popular. Memories of a 'Bush Dance' in Adelaide! Dan and Hannah play trombone and cornet with the Junior Silver band. I am learning to play the melodeon. We make theatrical intrusions

145

into the social dancing with our own brand of folk theatre and mummers dance. Last week in Chorley men who weld Vulcan bombers were 'Stripping the Willow' (a traditional dance) with, ironically, women raising funds for the Red Cross. In Nether Kellet rugged old Tories are doing the Excuse-me with the daughters of farm labourers. It's bizarre but maybe under the belly of the dying dinosaur a new sense of community is arising? In Burnley in our old wooden workshops which we donated to the local Youth Theatre punk bands are organising themselves into collectives to share limited resources.

On a frosty January morning with the mist rising, the damson hills across the Bay look like Kilimanjaro and despite the poison sea the dabs taste sweet as sugar cane.

Stan Laurel was born in Ulverston in 1890. I know this because Dan, our son, received his biography as a prize when he won the Stan Laurel Lookalike Competition (in the town's Charter Week in 1982). The mayor at that time, the late Billy 'Twin Tub' Cubin, signed it 'Well Done from Grand Sheik Bill Cubin'.

Dan looks nothing like Stan and never has done, but Bill Cubin was joyously filled with Laurelmania. If you join in a pub quiz in Ulverston, you might be asked 'Can you name three of the seven films where Stan does not cry?' (The answer is: *Lucky Dogs, Busy Bodies, Swiss Miss, Midnight Patrol, Me and My Pal, The Music Box* and *The Bullfighters*.) Bill Cubin's museum in Stan's honour still exists and by 2003 there will be a bronze statue of him and Olly staring across the bay towards the bronze statue of Eric Morecambe in Morecambe, staring back at us.

Ulverston reminds me of *Under Milk Wood* or *Clochemerle* (the story about the French town which is divided over a public urinal). Under every stone is a pebble – or perhaps chewing gum. Under every pebble is grit or a fossilised cobble and so on, back in history, so the town constantly confirms the wonder in every cliché.

It is a working-class, Georgian town (population 12,000) on the northern edge of Morecambe Bay. Halfway along the Furness peninsulas at the bottom of the Lake District and nine miles from Barrow and at the start of the Cumbrian Way. It now enjoys uncertain prosperity, dependent as it is on the biggest drugs company in the world, Glaxo-Smith-Kline, whose local factory makes anti-ulcer pills. Workers also commute to BAE Systems (once Vickers) and British Nuclear Fuels at Windscale. There are many small firms who make specialist components for underwater exploration or the armaments industry. One was convinced that it could bring up the *Kursk*. Another was conned into making a skilful electronic swordfish for Joan Collins to ride across Windermere in a film that never got made (the firm didn't get paid either). Like Glaxo, they, too, tend to get taken over by distant managements. A few small entrepreneurial shopkeepers struggle to maintain a living in competition with out-of-town stores and supermarkets, and there are two local and dynamic glassmaking firms (Heron Glass and Cumbria Crystal), a surviving slaughterhouse and weekly cattle mart.

The Georgians built pleasant terraced townhouses, one of which is now our home. Some of the bigger examples were for sea captains. Before the bay channels silted up, after the coming of the railway viaduct of 1880, Ulverston was a small port where boatbuilders constructed schooners. These sailed round the world, exchanging gunpowder (made from local charcoal) for spices and slaves who were sometimes chained in local cellars. The shoreline is perilous, with shifting channels and quicksands. Two or three people are drowned every year. A forty-five-foot whale from Florida was washed up in October 2001. In medieval times, after monks walked across Morecambe Bay, a Cistercian monastery was established at Furness Abbey, while in 1652 George Fox established the Quaker Society of Friends two miles away at Swarthmoor Hall. Although Ulverstonians threw him in the town beck because they didn't like his preaching, the Quakers are still doing well. In prehistory, our Bronze Age ancestors dug tumuli on the cusp of Flan How, where they practised sky burials or stored cremated bones in earthenware pots. In Victorian times, pole-vaulting was invented here, which appeals to us since we always seem to be reaching for the sky. The original pole-vaulters used to jump high across the Ulverston canal, which is the shortest and deepest in England.

During the First World War, at Dragley Beck, just down the road from Lanternhouse, the first ever women's league football team was begun. In the bay, which Turner and Constable painted, fishermen trawl shrimps from tractors. Legends abound of ghost stage coaches, travellers and horses sunk in storms and mysterious lights swinging at night. This is a place to rendezvous with stories. As you arrive near Ulverston by road from Lancaster, along the unpredictable asphalt serpent of the A590, a fat, green hill looms ahead. On its top, foreshortened by perspective, is the Hoad Monument, a lighthouse.

We never imagined Ulverston would become our home. At the time, we were performing a street show about a lonely lighthouse keeper. Every midsummer night, the last female dragon in the world emerged from the oceanic depths. Over the years, it came closer to the shore, until, one fateful night, roused by a foghorn, it landed on the lighthouse. So, like the dragon, the lighthouse drew us nearer to home. The trigger was a chance reconnection with the local Renaissance Arts Association, which had once contracted us to make a ceremony to reopen an historic corn mill refurbished through a job-creation scheme.

Carnival Night

Every July, there is an Ulverston Carnival, which never acknowledges Stan but often takes place on American Independence Day. One particular year things came bizarrely together, as they often do in Ulverston. On the large car park in front of the home we bought were many cars with raised boots and dozens of pairs of men changing into black suits, red fezes or bowler hats and sashes. I realised they must be Laurel and Hardy lookalikes. From their various 'Sons of the Desert' clubs round the world (many of which are in the USA), they were on a pilgrimage to Stan's shrine to celebrate his birthday. (Hence Bill as the Grand Sheikh.)

So many very fat, and some less fat, men from across the globe, paraded in our carnival as Olly and Stan couples, with their wives, carrying banners and singing 'The Cuckoo Waltz'. Unfortunately, this was also the year when the Young Farmers' Club blacked up as cannibals with chicken bones running through their noses and the parade marshals quite unwittingly arranged for their float to go next to the Trinidadian Steel Band from Moss Side.

In the evening, the drunkenness had no outlet except more raucous versions of 'The Blue Ridge Mountains of Virginia' or engaging with local youth on an equally post-carnival high. Great energy had been aroused but was spiralling into aggressive slapstick or worse.

So we decided to start a special Welfare State Carnival Night as a family gathering with music and a party to follow on from the town's carnival parade. Welfare State International and a few local volunteers erected market and food stalls (no bar, as there were two dozen pubs within a three-minute walk), flags, a stage for bands and occasional theatrical interruptions and parades. A loose narrative thread welded the evening together before one mortar shell was exploded from up Gill Banks, long before midnight, to signal goodnight.

It worked well, and we were making art on our own doorstep at last. These Carnival Nights carried on for a few years. Although the imagery was a little random, it was always celebratory. One year, we used our ice giant, left over from the *Titanic*, built the stage up as a ship's bridge and had gangs of pink fantasy flamingos on stilts stomping round 'the iceberg from Morecambe Bay'. To mark the official twinning of Ulverston with Albert in France, we used twin giant puppets. Once, we built a high lighthouse in the middle of the tarmac and the lighthousekeeper's wife was eaten by a white whale. Then the leggy spirit of carnival, dressed as a dancing lighthouse, chased away a boring wall, and so on. The poetry was usually found under our feet.

A favourite black-and-white photograph shows three or four hundred people of all ages and generations dancing together to a Winster Gallop from our barn-dance band. They are all holding hands, spiralling or making arches.

We try to step back and leave the event entirely in the hands of local people. This doesn't always work. Sometimes, because we have done things so well for so long, people never believe they can do it and indeed, sometimes they don't want to. Many work very hard at their own jobs and already have busy lives: with sports, hobbies, family, TV, fundraising for good causes and holidays, they don't have the time, energy or experience to take on anything else.

There is a debate to be had about the cloudy distinctions between amateur and professional roles and the nature of participation, access, ownership and origination of the art work, which community arts facilitators need to be clear about. Amateurs do it for love, we say, but in an ideal world we would all enjoy our work and maybe do some of it with and for love. Everyone is creative, but creativity can blossom in many public and private ways. Not everyone wants or needs to be a professional artist.

Most of the successful and fulfilled artists I know work at their play obsessively for ten hours and more a day. I do so myself. Why should we community artists expect the public to do the same? We don't expect our medical doctors or our car mechanics to be volunteers. These issues always come to the fore when we try to pass on our working methods and prototypes to local people. Do we hand them on because we have become bored with them but can't bear to see them disappear, and thus rationalise the good they bring to the community?

After ten years Carnival Night became a young person's band night, a useful showcase for a number of good local bands that had little access to a wide public. There was still public dancing, decorations and market stalls, but over the years it became less of a family night out and on occasion the sound-control desk blocked the dance floor. The organisers had to work too hard, with none of the resources we as a professional arts company had or could raise. Eventually, the official carnival, the local authority and the police raised so many objections and restrictions that it came to an end. I doubt the organisers – volunteer, unpaid, altruistic community artists as they were – will try again. Now, many townspeople regret the disappearance of Carnival Night. The spare energy of the daytime carnival has nowhere to run in the evening and the car park has reverted to dead tarmac. Other ideas for community celebrations, such as a Raft Race and New Year's Day door knockers (made in raku kilns), never took off in the same way as Carnival Night.

It is difficult to maintain energy and excitement in a small community. Maybe this is where the professional has a distinctive role. It is one factor that has carried the Lantern Festival through to its twentieth year.

Lantern Festival

We started the Lantern Festival in the second week of September 1983 as the company's contribution to the annual Ulverston Charter Festival. Ulverston received its charter to be a market town from Edward I in 1280. Regurgitation of history is a convenient way to reinforce the town's identity, have fun, bond citizens and extend the visitor season before the dark days descend. The lantern idea came out of our Japan trip (see On Tour). We started tentatively and were very surprised at the speed with which it spread and became an export. Lantern Parades become better and better. The event is frequently written up as if it were a long-standing Cumbrian tradition that has been there for ever. But, as Hobsbawm the wily historian has pointed out (mainly in reference to English royalty), any tradition can be started in four years. The Lantern Processions are now organised through a Lantern Supporters' Group, a voluntary committee of townspeople, who raise funds through coffee mornings and collecting coins in buckets on the night.

Lanterns are made with dried willow sticks, which are shaped and stuck together with masking tape to make rigid structures. These are then covered in tissue paper, coated with latex or PVA glue and lit by a candle carefully positioned inside, in a wire cradle.[1] They can only be used outside. One of their beauties is that they can be made very simply by novice, very old or very young makers, but they also lend themselves to the most elaborate of inventions and to a considerable scale. Photographs depict the first participants. Women (from the Women's Institute) are sheepishly holding little lumpy lanterns that look like sticky suet puddings. Many of our early experiments were conducted by Ali Jones and Mary Robson, who developed the basic prototype two-foot-high, four-sided triangular pyramid which has been copied in many places in Europe, Canada and Australia. Arts practitioners from outside the town receive grants in order to come and study our good practice, but in Ulverston itself the knowledge is embedded in the community. Some of the fifteen-year-old Girl Guides from the first parade now bring their own children to the workshops. Welfare State International artists run workshops on lantern-making for families at Lanternhouse in the run-up to the parade and others take place in community centres and village halls in the area.

But many parents are so experienced and ambitious, they just collect bundles of withies and jars of glue from us and return home to finish their considerable creations in garages and kitchens.

On the afternoon before the parade, as excitement builds, there is another tradition. We present specially made small 'gift lanterns' to unsung heroines and heroes, shop assistants, crossing keepers, district nurses and so on, people who give to the community but aren't recognised for their contribution. The visit is kept secret until our band parachutes on to each unsuspecting soul and their assembled friends, who frequently weep with joy (or is it embarrassment?) as we sing 'The Lantern Carol':

When it's drizzling
Grey as slate
When your feet ache
and you've put on weight.

When your mortgage can't be paid
When the bad news hits every page
You can light your lantern outside your room
You can light your lantern to banish gloom.

Oh it's gonna be sunny
It's gonna be fine.
In the light of your lantern it's fine fine fine.

People are proud to carry their gift in the parade. Theoretically, they are selected by the previous year's 'winners' but the town council tends to make the accolade corporate and we have to resist. Hundreds of big sculptural lanterns are made each year. Depending on the theme, fishes, lighthouses, spacemen, dinosaurs, *Titanics*, greyhounds, octopuses and many lyrical zoo creatures emerge from captivity to roam the night in one of four processions. Appearing from cardinal points of Ulverston, these four 'rivers of light' weave and bob down streets behind percussion ensembles like Blast Furness and the Ulverston Town Brass Band, switchbacking past old people's centres, pubs, the hospital, a graveyard and many homes.[1]

Children in pyjamas are held up at windows. Thousands congregate in the town centre. Tourists can't find a bed and breakfast between Ulverston and Hawkshead. Whatever the weather, generations celebrate together in their own streets in a

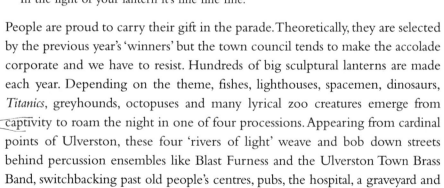

151

totally non–commercial event, in aid of nothing but itself, and an unspoken but understood agreement that we are marking the end of summer and the equinox crossover to the dark days of autumn. For funders, we have to measure outputs. We tell them the number of gallons of fuel sold at local petrol stations and the number of beds occupied on the night. The difficulty with the last statistic is that the more celebratory people feel, the more they tend to get into fewer beds.

The Finale of the Lantern Procession is a large-scale spectacle invented, made and paid for by Welfare State International as our annual gift to the town. Created by about a dozen Welfare State International artists and volunteers, working long hours for ten days, it costs £12,000 to £20,000. The money takes Eileen Strand, our dedicated and skilful business manager, a year to raise from a variety of sources. The event takes place on a central rectangular field which has so far miraculously avoided real-estate developers. All the processions, with their large following, make up a total audience of between three and five thousand, who gather in the centre around a marked ellipse, 100 yards across, lit primarily by the carried lanterns. In the distant corners of the field are the odd hamburger stall, festoons of coloured lights, a St John Ambulance, a meeting point for lost children, illegal pedlars of illuminated sticks (who creep in past the Lantern Supporters Group) and, so far, no toilets, which is one reason we keep the event short. Over eighteen years, we have tried various shapes and staging. Cinemascope, an end-on proscenium, circles and ovals, with the audience all, or three quarters, round them, plus central scaffolding stages depicting ships, towers, carousels and more, with amazing pyrotechnic sculptures by Dougie Nicholson (External Combustion), Caroline Menis and Roger Bloomfield.[2] Designs have changed to facilitate viewing (building images higher as the audience has increased), but also because our policy has shifted from providing spectacular production to lower-key participatory events where the big-scale sculptures are made by gathering scores of lanterns from the community. We might, for example, create a medium-scale fiery garden (with bicycle-driven roundabouts and burning paper rope images picking up on the theme), then collect community lanterns and hang them from cables which rise on various hydraulic lifts or cranes, creating maypoles of light or illuminated constellations. There is always a full sound score specially composed by Dan Fox, often played live with a choir and the town band.

In September 2001, a high, full moon sank into a blue-and-white firework sea with extraordinary Angel Fish made by Graeme Gilmour – from *Glasgow All Lit Up* days – and after a dance of sea-creature lanterns, a new moon was hauled high on a crane, followed by a cometlike tail or necklace of children's lanterns. This imagery was sweeter than we had originally intended. The moon was to have been shot down by missiles as a comment on George Bush's proposed 'Star Wars' missile-defence nonsense, but as the event came just after September 11th, we softened it by removing all fireballs and black smoke and ended with a gentle anthem for flute and percussion.

Imagery drops in from current preoccupations, but there are recurring motifs. The burning winged house on the cover of this book, for example (a detail from the 1996 Lantern Finale, directed and written by Hannah Fox) was developed from *Lord Dynamite* (see *The Flight from Spectacle*) As Nobel flew away in his shed, so did a shed on that Lantern Finale night. Laced with the lantern dreams of Ulverstonians, off it went over Morecambe Bay. Some swore blind it was a flying saucer, some said it was just a shed from any old working-class allotment.

Ten years or so ago, there was a sadness in Ulverston, with grumpy traders and many empty shops. Specialist grocers could not compete with a new supermarket and shops that didn't change simply died. Antiques, pine furniture, jewellery and stuffed novelties have moved in and, though some of the traders are just as grumpy, there is a sense of vitality, more smiling, rapidly rising house prices and probably more visitors and holiday lets. The town is frequently cited as an example of how to 'regenerate' a nice but once sagging market town, and has won a national award for itself and for Jayne Kendall, its patient and dynamic Town Manager. Things have changed, with restaurants, health-food shop, three art galleries, an excellent delicatessen, an outstanding bookshop, an upgraded railway station and many writers, artists and musicians settling in the locality.

The most significant change in the last ten years, though, is Ulverston's new-found identity as 'The Festivals Town'. A one-act-play drama festival, a youth drama festival and a highly competitive festival of musical instrumentalists and solo singing already existed, but the Lantern Festival increased the momentum and now we have festivals devoted to beer, complementary medicine, writing, printmaking, folk music and dance, walking, Dickens, flags and comedy. Working in partnership with local economic development officers and the Town Manager, Welfare State International can take credit for the last two and for triggering the festival explosion.

I wonder if these achievements will last longer than our artistic ones? Sometimes I find myself sounding more like a tourist brochure than the Dada manifesto writer of my primitive avant-garde days in Burnley in the seventies. This might well be the case. After serving on countless well-meaning and supportive committees, such as the Better Towns' Team or Ulverston 2000, arguing for too many days about double yellow lines, traffic wardens, adverts on parking tickets, dog shit prevention versus the value of art, my brain may well be addled. Or perhaps these practical considerations are the equivalent of a painter stretching the canvas, before beginning the art work. The Comedy Festival started off in 1996, with a week-long Welfare State International workshop in which the able and the infirm, the unemployable and the unsuspecting are dragged off the streets to be instantly drilled into a street-comedy troupe by Susan Clarke. Year one marked an arcane local rite called Changing the One Way System, which recurs every five years. No one knew where the main entry to the town was any more. So two eight-foot-high dancing traffic cones, a whirling Hoad Monument, a transvestite policeman with a whistle and the Hard Hat Band led the Mayor to cut five ribbons at all conceivable entrances.

We back all horses. One idea we tossed up at the Town Comedy Committee was the Convention of Pantomime Horses. It was a scheme for horses that found themselves unemployed outside the pantomime season. Now it runs and runs (literally) with sports and pub teams of well over 100 inebriated inner equestrians racing into the *Guinness Book of Records*. We often take an established form or theme – say, an agricultural show, or the World Cup, or 'They came in off the Sands' – and train novice artistes in appropriate (or inappropriate) role play which may include Wheelbarrow Obedience Tests, Parsnips on Parade, or a lonely shrimp weeping in Woolworths. A middle-aged bookkeeper (and grandma) leading the flypast of her Women's Ironing Board Aerial Display Team choked pedestrians with trails of orange smoke. The spin-off is unpredictable and often does not fit desirable economic 'outputs', like our accountant with his gala flea circus in an ice-cream tray. Clearly, underneath the image of the 'St Ives of the North', Ulverston is still a Lancastrian working town with Stan Laurel's music-hall in its blood.

We began the Flag and Banner Festival in 1997. It usually starts by reclaiming May Day and lasts for just two magnificent weeks. The town becomes a walkabout gallery – a cross between Matisse and the *Beano*, with flag trails and a children's Find a Flag Competition. In the first year, we put up fifty wondrous, big Japanese silk flags sewn by Shona Watt,[3] a flag artist of international reputation. We wanted to make the event as popular and participatory as the Lantern Festival, but in order to speed up the process, instead of starting with little flags and building up to bigger ones, as we had done with the lanterns, we went for a big initial splash.

154

A dozen long violet and blue banners, translucent in the evening sun, are erected on the A590 roundabout (this involved a year of arguing with the appropriate Highways Authority). Along the streets, many more colourful flags are located in specially made brackets which can also be used for small Christmas trees. The designs are graphic representations of trades and businesses. They are designed first by primary-school children and then developed by Shona in her workshop. They cost over £100 each but this price includes Shona's specialised technique of heat-cutting and making-up. Each year, thanks to the persistence and fundraising of the Better Towns Team, another fifty flags appear. In 2002, there were 250.

With the catalyst of this spectacular barrage, we are persuading schools, households and individuals to become flag conscious and to make their own, using simple printing techniques like potato prints. It is working. Some traders, just surviving on tight margins, with ludicrously high government business rates and parking charges, find the cost too high. One imported a job lot of £5 nationalistic flags, mainly Union Jacks and the cross of St George from Taiwanese sweat shops. Some want coats of arms, but overall we have maintained a wild spirit of nutty invention.

The children's drawings ensure this. They are fresh and uninhibited. The colours are electric. The gents' outfitter received a lipstick-on-the-collar design and the dentist (with his approval) a bloody tooth with a pair of pliers. For two hours, starting at 5 a.m. on a Saturday morning, the Better Towns team, lawyers, estate agents and businessmen, Sue and I, armed with trailer, ladders, gaffer tape, Stanley knives and pliers, are out there in all weathers. As the wind billows these shimmering silks in the early morning light, it's as if Stanley Spencer were painting the banners of Agincourt. It is beautiful, satisfying and extremely English,

Flag festival, Ulverston

and afterwards, as we trough our big breakfast fry-up in Lanternhouse, we are a little smug and well bonded into good-humoured citizenry.

Sooner or later, thanks to drunken japes, a few flags go walkabout and a few traders gently complain. One year, by mistake, the Animal Rescue flag was put up outside the butcher's and the butcher's partridge ended up outside the health-food shop. As their flag had disappeared altogether, we substituted a pink toaster on a black background, maintaining it was a picture of tofu at dawn. A badly drawn chemical flask looking like an erect penis arrived outside Boots the Chemist. The flustered manageress rang our answer machine at 7.30 a.m. to demand we change it immediately.

The Sky's the Limit

I was ambivalent about the Millennium. Very early on, I was involved in some relatively high-level discussions about the Dome and when I suggested running its community segment on a 'LETS' scheme with visitors and artists generating and swapping new work as they went along, I was never asked back. Initially, I wanted to hide in any desert, far away from the hype of our Western consumers' calendar. In fact, on the night itself, after playing some melodeon for a neighbours' gathering in a Girl Guide hut, Sue and I lit a small fire by the sea and watched other people's pyrotechnic displays miles away across Morecambe Bay. They appeared as sparkling anthills no bigger than our family fire.

The New Year, however, presented Ulverston with an occasion which could hardly be ignored. May 2000 was the 150th anniversary of the laying of the foundation stone for the Hoad Monument, the replica Eddystone Lighthouse sentinel above the town, built to honour Sir John Barrow, who was born here in a humble cottage at Dragley Beck and in 1803 became Second Secretary to the Admiralty, a job he did for forty-two years.

Devising the event in partnership with the town authorities was a challenge. It is always difficult, the closer you get to home, to find the balance between expected jingoistic reinforcement of a local hero, received history and the truth of carnival anarchy. However, apart from the Lantern Festival, which has become large by repetition and accumulation and is still an appropriate spectacle, we had never created one of our big events for the town. Maybe this was the right time? As I had moved away from this kind of work, we asked Peter Huby to be the artistic director. Eileen Strand, our business manager, raised £34,000 from many sources, including the Millennium Commission, the District Council, European Regional Development and Town Lands Trust.

Peter directed *The Sky's the Limit* with great aplomb and an inventive team concocted a mermaid figurehead, a Chinese pagoda and instant ships and icebergs as body costumes. We were inspired by a new source book, *Barrow's Boys* by Fergus Fleming, a stimulating account of Barrow's expeditions and fantasies, which if they hadn't been tragically true would have been pure *Goon Show*. Blimpish naval officers steered by Sir John from his Admiralty desk desperately searching for obscure sea routes, blundered into other peoples' cultures in China, the Congo and the Arctic and actually ate their own boots when they failed to find the geographical source of the Nile's nostril.

After a year of fundraising, planning (with Gail Dadson) and three months' intensive hard work with performing, percussion-making and special-needs groups in Ulverston and students from Lancaster, Sunday, 14 May arrived. A huge galleon built in the town centre was occupied by a Napoleonic re-enactment society with tales and samples of scurvy, replica cannons and weevil-infested biscuits.

Meanwhile, two Sir John Barrows emerged. Two actors: ours and one from the Heritage Centre. Such is communication in a small town. All morning, multiple charades with imaginary tribal people, demented explorers, paddlesteamers, arches, globes and the brand-new Big Red Drum Band spilled over the cobbles and the ginnels to entertain thousands. The tribal people were not easy to get right. We did not want to fall into clichéd caricature. In March, Susan Clarke, who was leading the street performances, faxed Peter Huby:

> Offensiveness. I do not want to have anyone in Welfare State International impersonating people of other races. I think it is a completely different matter to be ACTING or representing, but this has to be done in a very clear way, no one should be dressing up and thinking they are BEING a Nubian or an Inuit [we forbade the word Eskimo].

In the event, the tribal performers had a kind of surreal, non-specific nursery-rhyme quality, with faces and costumes in very unrealistic primary colours.

At 11.45 a.m., pubs mustered for the admirals' wheelbarrow race up Hoad Hill to raise funds for a heart defibrillator for Ulverston Health Centre in which very fat men had to be wheeled uphill as fast as possible. At the stroke of twelve and a half bells, the whole cavalcade of eventually five thousand people, led by the mayor and a six-person delegation from the twin town of Albert and the twin Sir Johns, suddenly changed course to navigate Hoad Hill. Winding in pilgrimage up its steep banks, they followed the musical compass of Blast Furness and the archery club with its heavy cannon (unintentionally) on fire. We all assembled in a mass picnic on the crown of the hill at the feet of the monument itself. Ulverston Town Band in their brand-new red uniforms looked totally the part as they sat elegantly blowing sea shanties. Those who couldn't walk, which included many old people, were ferried up a back route in four-wheel-drive vehicles.

With temperatures soaring into the upper seventies, the mayor, Ron Creer, who was smartly dressed in a suit and tie, announced that the original time capsule would be left in place – not that anyone could find it – and presented a new capsule to the caretaker for future burial in the monument's cellar. After firing a naval cannon, eight daredevil admirals abseiled down the monument and Sir John Barrow (a third one) climbed to the top of the hundred-foot-high cupola and stood solidly upright.

Peter Huby, a rock climber, had arranged for a climbing colleague to be tied on to a metal stake fixed to the top. All hell broke out round him with a Spanish-style firework display (*mascletta*) of ten thousand crackers, fat plumes of blue smoke and great unfurling blue and white silk banners leaping like languorous snakes around and down the stone phallus. One very long, thin, high white streamer, 'the longest in the world', we said, kept on coming, whirling high and then dipping low, almost to the crowd below. A cloth Catherine wheel spinning back on itself, it flapped so far above the lighthouse that it could be seen from Coniston Old Man. Big kites and big drums filled the air for hours as we picked up the litter and thousands of fragments of blood-red cardboard, the remains of the *mascletta*, to be cleared before cattle and sheep returned.

Our event was a great public success. Thousands of people hadn't been up Hoad for years, if at all, and, as in the *Town Hall Tattoo* in Barrow, we all shared in a temporary convivial community. We hoped it was as good as the original pageant had been 150 years previously, and wondered whether at the next millennium anyone would remember us. We received a letter from Putzi Smith: 'A big thank you for such a splendid weekend of celebrations in Ulverston. I will never forget the man who stood on top of Hoad while the fireworks and smoke engulfed him.' The mayor also said: 'Thank you. It was as good as the new Dickens Festival'. People love to dress up here. Gentlemen hire top hats and tails, ladies crinolines. In 2001, the Dickensian Committee advertised for street urchins with 'ragged trousers cut off below the knees' to parade round the one-way system.

My best memory of *Sky's the Limit* is 'The Hoad' written by Walter Howson, a local. He was born in 1929 in Ulverston and was the youngest of ten children.

He played the British Legion pantomime dame for nearly twenty years. He died in April 2000 just before *The Sky's the Limit* and his ashes are scattered on Hoad Hill. His daughter asked the mayor to read the poem as part of his address. It was perfect for the occasion. Its simple, if old-fashioned, evocation of one resident's life (and death) spoke more to me than the spectacular clutter and euphoria of most Millennium excess, including our own.

When snow has rested on her side
I've sledged her icy thigh,
I've britches torn on slippery 'scales'
And Kites flown to her sky

She's been to me an Everest
The range the cowboys ride,
A battlefield for heroes
The bush where lions hide

I've climbed her breast in howling gale
I've strolled her in the sun
And in her bracken boudoir deep
Oh many a heart I've won

And now in the autumn of my life
My heart is with her still
I know I'll find contentment
Each time I climb Hoad Hill.

Return of the Dragon

It snowed heavily and unexpectedly one February and many people instantly made elaborate snow figures. Not standard snowmen with carrot noses and coal eyes, but igloo lanterns, a life-sized cello player with an icicle bow and a Beryl Cooke fat woman staring into a handbag shop. Someone said: 'It's you lot. You Welfare Staters. You gave us permission to be crazy.' It would make a nice epitaph.

And what happened to the dragon who drew us to Ulverston in the first place? Well, it lies curled inside Hoad Hill and rises up whenever stasis rules. Once it was killed by a Viking king, they say, who is now buried with his long boat in a barrow at Pennington. Before that, it was nesting in Wasdale Volcano, near Windscale, until burning fragments were blown to Ulverston, where it reseeded itself. And goes on reseeding.[4]

The Sky's the Limit, Ulverston, 2000

Lanternhouse

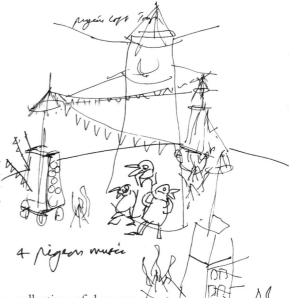

pigeons loft roof

4 pigeons music

I remember very little of primary school except for a collection of dens on a school playing field in Goole, the town where our family relocated during the war. Instead of the usual blank sports fields, this field was dug up and dotted with bits of corrugated iron, sheets of wood and fragments of packing cases piled to make scores of tiny home-made castles surrounded by their individual moats and personalised drawbridges. The image of that anarchic children's shanty town has stuck, to re-emerge in various installations. Our early nomadic fusions of embryonic architecture and installation were temporary. During the first twenty years of trucking, there was no thought either of settling in a permanent residence or making permanent art works. By the early eighties, though, we were looking to settle.

We had outgrown the caravans, and the lock-up garages, draughty hired rehearsal spaces and workshops had become tedious. Also, we had sussed, understandably late for a company who had named themselves after the Welfare State, that power and security in England is vested in property. This was certainly the case with us. If we had not purchased the Old National School in Ulverston in 1987 (thanks to an interest-free loan from the previous owners, Marl International), when it came to our near-bankrupt post-Barrow years we would have had nothing to mortgage and would have gone bust. Initially, the school provided a basic store, with offices, studios, a big meeting/rehearsal room, a canteen and parking for our vehicles. The idea of developing this fairly dilapidated Victorian school into a 'Total Art Work' and thinking of the whole process of building as an extended dramatic event with attendant ceremonies came much later. For years, we could afford only perfunctory maintenance. In common with most small touring theatre companies, except those touring out of the big reps, we had never had any capital grants except one from Housing the Arts in 1974, when we received £12,000 for a big truck. Then, in order to get the grant, I had had to argue it wasn't really a lorry but a mobile cinema projection room. My application to the capital grants committee included a brick on wheels (wrapped in the property page of *The Times*). This was wheeled (literally tabled!) across the Arts Council's vast mahogany boardroom table, and we got our money. Twenty-two years later, our second 'brick' was instrumental in gaining our Lottery Award.

Building Utopia

The idea of building a house started in Glasgow in 1990. Over many years, as ideas piled up like stones on a cairn, the notion grew beyond recognition. It was all part of our gear change. It reflected a need to move away from 'Theatre', where practitioners live in a bubble with a life span of six months at most (three behind and three in front) and a need to make something more permanent and substantial and maybe more necessary.

If part of our motivation was to improve society (as it continues to be), then it's a good principle to construct the alternative rather than theorise about it. Better to build, say, a house, than make a play about housing issues. Some issue-based theatre can change consciousness and encourage solidarity,[1] but there is always the danger of preaching to the converted, with the audience, after a good night out at a piece of didactic theatre, returning depressed and powerless to an isolated bedsit.

After *Glasgow All Lit Up* (1989–90), our epic Lantern Festival which had stretched us for eighteen months, we needed to hang on to something small and concrete. 'Like building a house?' someone said and we were off again, jumping quite naively into the unknown, to apply our creative and organisational abilities to an entirely new discipline.

Maybe that is how we have survived. Having a low boredom threshold and periodically changing our skin with new and sometimes ridiculous challenges. Ninety per cent of the time, we start from an idea and, however impossible it sounds, we usually find a way of making it happen. Ideas come very quickly. We have hundreds of them. People always ask 'Where do you get them from?' and we never quite know. *Raising the Titanic* came about because I quipped 'I suppose the next thing is we'll be raising the *Titanic*'. By the next day, it was in our publicity. The idea for *Glasgow All Lit Up* took eighteen seconds to dream up and eighteen intensive months to realise. We must be deficient in remembering the pain, I guess, or why else would we follow the next scheme?

We were still thinking about drama and audience. Ahead of our time, we imagined *Challenge Anneka* meeting *Changing Rooms*. We wanted to demonstrate our belief that self-building a house is not difficult. We novices could do it, and if we all learned building skills in neighbourhood co-operatives, or at school, we could outwit those banks, finance houses and other mortgage parasites who exploit our need for shelter and home ownership.

In Glasgow, we had planned to give the 'House', when we found one, to a homeless group. We had started to negotiate free land and services from the supportive Glasgow City Architect Chris Purslow, when everything changed. We realised that there was no housing shortage in Glasgow and that it would be more efficient and economical to build at our base in Ulverston, where we already owned a little land round the Old National School.[2]

Our school contains a microcosm of English history. It was first opened through public subscription in 1834 as the National School and remained so until the mid-1930s. We have copies of the log books. The times were austere and discipline fierce. Windows were high so that children couldn't gaze out. Inkwells had to be filled. A gallon bottle of ink once fell and broke over a child's head. We discovered this through contacting many of the old, often very old, scholars and, through occasional tea parties, produced *Capsule* (1994), an eloquent poetry book of their reminiscences and stories.[3] In those days, pupils were strictly segregated, with a playground wall between the sexes. To put matters right, we made a wall of cake, old girls on one side, old boys on the other, then we all ate our way to the middle. As the girls had never been allowed on a school outing, we took them on Coniston Water in the steam yacht *Gondola*, complete with sherry and violin arias to entertain them, sailing to Arthur Ransome jetties where theatrical Carmen Mirandas materialised, bearing tea and cakes and plenty more sherry.

We inherited a ghost. At night and sometimes during the day, in the old library corner there would be random creakings, doors slamming and the sound of footsteps. Someone had a fleeting glimpse of a hazy woman in white and once, in fresh snow, there were footsteps leading away from the outside door of the locked cellar. Even since the new build, unlikely footsteps are still heard. Maybe the source is the girl who, long ago, had fallen to her death down a steep staircase.

During the war, the old school became an army billet, then a Labour Exchange, where people were forced to queue outside in all weathers. To mark the 160th anniversary of the building, students from Wimbledon College of Art sculpted a life-size papier-mâché queue from the job pages of newspapers and placed it outside in the street. Eventually the building became a storage depot for Ordnance Survey Maps of England's motorways, a post office garage and an electronics factory making cockpit lights for Tornado bombers.

Within five years, by 1992, architecture had become the main plank of our creative policy and all we needed was the money to make our dreams come true. At this stage, we had no idea where it would come from but we had passion, a great belief in our ideas and boundless optimism. Rather than a normal venue for the arts, we saw our 'House' as an artwork in itself. Using a poem as a manifesto, in 1993 we made funding applications to Northern Arts for Visual Arts Year 1996.

A Centre for Celebration

As part of the Company's six-year programme, we will construct a new building for artists and tutors with a gallery, small-scale performance venue and a landscaped garden revealing the town beck. There are many poetic and functional aspects to this project which cannot be separated. It is a total art work. Artists from many disciplines will creatively reassess the whole process of building. Sustainable energy, new/rediscovered technologies and materials, good environmental/conservation practice are among the issues central to this symbol for changing social and environmental needs.

House provides a focus for many related projects. In the manner of a performance/sculpture we will convert and rebuild our existing base. With new studios, rehearsal spaces, living rooms, offices and small terraces for occasional events and concerts, we will create a functional base, a prototype, a symbolic environment and a total organic art work in the tradition of Schwitters's Merz Barns. The House project is the keystone of our dream. As well as being a practical accommodation centre for celebration, a poetry generator and store, it will provide a sanctuary for artists and a practical example for the realisation of ecological concerns through art.

Artist led, it will be constructed in an accessible, simple and cheap style to explore the links between art and work, poverty and surplus.

The building of House will be an extensive event in itself, but the accompanying ceremonies of orientation, foundation laying, roofing, hearth firing and opening etc., will provide further opportunities for demonstrating new vernacular rituals in performance.

This project will extend over at least five years and if financially viable take precedence over other projects. A significant stage will coincide with the year of Visual Arts in 1996.

On the edge of this poisoned sea
we are determined to devise
a haven for dreams made concrete.
A clearing in the uncertain storm.
Where windmills of the imagination
will gain a filigree hold
on the industrial debris of death.

Years before, I had read about a performance on a South Sea island, where the islanders stored huge masks for four years. These were brought out on the night of a full moon on a certain tide for one climactic event, after which they were garaged back in the long house for another four years. Some of our own theatre events had been very long by the normal standards of a two-act play; but the possibility of a continual performance over years was intriguing. Braque said that as you get older, art and life merge. Could this be another way to that elusive Utopia? Or would this too prove to be as transitory as that clumsy white bird which hovers, like our white ghost lady, in his late canvases?

Braque was a loner. Fine artists are still trained that way. I can sometimes be the Bloody-minded Loner, the Boss, the Long Stop, and, later, the 'Project Champion' which the Arts Lottery stipulated. I prefer, though, to work with a few project directors through dialogue and consensus. Duke Ellington wrote melodies and chord sequences, but after carefully selecting his team, he gave them space to play as individuals. The strength of Welfare State International is that it has exceptional players who can play brilliant solos but who create collectively with unexpected improvisations. The 'House' project epitomised this teamwork.

Unfortunately while Sue and I were in Australia again in May 1993, local councillors and planners agreed to the demolition of an historic Wesleyan chapel on the other side of the National School garden wall. We had been negotiating

Lantern Arcade, Glasgow Tramway, 1993

Candlehouse musical sculpture, 1995

with English Estates to convert it into craft workshops when a local builder asked permission to drive bulldozers into our yard. In a few months, he had erected three three-tier blocks of breeze-block flats with a ten-year guarantee, and collected a blue plaque of merit from the council.

However, he lent us his machines to demolish a brick air-raid shelter, opening up our garden space. In July, our bookkeeper borrowed two welding rods from the shipyard, bent them at right angles and dowsed for the exact line of the town beck which flowed under the concrete of our school playground. With the machines, we opened up the river, chased away the rats and revealed limestone sets, white and perfect as when first laid in the cut 150 years before. There was no vegetation, but ferns and lichen filled the channel in months. Trout then appeared there, too.

Our delayed opening ceremony clashed with our simultaneous Arts Council appraisal. While mandarin Officer Death was dissecting our business plan inside, we escaped to tie a red banner and a yellow smoke canister on to the builder's crane. As it flew high, we pulled a home-made paper swan along the river and I played a jig on soprano sax. The banner read 'Welcome home, Edna'. It was, conveniently, a colleague's birthday and she had always wanted to be called Edna. We returned to the critical meeting high as kites and giggling. Once the river was opened up, our desire paths had shifted permanently and there was no going back.

Weeks later, after the tons of rubble were cleared away, we built a small garden on the south side of the exposed beck. We first rescued the Wesleyan chapel belfry, which turned out to be made of rusting galvanised metal, then held an extended garden party. In a month, our artists made a Japanese iron bridge across the beck, a thirty-foot-high hazel screen depicting herons, a stripped-oak pergola, an arched limestone wall and, for story-telling and barbecues, an earth-banked doughnut ten metres across. Thirty visitors shovelled earth and covered this with squares of turf they had brought from all over Britain. After planting rowan and oak trees, we stood in the middle and sang joyously. The next day, a heron flew in from the bay and ate the trout.

By 1994, we were nudging closer to our 'building of the imagination' and planned a cruck barn, a wooden tower with dovecote and hanging gardens and later a permanent folly and communications centre with regular events and gatherings. The major difficulty was always going to be funding. We hoped that by making the construction phases part of our programme, we could use our annual revenue grant from Northern Arts to develop the concept in stages.

We had built a number of temporary towers and 'architectural' spaces before. It is intriguing to see how these motifs grew to become permanent in the new building. In *Scarecrow Zoo* in Bracknell, there was the mobile Tower of Babel. In *King Real*, the mountainous throne of pink cars. There was a siege tower in *The Golden Submarine*, and in 1994 in Bolton a cut plywood edifice that wheeled through the streets before it became a firework fountain.

In 1992, we built *Fragile Gift* in Glasgow. This installation, constructed inside the disused iron Victorian fruit-and-flower market in Candleriggs, soared into its domed roof with a series of withy arches framing an octagonal courtyard containing small shrines around a central brazier. It was a still secular space, a refuge to counter the hysteria of the downtown Christmas shopping. At regular intervals, we performed musical concerts, leading the audience in from outside with small parades of our 'klezmer' band.

In December 1993, four twenty-five-foot-high mobile towers were pushed by spectators on four railway tracks in *The Lantern Arcade* in the Tramway, Glasgow. Each made of cloth, wood, paper or metal, they represented four different civilisations frantically waving to each other but failing to communicate. For many years, too, we had variously used hydraulics, scaffolding, cables to raise maypole-like sculptures of light for the Ulverston Lantern Finale.

Initially, all we could afford was a new glass entrance, to be engraved with images from our shadow puppetry and maybe a small wooden tower. Two friendly architects helped. John Dryden formalised my ideas of a helter-skelter structure, which was inspired again by fairgrounds and included, in theory, a space for ceremonies at the bottom, a telescope at the top and an internet café halfway up. Hans Reymerink delivered some inspirational scale drawings of a wondrous but expensive scheme which fitted soaring glass colonnades on to the back of the National School. This ultimately fed into Lanternhouse. When we obtained planning permission for the proposed hexagonal glass entrance, the planners came back to say they had expected us lot to come up with something considerably wilder; an unexpectedly good omen.

A group of students from the Manchester University MA course on Arts as Environment led by Elsa Leviseur, a professional landscape architect, sketched a double-spiral layout for the site which would link across our Japanese bridge and bring together our two small gardens. We weren't sure where to locate our dream tower on site, so, in June 1995, at the same time as the Barn Project, we used the occasion of National Music Day and Midsummer's Day to make our thinking concrete.

The planners had agreed that we could designate our small site as a sculpture garden, meaning we could also leave structures for six months without planning permission, so we set out to build a 'sculptural sketch' called Candlehouse and try it in the middle of the proposed garden spiral on the south side of our river. Max Rosin, East German welder and engineer, turned up from the legendary Dogtroep. He was so daring with heights, he must have been capable of levitation, but he rather over-designed the structure. Rising from a circular wooden platform, our temporary tower, a thirty-foot-high 'sketch', was constructed with eight telegraph poles fastened to horizontal circular metal frames. A spiralling wooden staircase led to each platform and at the very top (designed by Hannah Fox and Jo Pocock) we placed a squat, revolving Tatlin-style edifice fabricated from bent steel rods and muslin. By adding gongs, drums, musicians and singers, the whole became a very tall musical sculpture.

The name 'Candlehouse' came from the original candle factory (1882–1940) with its sixty-foot chimney, which was once opposite our National School. It was demolished in 1960. Tallow candle-making was an essential trade before the invention of wax candles and gas and electric light. Animal suet from offal was rendered into molten fat to congeal around cotton wicks. The factory smelled, the hours were long, the work hard and the rats and the maggots prolific. A typical factory of the industrial revolution.

Between a Methodist Church spire to the south, the Hoad Lighthouse to the north and a chimney of an old cement factory to the west, and the last relic of the Wesleyan chapel belfry displayed in our garden, we located our Candlehouse Tower. Next to the town beck (now breathing easily after the removal of its concrete lid), herons, wagtails and dragonflies surfaced and were sculpted on the tower as flat-cut wooden silhouettes.

The 'world music' composition by Dan Fox which animated the site was a conscious fusion of different technologies. Pentatonic gongs specially forged in a small Balinese village (Dan had backpacked there to commission them) were played by wooden levers triggered by a mechanical steel barrel rolled in Barrow-in-Furness (the gearing was from a converted cement mixer). The resonant gongs of this giant musical box were balanced by Cuban rhythms played both on massive bass drums specially made by Dan and Tanzanian thumb pianos. Saxophones and trumpets were added, with an aboriginal didgeridoo, played with circular breathing. Tuned wheel rims taken from scrapped trucks on the M6 were tapped with wooden poles to boom beneath the tinkling of water wheels and whirring weathervanes.

Five concerts (one a night for an audience of 150 a time) signalled the start of our sculpture site; here were new candles for old. For the duration of the concerts, I put the green metal belfry high on a wooden structure and, to enhance the symbolic new fountain spouting from old traditions, used it to house water-pump valves and big hosepipes borrowed from our neighbouring fire station. With recycled water from the beck, we drove a crude bicycle-wheel fountain and other miniature streams which flowed elegantly over a staircase waterfall of horizontal recycled bus windscreens.

We had good audiences for the music, but in terms of our architectural dreaming we learned a crucial fact. The site for Candlehouse was fine for a temporary sculpture but completely wrong for permanent architecture. We discovered that it blocked the passage of the sun and dominated the garden. A big positive building requires negative space around it. We wanted a soaring romantic tower (and were eventually to get two) but, thanks to our tests, we knew they required a different location. We were learning the rudiments of architecture.

In the long, hot summer of 1995, with sixty volunteers and a few specialist and highly skilled greenwood workers, we constructed a cruck barn as an all-purpose workshop and extension to the rear of the Old School. Cruck barns are a centuries-old form of farm building for which trees, usually oak, are split vertically to form supporting arches linked by horizontal ridge beams. We had also recently discovered Walter Segal (1907-1985), an imaginative architect, who had championed self-build methods. After building a studio in his garden, he realised that with a modular system of standard sizes of wooden sheets, easily obtained from a local DIY store, anyone, with a little training, could assemble a simple house that touched the earth lightly and which could climb up rough, steep ground with minimal foundations. The two methods (cruck barns and Segal) came together and the barn was completed in about eight hot weeks.

We selected and bought five hundred-year-old bendy oaks which were still growing in a managed forest on the edge of Windermere. After these were felled specially for us, Chris Coates[5] sliced them up the middle with his chainsaw. Apart from a crane and a chainsaw to dress the trunks, the barn was made using hand tools. With three crucks (on concrete foundations), it is held together by 270 oak pegs. On topping-out day (a traditional point of ceremony when the roof trusses are in place), as we lashed a small fir tree to the ridge, the Ulverston Town Band played 'Hearts of Oak' (twice) and two neighbours in the new flats complained to public health that our female workers were not wearing bras under their dresses!

As well as rediscovering the regrettable xenophobia and youthophobia of a very few racist residents (who also called us Zulus because we played drums and employed a black worker), we learned a vast amount. Under the direction of our project managers, Chris Coates and Peter Wilshaw (foreman and engineer), we studied local cruck barns. They are an enduring form of vernacular architecture. About one hundred remain in South Cumbria, many two hundred years old and often still as solid as when they were built.

There were ceremonies along the way. Before the concrete was poured into the foundation trenches, about twenty of us gathered round the threshold area to throw in old keys with wishes. We also brought out a peace symbol, in the form of a bronze dagger bent back upon itself that we had been given at a Polish Theatre Festival in Wroclaw, twenty-one years earlier. As our business manager, Sophia Culbard, was half-Polish and as one of our blessings for the space was for it to be used for creative co-operation between nations, we gently added that, too.

By the track in the forest where the oaks had been felled, a woodcock and chicks had nested on the ground. Unaware, our tractor driver had on many occasions carted trees over the nest, the wheels either side. After discovering the nest, he drove the long way round the forest and soon enough the eggs were hatched. So we drank a toast in brandy from a wooden bowl carved in the shape of a woodcock by one of the volunteers. There was a further tingling moment, a dramatic end of the first act, when we tapped in the final oak peg to join the ridge of the big, ribbed, free-standing structure looking like a giant's toast rack. Our crane driver had lifted three two-ton crucks. Horizontal on the ground, their fixing pegs in position, was one thing. But to haul them vertical was another proposition. Would they hold? Thirty yards away, wearing our green hard hats saying 'Engineers of the Imagination', we held our breath. So did the crane driver.

After he had swung the ridge into position, Chris and Peter, thirty feet up, sat astride it and with one tap pushed the six-inch peg into two perfectly aligned holes. The crane driver gasped. Our street cred rose instantly. The woodworking boys couldn't contain themselves. They rushed into the barn space, leaping and shrieking and vigorously shaking cans of beer. As they ripped the ring pulls, beer splattered in arcs as high as the beams.

As we treated the volunteers well, giving them accommodation, travel, food, training, and seminars, it ended up costing as much as a professional job. We had planned to have eight at a time, week by week, but they were having such a good time – despite the very long working hours – that many would not leave and the numbers grew and grew. But we were committed to learning from working with amateurs. Maybe too many novices were better than too many consultants. They were to come, in droves, with the Lottery.

The Bid

By January 2002, the National Lottery was seven years old and stale. Camelot, the come-on kingdom of money, is no longer a shiny knight of our dreams but a rusty tin can of disillusion. In 1995 it was different. As the nation queued for tickets, millions of people rose above the soporific soup of the soaps to hand over hard-earned pounds to buy a way out of the endless cycle of uncreative work known as earning a living. We couldn't believe that the government was to give a dedicated slice to the arts. Our blueprints and computer printouts for our Shangri-La, our ingredients for an architectural Utopia were ready on the larder shelf and here was the gas for the cooking. Also, Northern Arts, with their clever and politically significant 'Case for Capital', were now backing us and other ambitious projects in their region as major players for the Year of Visual Arts (1996).

The Arts Lottery arrived just at the right time. Our heads were teeming with unarticulated 'House' ideas and the bid transformed our thinking. Initially, we hung back, guessing (correctly) that the Arts Lottery Board would be bound to throw out the first excess of nutty ideas, but we didn't hang about too long, guessing (correctly) that, once inundated, they would judge applications even more strictly and the money would run out. The detailed preparation took us a year. Then, in July 1995, a humble Amtrak van arrived at the portal of the Arts Council in Great Peter Street, WC1. Two men carried in a large, oblong parcel the size of a small tombstone. For a while, it waited in an anteroom until secretaries, Lottery officers, security men and a few art-form specialists gathered to witness the opening of our latest public art work, our Lottery bid.

The paper was old-fashioned and brown, tied with jute rope in reef knots round an Aberdeen Fish box tinged with woodworm holes, smelling very slightly of kippers. Inside the lid we had pasted a patchwork of brightly coloured snapshots of last year's work. Children beating drums, smiling punters and shadow sculptures of wayward herons eating trout. Inside the wooden shell rested a fake foundation stone. Mirroring the brick we had wheeled to Housing the Arts in 1974, it was a plywood box covered in terracotta plaster which divided into two halves. Along its central hinge I had painted a spiralling turquoise river/beck. Splitting along the length of the river, the foundation stone folded back on itself to become two filing boxes containing a total of twelve black files. One big photographic image of a pool rippled out across their spines. Six months later, in January 1996, after many re writes and many intensive interviews with Lottery assessors, we heard that our bid was successful. £1.6 million was awarded. Everything we had asked for. We had the mammoth task of raising an additional £750,000 ourselves. But we had a £2.2 million project on our hands, the chance at last to build our ark and our biggest project ever.

All our executive committee at one time or another rose to the occasion. After many fierce meetings and three intensive weekend retreats, often with twenty to twenty-five people, we collected a dumper truck full of flip charts, shopping lists, business plans, feasibility studies, scribbled sketches of dreams both grandiose and tiny and a pile of photographs of our architectural achievements to date. Over a year, with many research trips, masses of reading and the subsequent minutes, letters and e-mails, we had a fermenting hod. Initial discoveries were all distilled into the twelve black files, although after we gained the award and during the build itself, intensive meetings and research continued. The preparation of the gamble cost us £20,000.

Looking back, it is impossible to separate those many gatherings. Gradually, though, the notion of 'House' as a self-built domestic dwelling (already transformed into a 'Centre for Celebration') further metamorphosed into our 'Total Art Work' in its ultimate incarnation as Lanternhouse. As the good, the bad and the ugly, wise men and shepherds descended on our remote western town, we grabbed every building and business-plan expert in sight. John Faulkner, theatre consultant and once Arts Council Drama Director and grandson of a line of horse traders, wrote a feasibility study, put up shelves and quoted Kipling. As a fellow undergraduate at Oxford, he had rescued me thirty years before, when I was trying to invent and paint twenty scenes in twenty days for a musical called *All for Kicks* (starring Esther Rantzen). Every decade, John appears as the Archangel of the toolbox. Armed with immense practical knowledge of theatre spaces, he also knows the jargon of funding guidelines, market comparators and the difference between a tourist, a visitor and an income danglifier. He referred us to colleges and monasteries, the Bauhaus and Black Mountain College.

As a student of City University in 1972, Peter Stark had been our first administrator. Then, we did no bookkeeping and he ploughed through seventy-seven supermarket boxes of undated receipts piled in the loft of our house in Leeds. As the instigator of seminal art labs and centres in Birmingham and

Bracknell and ex-director of Northern Arts, he could sniff a seismic shift in Great Peter Street at the tickle of a felt tip. He wanted us to find a more green-field site. We argued that being next to a trunk road opposite a big garage and halfway between affluent north Ulverston and the poorer south was preferable to a remote Dartington-style ivory tower.

Roger Coleman is also a visionary thinker, who had started Welfare State International with Sue and me and his then-partner, the novelist Alison Fell. Now the director of the radical Helen Hamlyn Design Age initiative at the Royal College of Art, he is another first-rate carpenter who can think with his fingers. You can't get more skilled vernacular than the craftsmanship of his father, who engineered those delicate and intricate steel dies that cut thousands of paper doyleys. After lecturing on art history, Roger went on to build houses, direct housing associations for the GLC and edit *Innovations*, a radical movement inspiring green and socially aware buildings and technology. Early on, when we were thinking more domestically, Roger had the blueprints of Clive Latimer, who had designed and constructed a plywood house for £10,000.

Dermott Killip was the master of ceremonies at our weekend retreats. An arts consultant who writes mathematics manuals, Dermott has for years provoked, challenged and nurtured us with his own brand of inescapable logic. Wishing to be clear about the long-term purpose of Lanternhouse, I had written a polemic for one of the retreats.

The Vision Bite

On a better towns' committee an accountant grumbled that the thistles on a town roundabout were a disgrace. 'Not if we call it a butterfly park', responded an ecologist.

Vision is the envelope of imaginative references we set ourselves to give us an identity and our sense of place. A way of looking at the world which should centre all our daily tasks, but which is usually caught only in the tranquillity of time off.

So what do we do with our unlikely bag of gold beans?
I make three presumptions:
First, that our current excessive consumer culture with its increasing division between rich and poor (including the Third World within and without) is unsustainable morally, economically and ecologically. Secondly, making art is fun, stimulating, active and even spiritually uplifting and more people should have access to it every day – our job is to put ART back into an active social context. And last, with its ceremonies, feasts and celebrations and stretching of perception and

dynamic metaphors, art can change the status quo and move us to a more equitable society. This is a huge if not arrogant assumption. My belief is that by creating in Ulverston a mythic Utopian island, an art work between social engineering and carnival euphoria, clown catalyst of outrageous and imaginative acts, with trading and training and pull-yourselves-up-by-your-own-bootstraps magic, the pump will be primed 'til the fountain flows spontaneously. I guess somewhere in my kind of heaven, Maynard Keynes and Tommy Cooper are working it all out for us, except Keynes is wearing the fez.

If we can shape reality, if local distinctiveness is appropriate, if the community are interested, if we can make art concrete, if we can keep laughing at ourselves as we undercut Utopia, and if we enjoy piracy, then let's begin.

Dermott kept us focused; divided us into small discussion groups so that by the end of each weekend we came away with a shared sense of ownership and carrier bags full of invaluable practical snippets. Here's just a tiny sample:

What is the relationship between our public intentions and private needs? We may want a music edit suite and printing press but also, as artists march on their bellies and conversations, we need a big kitchen or maybe two big kitchens. The 3 Cs – Conversation, Coffee and Cuisine. We require good connections between outside and in. Places to sit, work, meet and talk. See plants and enjoy the rain. Surprise views. Nooks and crannies. Curves. Niches of special interest. Terracotta. Softness. Bike racks. Dustbin compound.

Lanternhouse should be:

Inspiring, spacious, safe, light, populated, unechoey, tidier than it is now, warm and welcoming, bold, striking, colourful, busy, peaceful, lively and a work-place.

It should not be:

Pretentious, pompous, intemperate (too hot in summer and too cold in winter), institutionalised (like some of the current toilet fittings), rectangular, miserable, neglected, corporate, cold, over-tidy, overfull, unloved or too posh so as you can't throw up on the carpet.

We workshopped practical situations:

I am a single mum from South Ulverston with pushchair calling in to ask about workshops with my older children. Who do I speak to?

We are 16, we've come over from Barrow. We have heard about your e-mail and internet set-up and would like a go now.

We have just flown in from the USA. I have a Master's degree in community outreach illusion. I am here for two days and want to learn from your archive. I want all you can teach. Where can I plug in my laptop? Take me to your leader.

The process of working out the ideas and their subsequent realisation was a good example of collective working. The full glory and garden of Lanternhouse, which finally opened three years later, in January 1999, on schedule and within budget, in time for our slightly delayed thirtieth anniversary party in March 1999, is testimony to the generosity, talent and dedication of scores of outstanding artists, staff and friends.

Fundraising merits a book of its own. Finding money and maintaining financial control was crucial. Fortunately, another board member, Steve Harris, who was familiar with the obscure practices of Lottery applications, could advise our administrators – first David Haley, then Sophia Culbard. Sophia worked obsessively for hundreds of hours to refine our bid and raise funds. Eventually she had to move on to other challenges. After writing an essay for our board, describing me as a wily old wizard with a clogged-up cauldron, she changed her name to Zosia Wand and left to become a full-time playwright and poet.

It often happens that our administrators leave to follow successful careers as primary creators. It isn't that administration is uncreative in itself, but it is very hard to continually nurture other people's visions, accept the grind of infinite form-filling and have the temperament to plan four to five years ahead. As it happened, the day after Sophia left I received a letter from Eileen Strand, an American with considerable film-production experience who wanted to relocate to the Lake District. She started a week later and has turned out to be our best fundraiser ever. If it had not been for her negotiating a critical deal for £57,000 of European funding under the Objective 2 ruling (meaning that Ulverston was in a run-down area, a victim of the 'Peace Dividend'), which helped secure a cliff-hanging £185,000 bringing the matched funding we achieved to £586,400 from 'English Partnerships', the whole composite lottery bid would have fallen apart.

Building Blocks

Once we had the money, we could put our vision into practice. We had been collecting architecture photographs and books for years. Out of the whole rattlebag, Nikki de St Phalle's Tarot Garden in Italy was a favourite. So were the carnival sculptures and fountains she made with Tinguely at the Pompidou Centre.

Then we discovered Le Facteur Cheval (1836–1924). *Le Palais Ideal* in Hauterives (Drome) is a staggering work, an 'extravagant and fantastic' monument to unfettered imagination. Visited by 100,000 tourists every year, it was built by one man, mostly after work, in thirty-three years, with 3,500 bags of lime and cement. Every day, after his twenty-mile postal round on foot, picking up stones and pebbles, he set to labour.

> I was the first to agree with those who called me insane; I was not a builder;
> I had never handled a mason's trowel; I was not a sculptor. The chisel was
> unknown to me; not to mention architecture, it was a field in which I
> remained totally ignorant.

Approximately twenty-six metres long by ten metres wide and ten metres high, this queen of grottoes is a joyous cornucopia of figurative imagery, a conglomeration of cement angels, ostriches, geese, eagles, flamingos and deer woven into a Khmer temple, a mosque, a Hindu sanctuary, a feudal castle and a Swiss chalet. Built on two levels, surrounded by small, pleasant gardens and full of laughing families, it was such an inspiration that I instantly scribbled five pages of free-form poetry notes. If only Welfare State International could make a building as rich and playful as this. Every spare surface was covered in cryptic slogans and poems. One of the many inscriptions read: 'This is Art, Dream, this is Energy'.

In September 1994, Sue Gill and I had visited the Matisse Chapel in Vence. It was a disappointment but a useful mirror. I had imagined this 'masterpiece' would be a remote Provençal chapel, romantic and organic in feel, but on the grey day we visited it, in its unexpectedly bourgeois suburb, it seemed cold, clinical and boxlike, with no east window to pick up the dawn. So different in concept from the warm embrace of even the medieval town hall with the Chagall paintings in Saint Paul de Vence. There, the tiles, the bricks, the wooden floors and the inviting entrance had gathered a recognisable patina. How much I preferred the soft ochres and earth browns of the town hall to the rather acid tones of the Matisse Chapel. But I did like its Miro-like spire of moons and planets and that fed in to our eventual spire, as did the Vence terracotta.

I had learned how important it was for me to celebrate the promise of a new day with the sun rising and to mark its passage during the day. I also wanted the totality of the Matisse Chapel, with its every last detail simply hand-designed. For our business plan, I could also point out that tourists will beat a path to a site, however remote, provided it is inventive enough and, of course, you are famous. Except that was in France, where people from all classes value their artists. Gaudí (1852–1926) had always been a hero, but I only knew his work from books. I could never forget that his death was mundane, knocked down by a tram while crossing the road next to his great cathedral, the Sagrada Familia.

In December 1995, the Fox family visited some old Welfare State International members, Bernie Armstrong, an inventive songwriter–singer and his wife Carmen, who lived near Barcelona. To see Gaudí's extensive coral-like fantasies for real was a total inspiration. I admired his ability to marry the best of vernacular traditions with his own avant-garde, egocentric, colourful and playful fantasies, which were in turn influenced by the European Arts and Crafts movement of the time. I also loved his knack of harnessing organic form with advanced technology, measuring stress flows and incorporating concrete reinforced with metal. But how would we match that Catalan sunshine and earthy spiritualism so locked into its Mediterranean climate and pagan Catholicism? And how could we adapt the big unspoken lesson of the Sagrada Familia? It is because the Cathedral is unfinished that millions of visitors experience the process and, inspired by its bubbling concrete plasticity, imagine their own architectural solutions.

In Barcelona, suddenly away from the congestion of Lottery thinking, we went into introspective overdrive. We had escaped, not just to study Gaudí but because only six months after putting in the initial bid we were already anxious and overwrought. Our executive had, quite rightly, pointed out that we had to be really sure that we wanted to be building-based and this was the last moment to pull out. Our staff had had to rework unbelievably detailed business plans. The potential change for the whole company was already becoming traumatic. Overwork and insecurity was affecting us all. In our state of retreat, doubts surfaced that we had not been able to articulate in public.

Did we fake gypsies really want to be responsible for managing a prestigious property? Would the ownership of a major architectural landmark be a millstone around our necks or a millstone to grind new grain? Where would we get the revenue to make it work? And would the sheer effort of driving through a massive unknown project give us all nervous breakdowns? There was enormous pressure.

I wrote a late Christmas card to Bill Blaikie, with whom we had worked so much in Australia:

> We consult daily with Goddess Chance, to ask if we really want to run a centre for cultural activists and creative anarchists and whether this is a contradiction in terms. You say you are acquiring a building in Bathurst as an Arts Centre. My anxiety is that your (and our) centres don't become institutions to sap energy. We have spent so much of this year on politics, meetings, number crunching etc. to convert our school into a wild folly that we have become 'zombified' and done very little primary hands-on creation.

> Capital money has become easier to get in the UK, but revenue for programme is difficult. The trick is (they tell us) to use the building to generate the income to facilitate artists to explore the edge. But when you are submerged under five-year business plans, tourist strategies, staffing ratios, job profiles, development directors, health and safety regulations, disability audits, general managers, administrators, wardens and caretakers, the edge disappears in a cloud of rationalisations and market economy bullshit and jargon.

The holiday was fortifying. There were sleepless nights and, armed with cheap local brandy, much pacing of marble floors. But when we returned, we were all committed to continuing. We had to find an architect as good as Gaudí, or Le Facteur Cheval, and the best administrative structure to liberate all the visions and skills of our own egocentric artists.

The contemporary culture of building in England is very inflexible, old-fashioned, totally hierarchical, male-dominated, deeply dull and entirely cost-driven. It is a microcosm of capitalism. It was a challenge indeed for us artists to engage with it at all. We needed a *fool*proof method! First, from our executive committee, we selected a Lottery Project Subcommittee chaired by Gilly Adams who met fortnightly.[6] We continued to channel our ideas over the next two years through our Artists' Forum under convener Chris Coates, who had considerable hands-on experience of building, including the Barn Project.

In January 1996, we made the most important appointment of all. Ten months before the architect arrived, Bob Hodge, our project manager, with his partner, Peter Thompson, took up the job. He came with an extraordinary pedigree. His last job had been to enlarge the dock gates in Barrow through which Trident submarines pass. Daring and innovative construction methods required a vast box of concrete (50,000 tons) to be lowered slowly into the ground while tons of sand were pumped out from underneath. To someone of such experience, our £2.2 million was small change. Just as well, because if we got our budgets wrong, we would go bankrupt. The next key step was to find an architect.

I wanted to be the architect. I knew that Rudolph Steiner had designed his own buildings and managed to build them by employing engineers when appropriate. This was a Walter Mitty fantasy. I had no training whatsoever and no architect worth a door knocker would be content to be my draughtsman or that of the Artists' Forum. Yet we had to find an architect who would be content to accept our pile of ideas and see-saw amongst a bunch of voracious self-willed creators all pawing the site under my 'Project Championship'. Ours was to be a different relationship from that of the normal client. Bob Hodge helped us write the architect's brief. Amongst many notions, it specified a total refurbishment of the main building, completion of the cruck barn (on which work had been stopped when we ran out of funds), accommodation, ceremonial space, a separate warehouse and extensive landscaping on two or even three sites.

'These bare details', I wrote,

> Do not give a sense of the mythic and holistic envelope of the whole scheme. This derives from the unique poetic vision which always informs Welfare State International's work. The company is used to constructing strong, often archetypal imagery, which can reach wide audiences but which can also be personal, idiosyncratic, comic and downright bizarre.

> In this case the whole single art work, the 'wild oasis' and 'functional folly', although stemming from an architectural focus, will be as much a 'symphonic' multifaceted creation as the earlier works. As Welfare State International generates prototypes this architectural exploration may become another form to be copied, as may the method and process of construction.

We were looking for someone who would be:

> A key member of the team able and willing to share specialist knowledge with creative and sometimes egocentric colleagues. Take risks with new ideas. Be interested in vernacular architecture, contemporary rites of passage and the nature of celebration. Enjoy an organic and hands-on style of collective working. Be practical. Prefer play, discovery and secular spiritual dreaming to the mad utilitarianism of the market economy.

We also specified principles for an ecologically sound design:

> We intend to pursue a low environmental impact approach to all design and build issues and wherever possible to: Conserve energy. Use renewable energy resources. Reduce emissions of greenhouse and acid rain gases. Avoid toxic chemicals and materials. Use natural materials from sustainable sources. Use products manufactured with low energy input. Recycle rainwater for flushing the toilets. Provide a low maintenance building. Integrate the building with the local eco-system. Source materials from within c. 75 miles of the site. Use local contractors and subcontractors.

We were also seeking someone with the right attitude to women and trainees in their practice with IT experience including computer-aided design and a hands-on approach. We must have looked like the clients from hell.

The selection process was steered by the Project Committee, the Artists' Forum and of course Bob Hodge. From a long list of fifteen architects, eight were invited to first interview and four practices were given £1,000 each to produce detailed submissions.

We must have daunted the interviewees. Ten Welfare Staters armed with notebooks and beady questions checked them out. Jamie Proud asked: 'Where would you send me to see one of your buildings that would make me gasp and/or giggle?'

Eventually, after considerable collective haggling on the Artists' Forum, we found Francis Roberts. He wasn't an obvious front runner. He built churches, had no IT skills and only a small practice. However, he was reasonably local, could draw elegantly ('thinks with a pencil', we said), but above all, he was a romantic, who loved towers and Italy, the English Arts and Crafts movement and art nouveau. He also designed like Charles Rennie Mackintosh – although he wouldn't admit it. Aside from his architectural skills, he played baritone sax in his own big band and as a child constructed immaculate model aircraft with sticks and tissue paper.

At interview, he said he hated our beloved cruck barn and suggested we demolish it immediately. We were outraged. But that clinched it. 'Anyone as arrogant as this must believe in something,' we chuntered, and so he did. His first concepts of knocking out the middle of the old school to make a courtyard covered with a glass circus tent were inspirational but too expensive. Eventually he maintained strong spaces linked with processional traverses and designed a separate accommodation block on our car park, with a linking bridge.

By raising the old roof structure five feet and lowering other ceilings, he conjured up a third floor where previously there had been only two. The barn was enclosed and enlarged with a sweeping, curvaceous roof of laminated wooden beams. We gained two big kitchens, a music room, a gallery, a lecture room, a sound studio, an IT room, a library and at last two towers, one for the lift, one for the stairs, and, best of all, we kept the sun, because he dreamed up an elegant roof garden. He distrusted interior curved walls and unfortunately failed to hire acoustic engineering or glazing experts, but otherwise he delivered and we have remained friends. As his Christmas card once said, 'Christmas is in the details'.

We had the ideas, the artists, the money (well, nearly), the structure, the project manager and an architect, plans his own regular team of attendant well-worn engineering and service consultants (later, we wished we had picked our own). All we had to do now was to find a builder to work within budget. In November 1997 (after three tenders), Leck, a local firm, were appointed. In December, they started on site, surrounded by a plywood wall with a mural conceived by our local Sir John Barrow Primary School. Simon Strand took the children's paintings and enlarged them so that our artists seemed to be dancing down the street with blazing pyrotechnics, bouncing lanterns and a few easels and berets thrown in. The stone caravan had been kick-started. The toolbox folly was going to emerge. By December 1998, we had the keys.

We had never worried so much in our lives. Every now and again, we surfaced to something of wonder, but most of the time it was just bloody-minded graft.

I realised I could never in fact be an architect facing all that hundred-year permanence. I couldn't travel past my baby every day and see the mistakes still staring me in the face. At least theatrical events, however poor, disappear.

After a last dinner for twelve of us in the Old National School, when we remembered to set a place for our ghost, we moved out for a year, fortuitously into that old mill we had opened in Ulverston twenty years before. When we were within a day of finishing our Lottery bid, I heard on the radio that Sadler's Wells Ballet had received £1 million to 'relocate'. Within an hour, I had scribbled down a six-figure budget which, as well as rents, telephones and removal costs, even included car-park passes for visitors. If we hadn't received that money, we would have been way over budget. As it was, I forgot furniture. We had always lived in such a culture of clutter, make do and mend (all relative poverty of course) that it never crossed my mind that we could include office equipment. Maybe it was a blessing. Necessity later forced us to saw up some of our old furniture,

improvise and achieve hand-made idiosyncrasies from flotsam and jetsam, unavailable in glossy office catalogues.

Planners hate change. In Ulverston, within artillery range of the Lake District, where it's 'Anything as long as it's Georgian and no Velux roof lights please', if you build a new warehouse on a new business park (as we did to relieve storage in Lanternhouse), it has to be painted in corporation colours to match the hills and the sky. Our warehouse was forced into air-force blue and is reminiscent of the dead bluebottle we predicted.

We were luckier, however, with our spire and microwave dish for sending and receiving digital information at high speed. We argued it through planning by maintaining it was the equivalent of a bell on a medieval church. Once, the bell called people to prayer. Today, the internet brings communities together.

We had written into the architect's brief that environmental issues were crucial. We did recycle the old radiators, acquire (thanks to Frank Mills, the service engineer) a cheap-to-run, non-hermetically sealed ventilation system with sectionalised heating which we could control room by room, decent insulation and an underground storage tank and pump for recycling rainwater to the main toilets. But try asking a builder about the toxic emissions from the industrial manufacture of PVC drainpipes and he will look at you as if you'd asked him to dance in *Swan Lake*. Materials and labour had to be gathered within seventy miles. Everyone nodded in pretend agreement because they wanted the job, but they didn't know, they didn't care, they had no intention of following our wishes and, worst of all in some cases, like the folding doors needed to improve the barn, the right product was not even made in Britain. The doors came from Germany. On a journey to Blackpool to study a lift, the lift supplier admitted he was only a distributor and that his product was actually made in Spain.

Which is partly why it was so hard to get a porthole in the lift. This and the toilets were my answer to the inevitable marketing plan. We now have the best lift and the best toilets west of the Pennines. Bryan Tweddle, a sculptor, engineered a tiny animated man who appears to be winding the lift up and down (and collecting and polishing the stars from the Milky Way at the same time). You look at him through a porthole in the wall of the lift. To acquire the porthole took six months of negotiation between Blackpool and the obscure manufacturing plant in Spain. To acquire curved corners in the steel shell of the lift compartment took three months. The inside of the lift is painted by Tod Hanson as a Tardis.

It is now habitable, but lift engineers, on an expensive service contract, still sniff at our inability to conform to their irrational desires for wood-grained Formica and chromium.

It is extremely hard to create anything original in contemporary England. I knew this before building Lanternhouse, but it was confirmed over and again in the process. Only because our terrier like Artists' Forum found a perfect project manager, a good architect, architectural team and an honest, solid local builder with a first-rate old-time foreman did we rise above the swamp, with me as an obsessional and slightly prima-donna Project Champion.

Take doorknobs as one minute example. You can commission a metalworker and design them yourself, but when budgets rule, you go to an unctuous salesman with catalogues of standard products all cunningly designed to fall apart (in the way of our market economy) the moment the guarantee runs out. So you waste a month in tedious argument and spend extra cash just to ensure that one tiny detail of a million-pound outfit is a mite less than ugly. Our taste was always way above our budget. Our audit trails, as I learned to call them, which examined furniture, ironwork, decor, light bulbs and disability access, were some attempt to anticipate gaps. In the area between architecture and interior design in particular, we tenacious artists clung to some vestige of poetic space, despite dull lighting manufacturers and sanitaryware dealers reared on English school toilets and time-served wash-basins.

The Artists

Jamie McCullough designed the lattice spire as a container for the microwave dish. Tragically, he never saw his last creation. He died suddenly in April 1998 during the refurbishment. The work was completed by Trapp Forge with guidance from Lynn Sanderson, his partner. The metal spire had a dozen strategic holes in its circular base. The crowning sphere was made from two woks welded together. The placement of the angle of the microwave (which is the first ever tidal microwave dish, affected as it is by water and air pressures across Morecambe Bay) was critical because it had to be lined up within half a degree of the transmitter twenty-two kilometres away at Lancaster University. Sixty foot up, builders hung out over the concrete parapet of the tower like masons in William Golding's *The Spire*, steering the crane to deposit the structure accurately over a dozen waiting bolts. Amazing theatre.

Duncan Copley, a poet in wood, created the curved and polished sycamore counter in the ground-floor café (where Frank Roberts had banned curves). He also designed its whole decor, balancing bright Moroccan colours with cut copper sheeting above the sink and the cooker. There is a subtle dialogue between the wave form over the sink and the ziggurat above the gas rings. The green copper echoes local mining, while the internally lit latticework flowers in the prow of the counter recall the lanterns that Lanternhouse is named after.

In the accommodation block, Duncan's designs for each of the four bedrooms ensure that there is no institutional uniformity. A bunk bed folds to the wall to become a desk in the family room, chestnut pale fencing frames bedheads and carved shelves support inviting ceramic washing bowls with copper faucets. In the roof-garden kitchen, he has invented ingenious cupboards which double their storage capacity with pull-out extensions. The doors are painted with a sprightly 'Kitchen poem' which makes a plea for artists' creations to be as good as their cooking. In the gallery foyer, his baroque desk pauses, curiously suspended on curved, crablike wooden legs, its surface scattered with laburnum slices inset like so many planets.

Martin Brockman made all the large tiles in two entrance foyers. Fired in rich red clay and impressed with representations of Cumbrian birds, they make an instant geographical and geological link with our Lake District hinterland. It is possible to make rubbings of the images with wax crayons, so visitors can take away souvenirs of the building. We took this idea from church brass rubbings and Tibetan monks who made woodcuts for pilgrims to rub in order to acquire individual prayer flags.

Derek Pearce,[7] Chris Coates and John Faulkner sorted out the library. A tree appears to grow through the shelves and there is a hierarchy of priorities underlined by the location and scale of each section. Poetry and picture books prevail, whilst art administration and fundraising categories are elevated to a top and quite inaccessible position. In addition, tall wooden ziggurats on wheels, which are also magazine holders, provide mobile screens for individual reading corners.

Hannah Fox customised lettering and signs with clothes pegs, seawashed colours and fragments of driftwood from Morecambe Bay, and, with Jo Kelly, invented numerous curtains which either match the soft ochres of undulating barley fields or contrast vigorously with vibrant silks like floaty stained glass.

In the music room and recording studio, the sound baffles are deep boxes covered in variations of traditional clipped rag rugs made by artist-in-residence

188

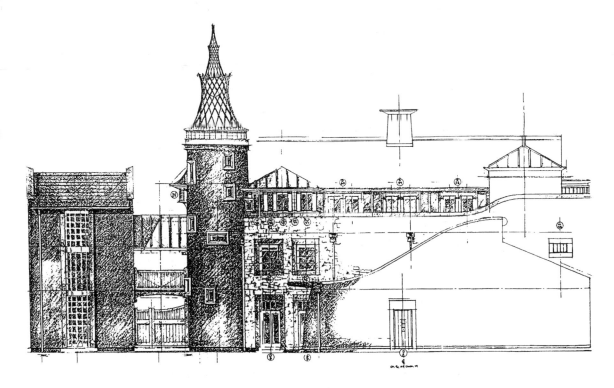

Ali Rhind. Their asymmetrical designs follow the motif of the barn crucks, while circular seats and corner cupboards were recycled by Matt Turley from the old school cupboards. On the top floor, some triangulated roof trusses from the original classrooms have been retained and on their ledges are rows of mysterious coloured chalks, which look like elongated Smarties. Disability access was monitored by Hilary Hughes and Gill Gill.[8] As a regular member of the Executive Project Committee, Hilary continually applied her experienced production manager's eye for detail and visitors with varying physical impairment have remarked on the high standard of care. The builders and selected specialised craftsmen also contributed beautiful work, much of which is often hidden or not noticed by the casual observer. The sculpted cement work of the main drains under the floor, with its very precise angles and slopes, for instance, is as good as anything produced by Gaudí's exemplary artisans. Behind the plastered walls of one of the towers are 65,000 cut bricks and scores of shaped breeze blocks which create 'battered' towers, i.e. ones which slope inwards imperceptibly as they rise, emphasising perspective to give a more elegant soaring effect. I had to haggle hard with Bob Hodge over the value of this. At £500 a tower, it was worth it. The leadwork by Neil Crompton is exceptional and is as good as any such work since the Middle Ages. It curves like a grey ribbed whale back over the humped roof of the barn and is fashioned into large rainwater hoppers, all hand-made on site, which punctuate the building at all significant corners.

Topping Out

The year 1998 moved as slowly as lead, but gradually we came closer to repossession. At the halfway stage, on 1 May (to reclaim the old Labour May Day), we staged the topping-out ceremony. We had thirty ceremonial mugs made, printed with the date, the occasion and the tower image and eight slightly posher ones in porcelain with a painted gold rim for the 'gaffers'. We left the posh mugs in an open site hut for ten minutes or so and they were stolen. Carrying on regardless, Hilary climbed high into the open roof space to fix a fir tree to the ridge, fire a red flare and let off silver waterfalls from the scaffolding. It was politically expedient to remind the workers that a woman could handle sticks of dynamite. Then Dan's quartet, wearing green hard hats labelled 'Engineers of the Imagination', paraded on stilts in and out of the half-completed ground floor. Border TV came early. The architect came late, so I did my speech twice. I praised the art of work:

> Work is despised in our society because it is rarely freely chosen. Artists are
> often envied because they have the luck or the audacity to choose their own
> way of working.

I also pointed out that I had learned two new concepts. The first was 'The Client', who is traditionally useless but has clout and cash, and the second was 'Poet's Day', which on building sites means 'Piss Off Early, Tomorrow's Saturday'. As I was both client and poet, I was in trouble. In the event, everyone got off work ten minutes early, so it was an undoubted success and Tom Jackson, Leck's boss, said wistfully: 'Maybe we could do this sort of thing more often on site, it was only ever work these days.'

We delivered on time and on budget, with two terracotta towers and our awards from the Royal Institute of British Architects and the Civic Trust.[9] In December 1998, to mark practical completion, we cut the cake, with an image of the blue lattice tower indelibly etched on white icing. The building workers, seduced by cake, beer and a slide show featuring Kodak highlights of themselves at work over the last year, were happy to stay on for half an hour after 4 p.m. on Friday – success indeed. In January 1999, we moved back in.

Building the cruck barn and the completed Lanterhouse

3

Rites of Passage

In the summer of 2001, there was a phone call. The male working-class Barrow voice rushed in:

'Can we have another one?'

As if he were ordering a pizza.

'You haven't produced another baby, have you?' I said, guessing.

'That's right. Can Sue do us another one, please?'

A couple of years before, Sue Gill had helped him and his wife to invent a baby-naming ceremony for their first child and now they wanted one for the next baby. After all that theatrical showmanship, here we were, servicing a local family with a simple and genuine need.

My mind went back to another phone call. On the last night of the Olympic Games 1992, I was idly watching El Comediants' closing fire show of fun and nonsense on television. Inflatable B-movie gargoyles, hovering in smoke and mega lighting, were entertaining the billions. For once, I was not concerned with those philosophical quandaries about the value of mass spectacle or even totting up the pesetas. Suddenly, the phone rang and a friend told me that his partner and our friend – a wonderful anarchic performer – had killed herself. The funeral was to be a purely family affair three hundred miles away, so we designed a small separate ceremony. Out in that bare expanse of cold sand of Morecambe Bay, we tried to sing a blessing from a mutual show of ten years before.

I am your guardian angel.

Spirit of the planet.

I will gently guide you through

the cracks of blackened earth.

I will guide you through the darkness.

Beyond the nightmare,

To the cave,

the cave of distant hope.

Compared with such life-and-death disruptions of reality, theatre seems a hollow distraction. Even the most cathartic public theatre production could not emulate this one small private ceremony. After a decade of researching many practical models of theatrical intervention, I was asking whether most theatre work, including our own, was too generalised, unconnected and given to mainly enervating containment and gladiatorial titillation.

Our moving between theatre and ritual was part of a consistent pattern which I can see more clearly with hindsight. As we travelled, we frequently created naming ceremonies for our own children, colleagues and acquaintances. At the time, we never thought of these as anything other than something we did privately. We certainly never imagined that, years later, facilitating ceremonies would be a major part of our work. We never defined these early ceremonies as 'Theatre'. We enjoyed making and seeing theatre; were flamboyant if not downright theatrical at times, and would, on a 'ceremonial occasion', chuck in an appropriate bit of theatre to entertain or make a point.

I realise that there was often an aspect of ritual or ceremony underlying our dramatic events. *Raising the Titanic* was a kind of ritual exorcism of capitalism. A drama was acted out and repeated twelve times to reveal and demonstrate a truth. But food and dancing were also shared in celebratory affirmation. In 1983 we were still receiving funds from the Drama Department and maybe we hadn't seen or couldn't admit that on occasion we were inventing rituals. I did once suggest that there should be a new Arts Council department of applied anthropology – with us as one of the tribes to be studied! Ron Grimes (a professor of religion and an ex-Methodist minister) was drawn to *Tempest on Snake Island* (May 1981), describing it as a 'celebration rite' (see On Tour and *Engineers of the Imagination*). No surprise, therefore, that Ron worked with us in 2000 on our 'Rites of Passage' courses in Lanternhouse, but in 1981 we were not that analytical about our purpose. I would often mumble about 'decompression' chambers to take our audience on unpredictable journeys from one world to another and I certainly referred to 'shamanistic flight'. But in those days we were definitely aiming at 'theatre' rather than 'ritual'.

Trawlers at Peace

In October 1993, we were commissioned by Grimsby Borough Council and the National Fishing Heritage Centre to create an outdoor extravaganza to mark the end of *Trawlers at War*, an exhibition at the Centre which had lasted sixteen months and attracted 200,000 visitors. It was a difficult brief. Many of the visitors (and potential audience) had lost relatives on trawlers battling in the North Atlantic. After some initial reconnaissance and pre-planning, we had two weeks to make and rehearse the event from scratch. Every rehearsal and every 'tech and dress' included transporting a thirty-five-foot haddock back and forth on a truck from a council workshop on the edge of town. The fish was made of welded 6 mm steel rod, rattan (flexible cane imported from Vietnam) and glass-fibre rods, which had been covered in stretchable fabric and spray-painted. The makers were Caroline Menis and Graeme Gilmour and Max Orton[1] and the project director was Hilary Hughes. We trod a fine line between creating a pyrotechnic celebration of a very successful exhibition (which acknowledged courage and loss) and a <u>requiem</u> ~~remberance~~ service. It was one of the most successful events (and best one-off rituals) we have ever designed. The council's sport and leisure officer noticed something special was happening during the preparations:

> There is a real sense of common purpose. It has drawn many parts of
> the community together, including schoolchildren and local companies.
> Everyone involved seems to have a deep feeling for the project.

We had learned by 1993 that you can't really do much worthwhile 'community art' in a short time unless you are invited in as a guest by a red-hot professional or amateur organisation on the ground. So *Trawlers at Peace* was a hybrid engagement; a professional host involving local bodies, like a sub-aqua club, plus a small number of invited young amateur performers.

It started at dusk at 7 p.m. on Sunday 3 October, in a car park outside the Heritage Centre. Thirteen young people, local schoolchildren and dancers from Humberside Dance Agency, dressed as mines, performed the overture; an aggressive and surreal dance around a carnival trawler amidst coloured smoke and firecrackers.

Meanwhile, in the Victorian-replica iron bandstand by the nearby Alexandra Dock, within a ring of big ice blocks, was a fifteen-foot trawler made of cloth and bamboo. Lit from inside with hanging oil lamps, it glowed a soft yellow. Alongside it, Peadar Long, a very accomplished soprano sax player and our musical director, played an exquisite lament.

The ship was then ceremoniously carried along the dock on wooden poles, accompanied by dancers, lantern-bearers and the Peace Artists street band. As a carnival atmosphere built up, the audience joined the procession over a few hundred yards, to end up at Freshney Basin. The Grimsby Council Leader Alec Bovil opened the next scene:

> This records a dark time in Grimsby's history. 260 trawlers and 11,500 men were lost during the war. Hundreds of local families still recall the fear of loss as if it were yesterday.

Then, with the assistance of local divers, the canvas trawler, its lamps still alight, was carefully launched down a slipway into the dock and manœuvred through the black water, navigating a flotilla of miniature floating mines. As each mine exploded, fire pictures of four blazing trawlers appeared in mid air, to be slowly pulled across the dock wall on cables and pulleys. After the model trawler hit a mine, it exploded on cue and sank. As the flames subsided, a roll-call of Grimsby trawlers lost in World War II was read out by veterans. Many had never used a microphone before and we had to rehearse them very gently. They read for six minutes over silence.

The giant finale introduced a more optimistic mood. The big haddock, lit up by a couple of very powerful follow spots, was lifted high into the sky by a crane on the dockside. It was lowered on to the water, to be met by a man and a woman in a small rowing boat. The jaws of the giant fish opened to reveal a crystal trawler made by Roger Bloomfield, which lit up as one of the rowers pulled it out of the fish. As they rowed round the dock, they held up the crystal trawler, accompanied by a song of hope for Grimsby. The same crystal trawler was lifted high into the air (using the crane again), surrounded by colourful fireworks as the band played an anthem.

Trawlers at Peace, 1993

Burning ships, *Trawlers at Peace*, 1993

We also used a silver waterfall firework that poured down in a column underneath the crystal trawler, which now appeared very tiny, high in the sky. The 'Song of Hope' which I wrote and Paedar arranged for a full band and fantastic female singer called Jane Coker was a gift. There was indeed a Hope Street in Grimsby. It was the longest street, too:

HOPE SONG
The longest street in Grimsby is called Hope.
You can see the stars in every pub.
You may fly up to the moon
on a force ten afternoon
and you can win a fortune
in the Iceberg Lucky Club

The longest street in Grimsby is called Hope.
Where Lady Luck comes under our control
Where we can hold the rudder
though drunk or going under
We'll sign on for the future
with an anchor of our own.

The roll-call of the dead
sings farewell and no return
While the rollercoaster sea
knows the tide will always turn.

Due to the confines of the dockside and fears of people being pushed into the water, the audience was strictly limited to 1,000 ticketholders only, although we had anticipated 500 gatecrashers, so the expected total was 1,500.

At the end of the performance, there was a stunned silence and then considerable applause. It stirred strong emotions. The mix of terror, joy, sadness and regeneration worked, and we left feeling we had been useful showmen – or maybe even shamen! Sadly, the Arts Council Drama Director did not agree, claiming it was 'formulaic'. He missed the ritual purpose of the event and could not acknowledge its genuine effect. The recognisable Welfare State International 'formula' that he referred to certainly involved big images, fire and lanterns. But that was the palette, not the painting, nor the reason for the painting.

On reflection, I realise that there was a big gap between our worlds. In a culture where most ritual or spiritual activity is claimed by the Church, the audience and funders may not understand or want to understand that they are participating in something like a ritual. If we, the practitioners, don't explain properly, observers can easily fail to recognise any underlying purpose and respond only to the theatrical decoration on the surface.

Hurricane Lamp

In 1987, in what came to be known as the 'Babes in the Wood' case, two young girls were murdered on the outskirts of Brighton. Not long after the murder, Same Sky, a community arts project then run by Pippa Smith, an ex-Welfare State International member in north Brighton, asked us if we would consider working on the traumatised and notorious Moulsecoomb sink estate where the two girls had lived. It was probable that the murderer had lived there too. A local man was in custody, but his case had not yet come before the courts.

We said no. We were too far away. We had no local knowledge and it was too close to the tragic events. A year later, they asked us again and, believing matters to have settled a little, we said yes. We agreed to work with the adults and children of the Moulsecoomb Drama Club, whose aim was 'to give the community, chiefly the children, the opportunity to express themselves through drama, music and dance'. The club had been set up by concerned mothers in March 1987, just after the murders had been committed. Most of the members were women with daughters about twelve years old; the same age as the victims, with whom many of the girls had been friends.

When we arrived, the atmosphere was very tense. During the year since the murders, residents' houses had been firebombed and families had moved away. Behind the foul accusations and rumours of drugs, child prostitution and parents making pornographic movies with their own children, there was poverty, isolation and rejection among the alienated, troubled (and troublesome) families. The violent tension had also resurfaced because the accused man had just been acquitted. Many believed him to be guilty (he was subsequently imprisoned for a separate crime) and there was an angry mood: they believed that justice had failed.

The Drama Club was a considerable testimony to willed optimism. There is a risk of being melodramatic about 'pure evil' and of making irrational connections between chance occurrences. For instance, when talking to one of the mothers in the Drama Club, I was sitting in the lounge of a council house looking out

203

on the wood where the children had been killed. Next to the window, I remarked on a crude but energetic painting of a bull and bullfighter. It had been painted by Ian Brady, the Moors Murderer, who had once lived on the estate.

Not surprisingly, my subconscious went into overdrive and powerful archetypes came to inform the event. Whatever our nightmares, though, we had been hired to produce a coherent 'show' and it was our job to maintain a rational focus and just get on with it. Reading Simone Weil helped. She points out that economic exploitation is passed down the line, ending with the economic brutalisation or entrapment of those at the bottom of the capitalist pile. Moulsecoomb was at the bottom, despised and scapegoated by respectable Brighton, although ironically customers from there were buying drugs and sex, and local gangs (and possibly some young women) were making more money than they would have collected from the DHSS. This Marxist analysis did not provide a justification or a precise understanding of the motivation of the murderer, but it widened the context and the logic was an objective antidote to hysterical fears of the 'mark of the beast' and any generalised neurosis about 'evil'.

The psychological context is a key factor in finding the purpose and the poetry of any site-specific work. Here, the stimulus was extreme and unusual, but it was still our job to connect, absorb and concoct some process of discovering images to distance the trauma. The company could not have been more dedicated to the healing task. My job had been to visualise the poetry, but, as always, it could not have worked without the unique talents of an amazing team. Our key move was to decide to work at the Gardner Arts Centre, which was just down the road. I knew this theatre well because seventeen years before, in February 1971, Mike Westbrook and I had played here with our multimedia Cosmic Circus production of *Earthrise* (a hymn to the Earth, incorporating a twenty-piece jazz band, light show, films, slides, inflatables, acrobats and Welfare State International clown astronauts). The Gardner Arts Centre space was similar to a TV studio. Designed by Sean Kenny, famous for his chunky wooden circular set for *Oliver* in the sixties, it was intended to be a totally flexible circular space, with multiple gantries giving access to state-of-the-art motorised pulleys and hooks supporting a mass of theatre lamps.

Like many 'totally flexible spaces', it wasn't. The Gardner was normally used as an end-on proscenium (via a big 'letterbox' stage stuck on at one side). Its full circular dance floor, empty of seats, would have been perfect for the planetary symbolism of *Earthrise*, but as usual we had to settle for a proscenium lighting rig, pre-set for the next celebrity, and the time/labour cost of shifting, storing and refitting seats meant that was out of the question, too. Nevertheless, the proscenium form might be ideal for Moulsecoomb Drama Club. If we could mount an original show with full production values in 'the largest art centre in the South East of England', which usually presented 'the best dance music and visual arts from Britain and the world', then people might take notice of this bruised and dispossessed estate nearby, which might as well have been in another galaxy. So we set out to do just this, with keen and sympathetic support from the Gardner staff.

As usual, I made a very detailed reconnaissance, taking photographs and scribbling ideas and drawings in my sketchbook. The Gardner Centre is set in extensive grounds. It is a circular, windowless building constructed with thousands of red bricks. Looking back at it from hundreds of yards away, it looks like a Victorian hatbox set in a moat. The flat roof was an interesting platform. There had been stands of large beech trees, but after the October hurricane of 1987, which had devastated southern England, most of these had been cut down. It was awesome to encounter century-old trees, elephantine, long, silent creatures, lying on beds of leaves. At what had been the base of each tree lay a pit, a self-contained world framed on one edge by the arched roots. Many images sprang to mind. Teeth ripped from gums. Lids of cans, slices of galaxies peeled back. Each vertical wall of tangled roots was the back wall of an earth proscenium stage. Fragments of moss hung from tendrils. Spiders had made webs and ants were foraging. In every black hole, the act of regeneration was already being performed.

Mesmerised, I kept returning to study them. I wanted to make a whole show here, take a guided tour through the dead forest, enact a story at each pit theatre and dress the roots in sparse fairy lights. I wanted to use delicate paper puppets and minute mobiles on invisible strings, I thought of tiny tin lanterns, Paul Klee paintings, jewelled stars and stations of the cross, or a pagan equivalent, where each tableau would be a delicate link in a new Creation myth.

On these recces, I never know what will drop into place. At the back of my mind, whether I liked it or not, were half-formed images of violation and girls' bodies lying in a dank wood. These became linked in my head to the brutal and elemental power of the appalling storm and the clear evidence of nature already recycling death. I could have written a set of poems, or made woodcuts, but we had to invent something apparently upbeat and optimistic to involve, engage and distract a particular group of people and an uncertain audience. The estate might come, but what about the usual theatre punters?

So the long process, complex collaborations and negotiations began. After the visit, I knew a little about the people, the place and the situation, and most critically, I had a strong glimmer of the 'poetic envelope' and even the title, *Hurricane Lamp*.

I can't explain where the site poetry comes from, but I know when I've found it and as long as I stick with it there will usually be an original and appropriate event. My first thoughts are nearly always the best ones and I hate having to tear them up and start again. In the best community work, if there is time, it is always better to workshop the ideas and allow the final script to surface through improvisations and discussion. The process can take many weeks. In this case, we didn't have the time or the budget, so I wrote a detailed scenario and a script to provide a useful structure which would also allow the community to write their own verses and dialogue.

Poetry should always comes first, though it does help to have a ballpark sense of the budget even before the recce. At least then you know the scale within which you need to conceive. After finding the poetry, we negotiate dates, times, money, spaces, accommodation, materials, insurance and so on. These days, I usually ask someone else to do this, either our administrator or a production manager, but I do it if necessary.

The next critical step is to book the team. Again, we needed a multi-talented core who would be happy to lead workshops, facilitate and complement the work of the drama group. There were a number of ideal people. Mary Robson, an excellent communicator and hands-on maker, with a working-class background, agreed to share the project direction with me. Then there was Tim Fleming, a long-standing friend, street performer, accordion player and first-rate songwriter and composer. There were makers like Alice King and John Vogdt, who were not only demon workers but people who cared about passing on their skills to inexperienced students. With these people and resources in place, the residency could start. Apart from the advance writing of the script for the theatre-based section, the show was devised, built and rehearsed, including the specially composed music, by a group of over sixty people, full or part-time, over nineteen days. The group only met together fully for the dress rehearsal. The first night was both world première and final performance.

Hurricane Lamp was conceived as a good night out, a catalyst and a healing poem. Skills, songs and objects were to be left behind for future use by the community. Other things fell into the mix. Many of the mothers in the Drama

Club were dinner ladies who, on top of everything else, were about to lose their jobs through privatisation of the school-meals service. Two days after the show was St Valentine's Day and many of the women had a few ironic tales of love in Moulescoomb. Heart-shaped pancakes (for a Shrove Tuesday in a leap year) also materialised (and we made a wild comic Valentine procession round the estate, in the form of an over the top singing telegram). But it was hard to find adult male performers. In the end, we discovered a secret seam of vicars. They had free afternoons, were good at projecting their voices and didn't mind, or chose not to understand, the pagan undertones of our work. We ended up with three of them making up half the company of our sub-plot archetype, the play within the play, performed by wandering thespians.

With great razzmatazz from our buskers in the bunting-filled foyer, we were led upstairs to the main auditorium. There was a nearly full house; a mixture of many people bussed in from the estate plus sufficient theatregoers from the Gardner mailing list. In the orchestra pit, a big band of professional and amateur musicians were tuning up. Throughout, there were cod but gentle self-referencing asides about making theatre. Tim Fleming, the conductor, was warmly applauded by the audience as he and the band ostentatiously stood up. He bowed, they sat, he then played a stirring overture. So, with full lighting, follow spots, scenery, big colourful props (the red spotty mushrooms were quite something), diaphanous kitsch angels, dark transformations and a rich score, we were off for fifty minutes of Part One of *Hurricane Lamp*, a rollicking musical and 'a series of tableaux, parades and performances in which the moon is captured and lost and a great storm comes to Brighton'.

In anticipation of St Valentine's Day, a group of dinner ladies were enjoying a hen night. Accidentally, one of them discovered magical powers and conjured up a whirlwind of animals and tree-spirits, goblins and angels who together gave warning of an approaching storm. The secrets of the universe were revealed via the Zodiac Square Dance but the spell was broken by a bunch of grotesque thespians who stole, tortured and hid the moon. A huge hurricane followed, in which everything was turned upside down. Luckily, the dinner ladies found a piece of the missing moon; then, in a song, the spirits of the trees revealed that a galaxy had fallen to Earth in the form of a collapsed forest. After lighting a chain of star lanterns from the fragment of the moon, the women and children decided to follow the paths of the fallen galaxy in search of the lost moon. Outside, in a processional journey of lanterns, the women, children and audience followed the galactic map of the fallen trees. They placed their star lanterns ceremoniously in the up-ended roots of the twenty-two beech trees felled in the October hurricane. At the end of the trail, they discovered the missing moon and freed it from the cage of an upside-down tree. As it was illuminated in a warming fire, a spectacular firework tree fountain of green Roman candles exploded in a joyous carnival image of rebirth, fifty feet high, from the flat roof of the Gardner Centre. On the outside walls, projections of stark trees appeared. The tree was sculpted by Tony Lewery, with pyrotechnics by David Clough. Back in the theatre, the orchestra converted into a hot dance band (with Sue Gill as a barn-dance caller). The celebration ended with a knees-up, complete with bar, food and surprises.

When storms were conjured up in Victorian theatres, they had stage machines involving cannonballs rolling down metal chutes to simulate thunder; hessian stretched tight round slatted drums cranked to imitate the rising howling of a screaming gale; pebbles from sieves rattling on to corrugated iron to fill the stage with rain. We did all this. But we chose to do it on stage in full view of the audience, with stage-hand goblins pushing sound-effect carts. We also flashed white light for lightning and wheeled on a big fan which blew up to the back row of the stalls and whirled dead leaves and flimsy rags into the wings. Backlit in silhouette, the demons' kitchen was a terrifying black-and-white cacophony.

Our script ricocheted between salacious ad libs, pantomime-style repartee, surreal nursery rhymes and ironic songs:

> I am a woman called Emily Smart.
> Married a man who fell apart.
> He likes spiders.
> I like jam.
> He fried his head in a frying pan.

> Who wants to be my Valentine ?
> My heart's behind the door.
> If you hear sad weeping
> It's not me. It's not me.
> So let me see your Valentine
> White lace and silver pink.
> Pin it on my outside door.
> I'm waiting at the sink.

BE MY VALENTINE

The sexual abuse of women was partially depicted through the brutal capture of the moon. Of course, the moon is often used as a symbol of female energy. It was obvious but not banal, I hope. Understandably, given the nervous energy and the time constraints, the show was a bit rough, but I think the healing process worked as much as anything could within the appalling trauma of it all. There was great laughter, bonding, sharing, social dancing and externalising, and the audience 'witnesses' seemed to enjoy it too. People were proud that for the first time they had been able to perform in the nobs' theatre up the road. We made a video of the show and a crowd gathered to watch it the following day, in another front room facing the wood. We drew the curtains and laughed again and drank beer. Suddenly, an adolescent boy who had been a pain in the arse and a sulky outsider most of the time broke down and wept at one song which seemed to resonate on many levels:

When I was a little girl
You were the tree by my window pane.
Your soft branch
brushed against
the frosty glass
scratching a secret sign.

When I was a little girl
You were the tree by my window
We shared dreams
Hidden treasure
Tucked down inside
Squirrels and winter nuts.

When I was a little girl
You were the tree by my window pane.
Remember
Your rough bark trunk
held my frail hands
Climbing so high so fast.

Tim Fleming tells me that, years later, this song is often used out of context at weddings and even funerals.

The opening image in the show was very risky. I was afraid it would be too sensational or melodramatic, given the sensitivity of the audience.

There was a small platform which rose out of an oblong hole in the black stage floor. Standing on it, three small girls (not two), one holding a lit hurricane lamp, rose very slowly out of the ground. Sharing the lines between them, unfalteringly and in their local accents, they said:

> I am the voice of the hurricane lamp.
> The still eye at the heart of the electric storm.
> I am the light of the hurricane lamp
> and the voice of the waning moon.
> I will show you a masque, a charade, a moonbeam in a jar.
> A dance round the edge of this cratered web.
> A pageant of fun.
> Conjured from ash.
> A filigree leaf caught in the wind.
> Like a moth on a neon sign.
> Listen (*gong*).

These rites based in 'theatre' were our response to public commissions from local authorities or arts organisations. At other times, we responded more privately to the circumstances in people's lives.

Funerals

When my mother was cremated, a fake nylon doyley under her chin was stapled to the rim of the chipboard coffin. The Catholic priest started the funeral service before we arrived. Under the plaster model of a Jesus that was deeply cracked across its chest, a Christmas crib was covered in creased black rayon. Six professional middle-aged female mourners all wore green hats. The priest told them: 'If you don't go to church,' like my mother hadn't, 'you'll go to hell'. No one took the flowers out of the cellophane. Maybe, as her son, was it my responsibility? The steamed-up plastic became a strong image. Here were tears trapped in the ineptitude of our culture.

When my father died in 1979, the ceremony was better. The undertaker worked hard. The coffin was in his front-room workshop, with pliers, staple gun and a mug of tea on the sideboard. More doyleys, but at least 'You can photograph your father before the lid is screwed down'. Bill Hall, as friend, vicar and now chaplain to the arts in Durham, helped. Instead of the piped music, I hired a cellist. My father was a sea captain, so the gutsy gentleness of the cello playing 'For those in peril on the sea' helped. Bill talked me down. Even if I wasn't a Christian, here was contact and real music instead of a remote tape. A year later, we conducted a more personal ceremony. My father's trade was in the North Sea. The Humber pilot ferried us out one misty morning, up the estuary between the tramp steamers at anchor near Spurn Point. To the strains of 'For those in peril on the sea', played this time by our family brass quartet, initially myself, Sue, Daniel (eleven) and Hannah (nine), I tipped his ashes into the sea. I judged the wind right. The pilot lowered the flag and the seamen's chaplain said a prayer.

The urn had been difficult. The anodyne plastic jar from the undertaker looked like it contained diesel oil. We decided to make one. But how big, how heavy and how wide the lid? Potter friends, Peter and Gill Dick, helped. We ended up with a small beehive-shaped slipware urn about twelve inches across the base, with a wide lid which I tied on with an old hippie silk scarf the colour of clouds and waves. The previous urns they had made looked like biscuit barrels or tobacco jars; inappropriate, we felt at the time, because of my father's love of biscuits and his pipe. But why not? Now it wouldn't worry me. In fact, I would welcome a domestic association rather than the meaningless fashionable or authoritarian ritual imposed by someone else's traditional values or aesthetic. Why not a big Toby jug, even?

Mick Ingman, the best man at our wedding, died of cancer in his mid-forties. He was a painter, a lover of impressionist sunshine and delicate spring flowers. A humorist, a boozer, a gentle aesthete, a brilliant teacher. In the stale church, men in black suits descended like polished crows on to his veneered coffin. Was this to celebrate the remains of an anarchist dreamer who once ate the Christmas decorations in a country pub? What did this sinister blackness have to do with life, or art, or us, or his family, or anything life- (or even death-) enhancing? The ceremony was everything he was not.

Why could he not be buried like that ancient ploughman in a running position behind his plough? Be sheltered in a circle of old hogs' hair paintbrushes? In a sprinkling of the red ochre used by so many cultures to symbolise the blood of the earth? Where was the bloody poetry?

Our administrator Howard Steel's death on 31 August 1989, aged forty-one, sent shock waves through the whole Welfare State International tribe. It nearly broke us apart. And it sharpened our sense of mortality and reality. All of us tried in our own personal ways to make his memorial service better. Mary Robson organised, David Clough did pyro and dug a perfect hole for the casket, Taffy Thomas told a story and Boris Howarth carved a stone. Remembering Howard's last trip to Florence, Pete Moser and John Woodward composed and performed music for accordion and guitar. I stripped the varnish from the standard wooden casket and repainted it in fluorescent enamel colours with lanterns, figures and a ladder. Then I transferred his ashes from the plastic jar into the casket and screwed and glued the lid down hard.

Frankie was a baby three months old. His was the most beautiful funeral and maybe the best art event I have ever been part of. The family had wished for the service to take place in a nearby country church, near their favourite picnic spot, but the vicar refused to allow her premises to be used unless she was in charge of the entire service and had the last word. She would allow only one family member to speak. Seeking the right venue for Frankie's funeral, his parents approached the local Quakers, who, with their usual generosity, offered them their meeting-room with its gallery.

Hannah and Sue prepared the space. They placed bowls of cream roses at the entrance. Duncan Copley made a small coffin in the shape of an egg. He wrote:

> The coffin I made had a rawness, but radiated a delicacy and simplicity. Hand carved from English lime, I chiselled a seed-pod, a nut, a foetal nest that would cocoon the baby. The interior remained rippled from the tool, the exterior became a smooth skin that was stroked by the children present at the funeral as we said our farewells. The process of this making felt entirely sacred. The focus I gave to its creation intensified as the day drew near until in the final hour the charging of an energy into the vessel was tangible as I burnished the outer surface to a flawless creamy sheen with the shavings of lime gathered from the workshop floor. I believed that the energy I exerted from the labour of work would help the release of a spirit that was departing.

> I had made a vessel for the journey from this place in time to another, a vessel that could contain a joy and the wild energy of a newborn child. During the labour I was filled with the question of where does the spirit go to?

Within the meeting-room, this coffin, with Frankie inside, was placed on a glass table top resting on two pale wooden trestles. Small night lights in cones of sand with sprigs of mistletoe were lit around the coffin, making soft reflections. The congregation sat around the table within the oblong pattern of the room. Behind us, all around the walls, was an outer perimeter of candles. Members of the family read poems and told stories. Two choirs sang. One harmonised carols from the balcony, including 'Away in a Manger' and 'Silent Night'. From the floor, Bella Acappella, a local women's choir (which included Sue and Hannah and usually Frankie's mother) sang 'Your children are not your children' by Kahlil Gibran. At the end, we trod carefully into the dusk, leaving Frankie to the family and the funeral director, who all travelled with him to the crematorium. The event was a perfect fusion of people, purpose and aesthetics. The child was dead, but the gathering and the ceremony, mainly because of its direct honesty, coupled with the fine yet simple aesthetic qualities of the artefacts, music and organisation, were healing and enriching.

One day, a quiet and shy family came into Lanternhouse: a middle-aged woman, her husband and a teenage daughter. The mother had been diagnosed with a terminal cancer and she wished to make arrangements for her funeral. After considerable discussion and the engagement of Caroline Menis (who had painted our sample cardboard coffin with resplendent sea creatures in flowing waters), they planned a painted coffin to reflect their environment and her interests and passions. On one long side was the view they saw every evening on the way back from work, with wader ducks hunched in the foreground. To her, it meant 'coming home'. On the other side, there was a Portuguese scene of fishing boats from their regular holidays. In their village, she taught children badminton and played golf. So golf sticks and shuttlecocks appeared too. Two flying shuttlecocks and a tennis ball with its S-shaped seams became eloquent symbols of loss and ying and yang crosscurrents. The husband wrote to say how well the painted coffin was received at the funeral and how well the process and the articulation of grief had helped them all.

Alexandra, a baby girl, had been promised a bike ride on the back of her father's bike, but she died before this could happen. Her last journey, to the funeral chapel, was in a small coffin strapped on to a bike trailer which her father cycled over Urswick Common. The white coffin was provided free of charge by an Ulverston undertaker. It was painted with rows of yellow roses, at very short notice, by Katriona Stamp. In a case such as this, the artist's job is to service the family and on this occasion Katriona just painted perfect realistic yellow roses.

As we attended many more funerals, we gradually gained experience and confidence. We learned that you could be interventionist. You didn't have to accept

the standard, often formulaic, practice of the conveyor-belt twenty minutes in the crematorium; the Christian artefacts; the seating plan; the taped or irrelevant music; dull, Victorian-style, fake-oak coffins with 'brass' plastic handles that you can't use; chipboard coffins that turn to mush in the grave before the corpse; priests who take over and use your friend's body as propaganda for their religion; undertakers who overcharge for items you could have made yourself. All this and much more can be challenged.

We realised that with all our aesthetic and theatrical experience of stage managing, directing, writing, designing and even organising theatrical rituals, we could on occasion improve a ceremony. There was a vacuum. Very few people were working in this area. We had identified both a need and a situation to which we might apply our skills and knowledge outside the self-referencing and self-reverential emperor's-new-clothes world of the arts. We started in small ways, finding poems, writing services, discovering poetry, painting images on ecologically better (and cheaper) cardboard coffins, and above all helping people to write their own celebrations to mark the deaths of their family members.

As Sue Gill and I read and researched more, we organised small courses to improve funeral ceremonies. We met more people, found common stories and realised there was a groundswell of those facing and challenging the taboo of death.[2] Paradoxically, the radical questioning gave people strength. Confronting death and dying became life-enhancing. People frequently changed directions in their own lives and, faced with new priorities, couldn't always return to a poor relationship or an unfulfilling job.

In 1996, Sue Gill and I wrote *The Dead Good Funerals Book,* which is a nuts-and-bolts manual of all our thoughts, experiments and practical examples. It covers legalities, standard practices, rights, definitions and forms of rituals, and the theory and practice of rites of passage, religions and customs, plus diagrams and instructions on how to make funerary objects, including shrouds, lanterns and paper cuts and assembling flatpack cardboard coffins. It also explains where to find musicians and celebrants and gives many inspirational case studies of inventive ceremonies created by many people, most of whom are not experts. It has helped improve some funeral ceremonies and also slightly shifted a few attitudes to the taboo of death. Above all, it demonstrates just how much choice we do have and how, when necessary and appropriate, we can take control of the process of the funeral ceremony.

Although we have been engaged in funeral research since July 1993, which was when we first imported a Swiss cardboard coffin and asked Caroline Menis to

John Fox stapling a painted coffin

paint it, there are still very few theatre practitioners engaged in this work. We have found health workers, therapists, counsellors and a few artists, undertakers and ministers of religion who have been influenced by our practice, but there is still a long way to go before a majority of arts and theatre workers make the connection.

Five years after the publication of *The Dead Good Funerals Book*, we were amazed to receive a call from the Great Ormond Street Hospital, who use the book as one of their regular resources.

The media spotlight on retained organs (Alder Hey, Bristol) means that every hospital is required to review its practice and consider its protocol with affected families. In November 2001, Sue Gill, who is now Welfare State International's Director of Ceremonies, helped to devise and conduct a ceremony of remembrance on behalf of the congregation of three hundred bereaved parents at Great Ormond Street Hospital. Sue Gill writes: 'Following publication of *The Dead Good Funerals Book*, Great Ormond Street Hospital got in touch with us in the summer of 2001 for advice over a ceremony they felt the need to offer to families affected by the retained organs issues. They were planning to invite families on their files going back as far as the mid 1950s whose children had died, to attend a secular Ceremony of Remembrance.

'The venue was a new lecture theatre in the Institute of Child Health with strident colours and business-like lighting, which had an open atrium adjacent where people could mingle afterwards. As ever, the site was the starting point. I had stressed the importance of the invitation, which would set the atmosphere, as it would be the prologue to the whole event. I dreaded an institutionalised NHS letter but my fears were groundless. The heart of the ceremony was the roll-call of children's names, to be read by two bereaved parents who are involved in the volunteer telephone helpline counselling service. Two weeks before the event the co-ordinator asked me to lead the ceremony. Their new Chief Executive had vetoed the idea of a celebrity, a national worthy, to present it. Much editing of the draft needed to be done, which Gilly Adams helped with immensely, giving me the courage to delete some of the judgemental readings and replace them with text and poetry that dealt with innocence, that spoke about children. My rewrites were accepted. There was a lot riding on the day, both for the staff as well as the families. It needed to strike the right note of acknowledgement as well as witness the need to heal and move on. I had been involved in infant funerals before, but here the challenge was how to hold the brokenness of four hundred strangers.

'Before we knew it, the families had arrived, clamouring to be let in to take their seats, bringing with them their stories, shells and pebbles to contribute to the cairn we would build afterwards. People of many races, cultures and religions, a surprisingly vast age range, some elderly people and some with young children and babies. One couple had travelled from as far as Iceland to attend.

'After my welcome and introduction, the Chief Executive of Great Ormond Street Hospital Trust made a clear and direct apology for previous professional conduct and attitudes which, although in good faith, were misguided in causing distress to the families. The ceremony included eight short readings with eight different voices, four songs, instrumental music. The reading of each child's name was sensitively paced and took almost twenty minutes over gentle music. It began by bringing to the stage the basket of cards on which each bereaved parent had written their child's name, and concluded as the readers added the final card bearing their own son's name. Drifts of sadness, grief, anger, betrayal and reconciliation rose and fell across the auditorium during the roll-call and settled into a sense of peace through this symbolic completion.'

'My job was to draw together this disparate community of loss, to rebalance the energy as I spoke about the cairn and encourage everyone to contribute to it before they left. The committal brought it all to a close on time:

Child of my flesh
bone of my bone
wherever you go, I will go,
wherever you live, I will live.
As you go into the mystery of life before us
may you be at peace.

'The cairn became the focal point of the gathering over lunch after the ceremony. It is still there in that internal courtyard, open to the frost, the wind and the rain – a memorial that will not last for ever, a validation of that autumn gathering, a milestone on a shared journey.'

Namings

As with funerals, our motivation for namings came from personal experience; indeed, most of the art works and the poetry on our journey has started from a subjective need which eventually becomes public.

We attended ceremonies, especially funerals, but also weddings and christenings that were inadequate, ugly, expensive, exploitative and unconnected to the participants. In the case of namings, we and other parents wished to celebrate and mark the birth of our children, but there was nothing available except the standard Church baptism. This is fine if you are a Christian and agree to appoint the required 'GOD parents' to ensure the child is reared in the Christian faith. But it is not valid for everyone. Often, people with strong moral views feel embarrassed using ceremonies they don't believe in.

In 1996, Sue and I oversaw another book, *The Dead Good Book of Naming and Baby Welcoming Ceremonies*, in our series of Dead Good guides. Edited by Jonathan How, it contains many collected case studies and the wisdom of umpteen parents and artists who have named children and other entities, like animals, houses and boats. In a collage gathered from practical experiences, other cultures and our own traditions, the book (which also explores notions of identity and philosophical ideas about conception and birth) contains many practical suggestions, poems and useful legal information.

> A naming ceremony is a marking, usually public, an affirmation, a declaration, a witnessing, demonstrating at a particular moment, usually celebratory, in which some person or thing is given a name by some person or persons. In a rite of passage the recipient moves through a symbolic gateway from one state to another and their friends acknowledge this changed presence within their community: 'We call our daughter Spicy Pankhurst Amethyst Montgomery or SPAM for short.'

We began with naming our own children. We named Dan in 1969. A Chinese New Year story seemed a good starting-point. It told of a poor man who lived outside a city and earned his living through selling fireworks. At New Year, unlike his neighbours, who spent their money on food, he bought a statue of a beautiful girl. He took it home and honoured it with food. In time, it came to life and she began to prepare his food and care for him. They lived together and had a child. But an inescapable longing overcame her to return to her former state and he was left with the child, who in her turn honoured the statue with flowers. We made the story into a simple mime play, with a narrator and specially composed music and songs. As the performance was planned for outside, the actors and musicians rehearsed and played music all over the dale – particularly in the chosen spot, a sheltered clearing dotted with foxgloves, bracken, wild roses and butterflies. Everything depended on the weather, and the day was perfect. About sixty people arrived, including several other babies to be included in the ceremony. We sat on grassy slopes and waited. Firecrackers went off on the hill facing us and singing was heard from the wood on our left as the band approached. The poor man, in oatmeal robe, white wooden mask and enormous canvas shoes, appeared near the straw bales (indicating his house) and the slow, dreamlike play began. The movement was closer to dance, gestures were kept to an absolute minimum and, frozen in the pauses, they looked like life-size puppets. It took over thirty minutes, during which time the score of children who were watching were enchanted.

At the end of the play, as the father held his child triumphantly, priceless Japanese fireworks were again released on the opposite hill. The poor man began the procession to the top of the hill, and we followed with the musicians. A bonfire blazed, a red banner flapped and coloured smoke billowed up – this was to be the naming. At the sound of a gong, the first parent went forward, held aloft his tiny son and shouted his name into the wind.

We named Hannah in 1971. In the context of the National Students' Drama Festival, this was a more anarchic, theatrical and public affair acted out in the Wool Exchange in Bradford. We set up our circus tent's crimson seating, rather precariously, on the historic wooden and overpolished floor. Alchemical and zoological curtain-raisers included two colossal glass flasks of clear water which were wheeled in by Steve Gumbley[3] to be dyed a pungent magenta and two goats who were rather swiftly married. With Diz Willis in drag and Jamie Proud in a wonderful priestly King Mummer's cloak of bones and feathers, I pushed in a springy silver pram which I had turned into a boat with a mast and a rigging of silk ribbons. I made a silver suit to match and stitched two emerald mallard's wings on to my red check flat hat. Mike Westbrook and Phil Minton played fanfares and Sue and I shouted, how we shouted Hannah's name to the old rafters. And we meant it. In the context of this festival, it was also a propaganda exercise to show how theatre could be given a different context.

Hannah now has misgivings about the way she was named:

> My naming was alternative but how personal was it? Was it an experiment and a statement or a genuine gift to the child?

I have never dared tell Hannah the worst and maybe most memorable bit. As we were committed to a drama festival where products are always repeated, we had to go through the motions on two more occasions, saying: 'At this point we held Hannah in the air and shouted her name.' The third time round, the seating collapsed. From about six feet up, the triangular trestles which were designed to be embedded in grass but had been set up on the slippery wooden surface very, very slowly went splay-footed. Quite suddenly, a considerable number of England's subsequent famous playwrights, including David Edgar, found themselves sitting on the floor. However, they all lived to tell the tale and their experience probably found its way into a play.

We have been involved with about fifty more naming ceremonies in Britain, the USA and Australia. The elements have always been a starting-point. Thus, a gathering in a chilly Yorkshire landscape might involve the outdoor firing of a kiln containing clay birds or animals to be given to the children as mementoes of the day. In Australia, mangoes and parasols are more in keeping. Each ceremony is distinctive, to respect the personal wishes and feelings of each family and respond to the local materials, climate and culture. Children have been named on a beach, in a cave with an underground waterfall, in the garden, on the open moor, in the living-room, on a college campus and in woodland. At different times of day, from dawn to dusk, whatever felt right, and in all seasons of the year. The ceremonies have included shadow theatre, live music, specially written songs and words, food, gifts, surprises and sometimes a gathering of people taking a short journey together for different stages of the event.

Once again, the training of theatre practitioners and some artists may be applied to this area. There is a growing need and a real context. It just requires a leap of the imagination to take drama and visual art into these person- (and site-) specific areas.

Everyday Ceremonies

In addition to the traditional areas of funerals and namings there are many other crossroads where ceremonies and rituals are appropriate. Many people believe that today we live in troubled times. We always have. The trouble varies with the scale and the purpose of the ditch, the bullet, the spade or the rescue remedy. We are persuaded that it is worse than ever. The story goes that we live in a post-religious age where our community or society has gone, isolating us in a violent and polluted environment with at least a rampant axeman and a rising sea level outside. True or not, media gossip reinforces our insecurity. Most escape routes, such as sex, religion, alcohol, gardening, TV chefs, exercising, birdwatching, writing autobiographies and all the others, are a pleasurable mix of sweat and illusion. Ceremonies and rituals are no different. They can be equally addictive, sentimental and nostalgic reinforcements of outmoded tradition, or they can be life-enhancing celebrations of our shared humanity, a magnet to draw families together in community, a rope bridge over the dizzy void, or a memory bank of mutual experience.

At critical moments, we need all the support we can get and it can be useful to shout or share our being with a wider congregation. Retirement, leaving home, stopping work (either through choice or redundancy), changing jobs, changing status, reaching a birthday decade, moving or building a house, divorcing, becoming a grandparent, getting over illness, burying a time capsule, as well as all the traditional areas of birth, puberty, marriage and death, are points where some of us can benefit from considered declarations of our position, with our declarations made privately or publicly to a sympathetic group.

As some traditions die, new ones appear. Many rites of passage, like adolescent joy-riding, evolve spontaneously and don't need formalising by 'experts', and some can be repressive and reactionary. The question for a moving, fragmented and, to some people, rootless society is not whether we need rites-of-passage ceremonies, but what form should they take and who should provide them. Should there be training for new groups of specialist celebrants, or should people learn to do it for themselves, perhaps even at school? The experience of writing our *Dead Good* guides and learning from the participants on our many subsequent courses has been humbling. Once we stopped assuming that religion had to be the stuff of deities and pieties, institutions and retributions, and realised that there is a common need to reclaim a sense of the sacred to inform secular rites, we came to understand that many of our neighbours have their own 'religious' and 'spiritual' sense of the inexplicable.

People experience great wonders not just when their children are born or they fall in love, not just when they are faced with strange coincidences or are overawed by 'Nature', but also in everyday surprises and communication with friends. For many of us, the daily grind, ambition, our careers, September 11th and other news and the welter of the trivial obscures the central focus. But once removed from this clutter, many of us have a sense of the miraculous in the mundane. The basic forms of rites of passage are similar in different cultures and centuries and perhaps, more surprisingly, are also similar for varied occasions. The underlying structure for a funeral ceremony need not, for example, be very different from that of a wedding. In 1890, Arnold Van Gennep pointed out in *Les rites de passage* that we are marking the transition from one cosmic or social world order to another and that we naturally follow a three-part structure of separation, transition and reincorporation, taking us from an old position via an interval to a new status. The bereaved have to disentangle themselves not only from the past but from the previously envisaged future. Such sequences can work in real time and space, within a self-contained invented world and quite mysteriously and cleverly in both at once; similar to the process of transition and transformation provided by all good art.

Peter Cheeseman is Mr Theatre-in-the-Round.[4] Following Stephen Joseph's theories, he designed and raised funds to build the New Victoria Theatre in Newcastle-under-Lyme. Perfect for playing to an intimate, wraparound audience, it would not exist without the same bloodyminded tenacity he used in his innovative documentary dramas. On 31 January 1998, the time came, brutally, for his retirement; this was his last night as the director of the Vic. The house was packed with an affectionate array of supporters. After many speeches, bowed down with gifts, he was as still as King Lear, blinking and a little fearful in the spotlight. A clutch of excited actors in smart tuxedos steered his last exit by wheeling in a pantomime sedan chair.

'Time to leave, Peter.'
He climbed in and the actors heaved, pretending they couldn't lift it.
'Must be the weight of the keys . . . ?'
Peter descended.

Hidden in the upholstery of the cart was a huge bunch of theatre keys. In a daze, Peter was persuaded to hand them over to the youngest actress in the cast, who acted shock and surprise in the round. After mock appealing to the audience, she returned one key to the master.

'You are only permitted to have the key to the archive room.'

As Peter returned to his chair, drums reverberated from the back of the auditorium and a tacky bunch of 'Welfare Staters' and 'Beavers' dressed as pink fairies with wire wings in samba percussion hobnailed down the aisles to the stage. Hurriedly, an overcoat was slung over Peter's hunched shoulders and we all escorted the sedan chair in procession through the warm foyer to the chilly car park outside. In the furthest corner of the asphalt, we had erected a giant golden boot (Peter reckoned he'd been given one). A glowing lantern, big as a donkey, it was wired to a fake dynamite plunger. Betty Buffer (Susan Clarke), a comic (and motorised) cleaning woman, proclaimed a pantomime speech.

Betty Buffer is my name
For speedy Cleaning I am famed.

Corridors of power
Carpets full of dust
Betty Buffer's broomstick
Sweeps away the rust.

New brooms. New looms
New carpets roll before us.

Now, Peter KING. King no more
You must lose your office
But a king without a castle
Is a rascal full of promise.
Take this plunger. Show the truth
Blow up the dreaded Golden Boot.

Peter grasped its handle and pushed with glee. Two hundred of us cheered as the boot exploded in worms of greasy smoke. Carnival drums rolled and rockets spiralled over the telegraph poles of the encroaching housing estate. Pigeons flew, beating, from the oak tree he had planted to herald the new build in bare land on 23 November 1981. Betty B, waving her mop wand, spirited him down an avenue of crimson Catherine wheels towards a burning wooden arch perfectly made by Roger Bloomfield. Dressed as mock gardeners, Peter's long-standing mates (working colleagues from stage management and the carpenter's shop), removed his overcoat and re-dressed him in a large gardener's smock which he had used in a mummers' play at the original ceremony marking the leasing of the land. A straw hat was placed carefully on his head and a wheelbarrow containing a cardboard model of his beloved theatre was passed across to him, along with a cherry sapling to be planted in his retirement garden at home.

As he steered the heavy barrow away from us all, courageously wobbling through the fiery arch, pinpoints of blue and silver rain sprang from behind us, spelling: 'GOODBYE, PETER'.

When he arrived at the stage doors (in some shock), he was given a bottle of good malt whisky. He stayed a while in the carpenter's shop until the finale barn dance began, back in the studio theatre. Here, he was nurtured by his family until the bewitching hour. Out on the asphalt, it was drizzling. It took a long time for us to go inside to the dance. A fiddler was still playing, and besides, looking towards Mark Fisher (then Arts Minister), I realised the minister's trousers were on fire.

★

Before he became the Chief Executive of the Arts Council of England, Peter Hewitt worked for Northern Arts for fifteen years including five as chief executive.[5] In February 1997, he left for a new career in the Tyne and Wear health authority. We were invited to invent and organise his leaving ceremony. After many discussions with his staff, it became clear that this had to be a two-way event. For Peter, of course, but also and maybe more so, for his loyal and supportive team of forty people.

The ceremony took place on 7 February 1997, between 5.30 p.m. and 7.30 p.m. in the Pitcher and Piano, a new wine bar for the new Tyneside, opposite the shell of the Baltic Flour Mills (now developed as the Tate Modern of the North) and half a mile to the east of the great Tyne Bridge. On the evening, it was cold and the river was swollen dark. There was a new moon, so on the second-floor veranda we strung cut-paper moons which flapped like distraught ghosts. A few mushroom Calor-gas heaters hardly penetrated the chill and office guests, preferring the warmth of the bar, merely popped in and out, clutching aperitifs.

Peter's three daughters, Katie, Anna and Laura, were recruited to wait for him in an ambulance on the far side of the river. Also, the river pilot offered a motor boat for transport. It took time, letters and phone calls, plus (legal) donations and a bottle of Scotch, to persuade the Health Service and the River Authority to join us. But they were willing and generous.

The plan to lower Peter off the parapet thirty feet to the dark dockside below nearly went adrift when we discovered, quite late on, that he had no head for heights. (I should have checked.) However, with ropes and three strong men, we achieved a safe exit with an illusion of real danger. Peter was politely scared but, laden with farewell speeches, poems from me and Peter Mortimer and a ceramic plaque of the view from his old office from Paul Scott (all jammed into his backpack), he stood ready.

As he was lowered, Alistair Anderson played a lilting lament on the Northumbrian pipes. A glittering life-size lantern crescent moon came dancing along the quayside to lead the way to the steep steel ladder down to the swaying boat which soon roared off north across the river. The looming Baltic Flour Mill dwarfed the bobbing of the moon lantern on deck. Ozzie Riley of Dodgy

Clutch Theatre and Events Company lit a firework arch of red, green and silver rain, which sprang up in the darkness. And that was that. Or so the guests thought. Until, just minutes later, Peter was back. Transported fast along the dock edge from the other side of the river in that NHS ambulance with his daughters inside. Siren making whoopee and blue light rippling across the foaming river. This sentimental part of the rite of passage – a wayward return after the apparent exit – was added to satisfy the genuine trauma of some of his staff, who needed to dance and drink with their ex-leader in a final unbonding. While he was speeding across the river, not knowing where in the night he would end up, they fancy-dressed themselves into TV doctors and nurses. My script read: 'cliché NHS doctors and nurses with umpteen white coats, surgeons' masks, pinstripes, pince-nez, fake beards, starched bonnets, surgical saws, colourful pills and false promises'. On re-entry, he was treated with mock severity, pretend-ostracised and obliged to sit at a fake hospital Formica table sipping hospital gravy from a fork – until a kindly anaesthetist slipped him a 'Newky Brown' and he was allowed into the feast proper.

Rose Fenton and Lucy Neal direct the London International Festival of Theatre (LIFT). At midsummer 2001, art was never such a holiday. It is hot and people stream over Blackfriars Bridge to Tate Modern. Some say they come for the views and the cafés, and that the art is just an additional novelty. Certainly on this midsummer's afternoon, with many couples and families lying on the lawns, staring up at the massive square chimney of the old power station, and many queuing for ice-creams at the (unlicensed) vans on the riverside walk, there are more people outside than in the austere and sparse rooms of Morandi paintings inside.

Morandi (1890–1964) is an old favourite of mine. His small, perfectly judged still lives of regimented bottles and bowls in tonal greys that ooze with colour offer the perfect calming antidote to the scramble of today's art world. Morandi took a lifetime to organise chaos in a shed at the bottom of his garden, finding personalities and planets in random dusty domestic objects.

Outside on the shingle and mud bank of the Thames by a corner of Blackfriars Bridge is a remarkable pile of remains, still immaculate. A century and more ago, people smoked clay pipes and tossed their used stems into the river, as we would tab ends. Despite so many sweeps of the river, hundreds of these fragments remain today. We are inserting them like small teapot spouts into crude red clay egg cups which we are rapidly fashioning to dry in the hot morning sun.

It's 8 a.m. and we are back to camping as 'gypsies' in caravans outside Tate Modern. At 2 p.m. we shall fire the egg cups in a large home-made kiln we have been fashioning for the last week. The kiln, designed by Martin Brockman, is in the shape of two entwined chickens. Reaching for the sky with two mouths stretched open, they are emblazoned in red, white and yellow ochre clay feathers with black scratchings. Next to the soaring modernity of the powerhouse Tate Modern, they appear crudely primitive, from elemental ancient landscapes. Yet the process of public making on a lawn behind a rope has drawn crowds and conversations for a whole week. Spectators enjoy seeing artists at work and talking demystifies what is often obscured both by artists and critics.

The occasion is the twentieth anniversary of the London International Festival of Theatre (LIFT) and a birthday rite of passage for Rose and Lucy, its two renowned and intrepid founder directors, who have, more than anyone else, brought stunning and original theatrical events to Britain for two decades. We have worked for them before with large spectacles: in 1983, with *Raising the Titanic* in Limehouse, and in 1991, with *Lord Dynamite* in Newham. Our current move to this kiln party, a relatively small-scale event in the context of a semi-domestic tribal rite, mirrors our bigger journey and it is fitting that it should have a public outing in the context of LIFT 2001.

Rose and Lucy intended to shift the dynamic of their festival so that it would no longer be concentrated in one block but scattered over twelve months into specific events in varied locations in and outside London. They too wish to make connections across disciplines and explore new creative partnerships, maybe outside the sometimes narrow constraints of theatre product and performance art. A crossroads and a mutation to be marked.

Our plan is to use the chicken kilns to fire simple egg cups to be revealed at dawn for a celebratory egg breakfast with friends and supporters. Some weeks before, parcels of dry clay have been posted to their mailing list, with instructions for the clay to be soaked in water, sculpted into egg cups and air-dried, ready for insertion in the kiln between 12 p.m. and 2 p.m. on Saturday, 23 June. Not all is perfect. Some cups are wrapped in polythene and are still wet, some arrive after the kiln is sealed, and, as always, many wanted to give of their best but forgot or were too busy. For these, we make the forty extras with the stems of the fragile white pipes inserted to let out the water in the clay which will turn to steam as the temperature rises. If they don't explode first.

We are on schedule. Martin Brockman, our master kiln-builder, is true to form. So as not to burn the fresh lawn, the kiln has been constructed on a raft of house bricks, then built up with more bricks, iron stakes, firebrick shelving, hundredweights of clay, dried willow sticks and, appropriately, chicken wire. The brick arched firemouth is laid at an angle to the river to pick up the prevailing wind and a large pile of pallets have been sawn to firewood length to feed the fire we must tend all night. Martin's calculations, as usual, prove accurate, and exactly on cue, just before midnight, great cones of deep orange fire project from the throats of our demonic fowls.

With the edifice of the Tate Modern chimney looming high behind us, the stretched necks of the two chickens make a V in the middle of which St Paul's appears floodlit, glowing wedding-cake white across the Thames. Fistholes of fire, reaching 800 degrees centigrade, lace the upper bodies of our birds, but their sinews hold. This is amazing, given their very basic construction from wet clay bunched on to braids of hay, and awe-inspiring given the primeval power of the inner furnace. Spectators have to be kept well behind the safety barriers. All goes well, however, and slowly we seal the kiln to slumber, to cook and slow down to cool, to await the dawn opening. Despite the distant roar of traffic, everything seems quiet except for the crackle of two braziers.

Jodi Watson, our tireless site manager, had designed a fifty-metre encampment round the kiln. On the outside, lines of young silver birches were gently lit in bronze, pink and blue; then came a semicircle of twelve elegant vertical silk banners (made by Shona Watt) in deep yellow or violet-blue. At dawn, these became luminescent in the rays of sun shooting up the river. Scores of LIFT devotees have gathered and we wait for the breaking-open of the kiln. Our diminutive marching band have only just met each other. A small woman (Dini Presman) with a big and battered sousaphone and a fat man (me) with a tiny reedy melodeon improvise fanfares and folky good-time tunes. The blessing is auspicious and all the pots, bar one, emerge unscathed in their fat pink chunkiness. Under a festoon of coloured bulbs, as people find their personal egg cups, four cooks serve a feast of succulent salamis, hams, home-made jams, country butter and slabs of fresh bread with boiled eggs and perfect coffee. With characteristic attention to detail, Rose and Lucy have purchased red flowers with matching gingham tablecloths so that over one hundred long-standing fans can enjoy a stylish and a memorable celebration.

A colleague from their office gathers us together for a speech and Lucy and Rose set off towards the river with a wobbly wheelbarrow supporting a large bundle under a yellow blanket. Gripping one handle each, they stagger some hundreds of yards, led on by the small band and some enthusiastic but rather English clapping and cheering. About 5.45 a.m., downriver, in the direction of the Globe, past the still out-of-commission Millennium pedestrian bridge, we parade, waking up a naked man who peers at us full-frontal from the crystal

227

windows of an expensive Georgian mansion. Or was he an actor's ghost from the old Globe, tracking the course of theatre history as it lunged back to its original roots of ceremony?

As the jetty looms, we dance down its slope to the fast, mustard-coloured river. With additional speeches about eggs and hatching and unpredictable futures and voyaging out to further unknown seas, we toss ladles of water, anointings from a big bucket, on to the steel deck. The duet play an expedient Cumbrian–Cuban gig as the blanket is removed from the lump in the wheelbarrow, revealing a metre-high speckled egg tied in shiny ribbon (made by Jodi). The label says 'free range' and inside there is a plentiful bag of greetings and wishes from the LIFT inner circle. Finally, our two leaders leave the jetty to enter a small motor boat. As it swirls and circles away in the fast current, silver-rain fireworks jet backwards from its gunnels. Together, Lucy and Rose clutch their egg. Fortuitously, a hundred metres downstream a dolphin spirals up and round their vessel in an exotic figure of eight.

My poem to them (which was also inside the egg) says 'search for tidal waves', but 'never ignore the wake of your own boat'. Morandi found the solution in his own woodshed. Doubtless he found many galaxies and dolphins too, even in Bologna.

By 2001 we had documented enough material to mount three exhibitions to do with Rites of Passage.

Hatch, Match, Dispatch[6] was first mounted in Lanternhouse before transferring, in an expanded version, to Tullie House in Carlisle from December 2000 to February 2001. It contained many vernacular artefacts from old and new ceremonies, including Bronze Age burial urns, christening robes and the 'top ten' wedding presents from a local department store (mainly tableware and bed linen).

Picking Up the Threads, which ran from August to September 2001, featured farmers from the Duddon Valley and local artists in an exhibition of Herdwick wool rugs, wall hangings and jewellery, photography and installations. Curated by Alec Bell, the Centre Manager of Lanternhouse, it was part requiem, a reflection on the foot and mouth devastation of Cumbria, and an affirmation of a future for local distinctiveness and well-made imaginative products. The Cruck Barn gallery space and the occasion presented an opportunity for us all to take stock and to swap stories. It demonstrated the celebratory role that could be appropriate to a site-specific gallery; a role, indeed, that might at one time have been filled by the parish church.

Dead was our major input into YOTA (the Year of the Artist).[7] Under the guidance of Andrée Cooke, a dynamic and knowledgeable curator, we invited seventeen artists, many of whom were well known in avant-garde circles in Europe and London, to respond to the challenge of Death by making a real artefact for a real funeral. *Dead* was presented for a week in March 2001 at the Roundhouse in London, and then for three months at Lanternhouse. In February 2002, all the works were auctioned by Bonhams at the London Institute, hosted with great generosity by Mark Lamarr, the proceeds intended to raise an annual bursary for artists to study at Lanternhouse. Unfortunately, we didn't sell anything.

The work varied from the delicate and almost domestic, such as 'To rest', Jessica Ogden's antique linen pillow for her father made with eight layers of cotton wadding and cotton quilting thread, to the provocative coffins of Bob and Roberta Smith, made with discarded fruit boxes and filled with colourful badges proclaiming 'When I die, bury me in a fruit box coffin'. Owen Gaster made a spectacular diamanté shroud, Gavin Turk a large glass-fibre egg, George Shaw painted (exquisitely) two tiny cardboard foetal coffins, each with a *trompe-l'œil* picture of a dressed child, and Duncan Copley made Coombe, another vessel which, like his seed-pod for Frankie, was carved from common lime.

> My hands-on interest in this area of work began when I was asked to make a coffin for a child who was to be cremated within the week. Prior to this, carrying a coffin, lowering it into the earth and the scattering of ashes was the closest I had come to any involvement in the creation of a funeral ceremony.

> In the heart of Coombe is a secret vault – a gilded chamber – just large enough to hold the cremated remains of a person. The ashes are poured into the interior through a channel from the outside. Finally the channel is sealed. Coombe is an object for contemplation. Sited in a garden or a wilderness, it too will decay, in time.

Tord Boontje created a deep-blue crystal container in which the cremated remains would give life to a plant – in this case, rosemary (for remembrance). Lawrence Weiner made One Dead One, a canvas body bag with aluminium painted text; Linder Sterling a delicate soundtrack on CD which included specially composed requiem music interspersed with inner-city helicopters; Hussein Chalayan constructed a mahogany boat; Peter Friedl a wicker willow 'dead duck'; Dunne and Raby a Memorial Kit – Final Breath (a small inflated white balloon with a luggage label); Padraig Timoney a large hanging shroud/banner printed with infinity signs. Simon Periton cut perfect small anarchy symbols from shocking-pink kite fabric to create 'lace' for his 'Anarchy Veil'; Milena Dopitova an iron and blue velvet fish-shaped coffin; and Rose Finn-Kelcey's Return to Sender was a large white paper envelope containing a life-size mannequin wearing sunglasses programmed with moving sparkling LEDs saying 'I am happy'. Finally, Inventory's Burial Kit for the 21st Century was a dense and powerful manifesto printed white on a black biodegradable plastic body bag. It linked well with their image used on the cover of the catalogue; a random person in a crowd wearing a jacket with a skull and crossbones on the back. There was also an arrow pointing to the words 'Work, Buy, Consume, Die'.

The works looked particularly good in the Roundhouse. Designed by Adrian Winch of Design Unit 21, we achieved what I had hoped for: a sense of this Victorian engine shed as a massive stone and metal universe. We placed all the objects in the middle, some on the floor, some on discreet stands, and lit them quietly with hanging shades and unobtrusive spotlights. Although the outer walls were carefully illuminated in a cold blue, we managed to avoid the dominance of theatre lamps so that the inner perimeter of lit artefacts became a glowing, hovering encampment of stars.

Roger Coleman sent me an e-mail about the show: 'The Roundhouse show was full circle for me because once again here were young, very creative people pushing the boundaries within an agenda which was about connecting art with people in the context of their lives. It wasn't political, but as I said earlier, the Welfare State was born in political times and today is not like that, at least not in the same way. It was also exciting to see that the Welfare State agenda continues to be relevant and give social meaning to art in the sense of connecting it with people, in an era when fine art has largely vanished up its own iconography. The young designers and craftspeople involved in the show - at least the ones I know - are now invading the space vacated by the fine arts, by the ones that stayed on the walls and in the galleries, and working at making objects with humour that engage and interact with people in new ways. That is a very positive direction. *Dead* made the links, offered the bridge, and for me brought a lot of this new "stuff" into a context that was suddenly meaningful, and gave me a hope.'

Frankie's coffin

New Generations

*unspeakable processions of
arbiters of Taste led
by the laughing mule of History.*

*Dangerous & Doubtful Processions
of the Museum Beast.*

Wireman (1997), a peripatetic show, was created by a younger generation of Welfare State International artists who valued and revived the challenge of traditional touring but who brought in new ideas and electronic expertise. Their programme note read:

> As well as establishing a firm anchorage and international beacon in Ulverston, Welfare State International also intends to project *Wireman*, a satellite 'event' which will tour extensively at home and abroad. Following a pilot project in 1997, *Wireman* will be a self-contained series of changing performances, a rolling diary, a showcase of the high-tech with the home-made; a catalyst designed to parachute into diverse non-standard venues.
>
> *Wireman* will draw members and fans back to gatherings in Ulverston. Contact will be maintained and extended through IT communication and periodically there will be elaborate performances and exchanges at the Lanternhouse Home Base.

In 1997, this was a little premature because Lanternhouse was not yet built and it was hard enough to raise the funds for the main scheme without taking on the additional expense of an unpredictable chain of residencies with an uncertain satellite. Nevertheless, *Wireman* was a key transition and an important acknowledgement of the needs and work of younger and very imaginative artists.

A relatively small-scale work, it was invented, made and performed by Dan, Hannah and Roger Bloomfield and subtly directed by Mette van der Sijs, a Dutch

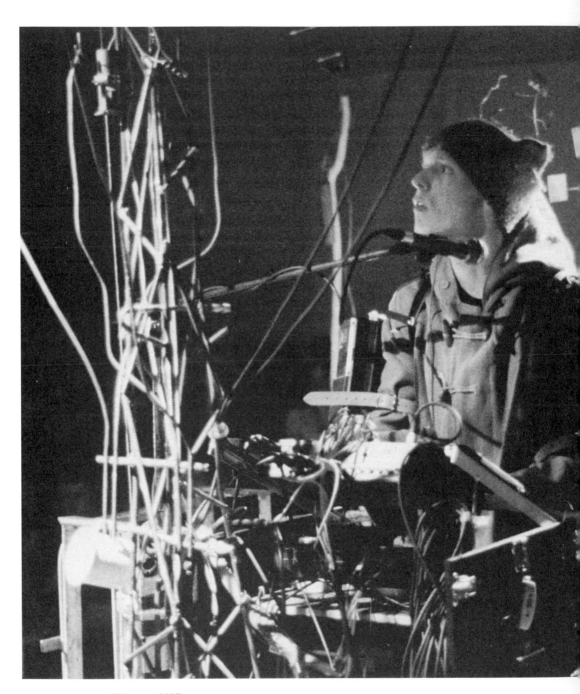

Wireman, 1997

choreographer. It toured on a pilot run within Cumbria. As well as the usual village halls and visitor centres, unconventional non-art venues included a youth club, a marquee, a drill hall, a cattle mart, a walkers' hostel, an outward-bound centre, an embryonic eco-village and a late-night disco. The tour was designed to test audience reaction, particularly that of young adults, and with discussions and a good return on questionnaires we did learn that there was potentially a large audience for strong, original visual theatre in unusual places and a potential for drawing a following of fans and artists who would communicate with IT. By early 2002, we ran a considerable number of IT training courses.

In May 1997, in six weeks, the team devised and rehearsed the innovative show (including constructing the set, composing and engineering the soundtrack and making the costumes) and took it out for two weeks with two preview shows and eight performances with an average audience of about eighty each time.

The story was a pre-millennial and disturbingly fortuitous science-fiction fable about two local farmers who were abandoning their farm to take up an all-consuming hobby, running a radio station. As they became distracted by the pleasures of an 'artificial' media world, they forgot the land under their feet.

Suddenly the ground (a desert made from brown paper) erupted and a demented woman (played by Hannah) emerged like a mole in welding goggles to present warning parables. She sang, played the ukulele, made puppet personages from wire and vegetables, turned, radio masts into trees and like an archetypal Mrs Noah, gathered her wire animals around her. These also literally sprang up from under the ground. She had been journeying to discover the oldest rocks on earth, while the men had been listening to radio waves. Their worlds collided in a cloud of suspicion and misunderstanding.

The set, constructed by Roger from corrugated iron and other farmyard junk, was a cross between a disintegrating cattle mart and a forgotten bunker. All the sounds (composed by Dan) were played live in a cunning mix of melodic trombone, melodeon and percussion, with digital sampling, echoes, atmospheric effects and voices triggered from foot switches and others hidden in costumes and boots. The episodic sculptural cameos were a kind of simple but strong 'performance art'. But one that spoke clearly and comically to young audiences who had never heard such jargon. Well before the foot and mouth epidemic, sounds, images and clowning were strongly integrated to make a punchy, surreal comment on the undercurrents affecting farming.

Wireman found many non-standard venues blissfully free of standard theatre expectations. Reaching audiences who would normally avoid theatre, it mixed 'home-made' imagery and performance with very sophisticated high-tech sound played live. Produced entirely by a second generation of Welfare Staters who had learned the language and acquired the skills to create and present their own personal and sensitive poetry, it worked as a show. However, we still haven't made full use of two key ideas: the rolling stone which gathers, changes and expands as it rolls (a concept left over from *Hollow Ring* in 1993) and the network of exchange which energises, partially through electronic communication, a club of participants who may visit Lanternhouse for extended gatherings. A post-tour meeting reconfirmed some of the essential ingredients of our method: playful improvisation in devising and presenting; supportive teamwork; a strong mythic narrative performed (rather than acted) and the construction of a practical and emblematic circle.

This method of collective dreaming, intuitive playing and working generously is totally dependent on trust, but with the right team it can evoke strong archetypes which may complement each other. As Roger put it, 'Dan was like a man made of his surroundings, a living museum of sound, each part of his body reflecting a bit of the world as if he were a receiver and transmitter for all the stories in the world. Hannah was the spirit of mischief and change, a female ringmaster conjuring up wild colour, plants and animal ghost dancers.' Roger saw himself as 'a man of the soil, a primal energy, endlessly tinkering, keeping the balance between earth and sky'.

> The world of the circle was a parallel self-contained universe where the performers literally struck powerful musical (and metaphoric) chords communicating more subliminally than through thrusting information.

In another era or another culture, Roger would have been talking about magic or shamanism.

Satellite House

In 1998, another team of five artists,[1] which also included Dan and Hannah, continued to place art works in an unusual public venue, using sophisticated electronics for Christmas in Ulverston. *Satellite House* was an installation in the front window of a disused gas showroom in the middle of town. We had no problem collecting spectators. We had expected drunks to kick in the shop window but, far from it, gaggles of lads would gather late on, to laugh and wonder at fine-art magic. One even told us it was the best part of his day, every day. In the manner of peepshows in an old-fashioned amusement arcade or secular advent calendar, Hannah designed it to include over thirty separate images. The whole window was first covered in tracing paper printed with old maps of Ulverston. This skin was then pierced with framed boxes up against the glass. Some tableaux in shallow boxes were placed in the front of the window, but others were in 'deep space'. On the pavement, the audience had to queue before peering up one of a number of cardboard tunnels to an animated scene seemingly hundreds of miles away in the back of the shop.

Inside was an elaborate array of pulleys, motors from mirrorballs and windscreen-wiper motors, fairy lights, small-scale halogen lamps, a computer, a sampler and CD player; an Aladdin's cave of electronics all driving the various scenes. These included oblique and poetic references to the Christmas shopping season. Fragile paper sculptures depicted a woman who had missed the last bus, while gossipy neighbours hung out their washing. In fairy-tales and nursery rhymes, people (including a whole tiny paper football team mounted on the turntable of a record player) danced up to the stars while various incarnations of bowler hats and Stan Laurel, drawn in black wire, joined them in comic dances. Dan composed a cartoon soundtrack that was amplified to the outside and triggered by an electronic beam as shoppers passed by. An old-fashioned car horn with a rubber bulb outside the shop window could be squeezed by spectators. As it honked, a giant hairy spider dropped on a string and ate the Hoad Lighthouse. Over three weeks, with the installation on display for twelve hours a day, we got through four rubber bulbs and five electric spiders.

When Lanternhouse opened in 1999, we suddenly had an anchor, and for the time being the need to tour or work in shop windows evaporated. Having our own staffed and heated toolbox with multiple spaces on site meant we had far more control. Lanternhouse is our own. So as well as being a community resource on occasion, as it was for Alec Bell's *Picking up the Threads* exhibition (see Rites of Passage), when it incorporated healing, release and reconciliation, it can also offer a centre to escape from the mundane; in the way churches or even non-commercial art galleries once offered architecture and art works as symbols for spiritual focus, contemplation and meditation. A number of our installations have explored the possibility of a centre for secular prayer and a gallery to hold stillness.

Sand

Sand was a special installation. It held and brought together many strands of the journey. It was part of Welfare State International's 100 days, a rite of passage across the millennium which started on 7 November 1999 and continued to 14 February 2000. In our publicity brochure we posed the questions: what is the Millennium about? A rough mark on a religious calendar? A celebration of consumer culture? The biggest, brashest bash of all time? The cover of the brochure itself, based on a small painting on wood by Hannah, evoked obliquely the tentative and ironic existentialism of our answers. In a soft and delicate pink, blue and white universe, two planets are linked together by a drooping tightrope. A winged insect, a decimated fly or a wasp sets out to walk across. Below lie the corpses of dead insects. It was a time of uncertainty and doubt.

> 100 Days is a public Rite of Passage to dump debris and build new jetties for voyages and arrivals. As a refreshing alternative to legless wipe out on New Year's Eve, Welfare State International propose an active contemplation to mark the transition across the centuries. 100 days is a total poetic work, with markers along the way. There will be stories, songs, sand paintings, tableaux, gardens, flags, ice sculptures, a grotto and a stone beach. Inspirational speakers, poets, artists and songsters will animate 100 days – re-awakening the imagination, analysing violence, pondering ecology and dreamtime in local ponds – powerful medicine to undercut consumerism. Above all there will be singing and SAND between toes.

Over the years, we have learned a little about setting out bubbles of the future to convince promoter, public and indeed ourselves that we know what we are delivering. We try to set a convincing atmosphere but keep the details as open as possible. Highlights of the 100 days included two week-long courses and workshops in contemporary ceremony, rites of passage and new celebrations, a Winter Beach Café with monthly soirées for conversations, poetry, food and wine. A performance of the Burma play (see Rehearsing Utopia, note 9) and the new Breakwater Choir (a group of women who continued choral singing following one of our workshops).

At the heart of 100 days was *Sand*, an 'environment of enchantment' created in the Lanternhouse Cruck Barn. This was to be in two parts with special openings, closings, vigils, performances, ceremonies and wild walks. Art and the family came together. Both Dan and Hannah are normally so busy with their own work, their own theatre companies and bands that they haven't time to be with Welfare State International or me over an extended period. In this case, I booked them a year in advance. Hannah as joint artistic director with me and Dan as musical director. Sue Gill, with her love of cooking, nurturing, inventing and teaching rites of passage and comic performing, would have a major role. And, treat of treats, I could work with my hands as one of the key artists on the ground rather than just being my usual Rushabout Lasso.

Hannah and I divided *Sand* into two 'Movements'. The first, 'Letting Go', a focus for dumping baggage, took place inside the Cruck Barn before Christmas and the second, 'New Journeys', was staged outside in our garden in the New Year. We offered a series of images and sounds to trigger thoughts and emotions and provide points of reference for visitors to do their own dreaming. We agreed to keep the materials simple: sand, paper, wood, string, salt, etc., and we shaped things to work together, with the right scale, colour and atmosphere. As in a church, when the architecture is right, you are steered physically and spiritually to a receptive frame of mind.

In Part One: 'Letting Go', 7–22 December 1999 five of us worked for two weeks in the Barn to build an elaborate garden grotto. Moving up from the ground, three different worlds, in three different universes, co-existed in their horizontal planes. An earthbound world of tiny wooden shacks on stilts, in dunes of silver sand (which Hannah made), a flying world of bone prehistoric animals (which I made) whose projected shadows entangled with the bigger shadow of a disturbing Cherub of Death and, high above, a satellite whirligig of revolving space stations by Rob Hill. Tableaux in the corners included 'The Whingers', dreadful, bored old men who contributed nothing except moaning and belching (made by Vivien Mousdell, who modelled black clay on the tips of vertical wooden organ pipes), and emerging from underground a black dragon made from industrial junk.

The audience was given a map. As they walked round, they connected with many vistas and sounds. Dan designed six trigger pads, twelve-inch-wide discs covered in black rubber which when tapped by the audience played short sampled loops. The sound collage ranged from wispy rock'n'roll emanating from a lonely shack to fragments of distant choirs clinging on to forgotten requiems, radio news pips and the shipping forecast. Cleverly, however many sounds played at once, they were all in interlocking keys and tempos, blended to give moods from empty anguish to full-on frenzied party. There was also a 'Millennium Window' decorated with brief texts to which early year teachers were invited to contribute. What would they like to leave behind? What values did they wish to hang on to? I found their autobiographical remarks quite shocking. Many felt they were overworked and overweight, undervalued and in debt. What they wanted was more time, better health and less stress.

In her review, Josie Bland quoted Suzi Gablik's suggestion that Art should be for 'Re-enchantment'.

During the dark days of December 1999, the group has created 'Letting Go'. It is the first part of a two-part installation; a whirl of light, shadows, sounds and objects, which create nightmarish, beautiful, literal and allegorical images of this terrible century.

The work evokes Goya, Miro, the Dadaists, Tinguely, Boltanski. Its surface fun gives way to reminders of the deeper unspeakable horrors of the last hundred years. The viewer walks around the edge of a sand-filled area. Sand, a changing medium with myriad grains, suggests the millions who have occupied this century. Shoes of sand and suitcases of memories recollect those who were lost, destroyed or forgotten. Tiny candles, lit in the shoes at dusk, create a memento mori. Overhead is the dizzying whirl of a skeletal boat containing a gamut of harpies and apocalyptic horrors straight out of Bosch, Brueghel and Bacon. An angel of death projects its shadow on to a suspended screen etched with the gates of Auschwitz. Headless mechanical soldiers march along one wall. Organ pipes topped with Easter Island totemic faces howl eerily. A suitcase of crucifixes recalls the two World Wars and all the needless deaths of this epoch.

There are images of hope – tiny ladders pointing to the moon, houses on stilts with lights within, but elsewhere, similar fragile constructions have been destroyed. Not surprisingly when we look through the windows of the nursery rhyme screen we see the words of the Big Bad Wolf, I'll huff and I'll puff and I'll blow your house down.

The German philosopher Theodor Adorno stated that after Auschwitz there could be no more poetry, but this piece proves him wrong. Welfare State International have shown that it is possible to represent the unrepresentable, their poetic imagery acting as an antidote to the moral, emotional and visual bankruptcy of much post-modern practice.

240

Before we started working in the space, we talked and read a lot. The last Millennium proved too vast to examine, although we did visit the Bayeaux Tapestry and I made a bone boat similar to the Viking Longship discovered in Newfoundland in AD 1000. We asked ourselves many questions about the key points of the last century. War, AIDS, genocide, Hiroshima, technology, science, famine, exploitation of the third world, fear, isolation, and so on. In particular, following Hobsbawn's essay 'On Brutalisation', we asked whether the human race has become hardened to cruelty and torture and whether commodification and demonisation of people, with the killing of civilians, had become inevitable.

We looked at many art inspirations, from the Lindisfarne Gospels and Goya's etchings to nursery rhymes and Anne Michael's 'Fugitive Pieces':

To remain with the dead is to abandon them.
 I see I must give what I most need.

We are always searching for resonating images and sounds to tell a story that is truthful but not didactic, clear and simple but which does not destroy mystery. Above all, to find a joyous and celebratory vehicle for an audience aged eight to eighty. Hannah and I both filled notebooks with lists of our preoccupations:

HANNAH'S LIST
shacks/shack in the head
the beast inside/outside
debris driftwood
blowing the sand away
the bay
sands salts
rocks gardens
invasion
boundary
distance
going up
encampment
expanse
seeds in the ice
where the wild things are
Little prince

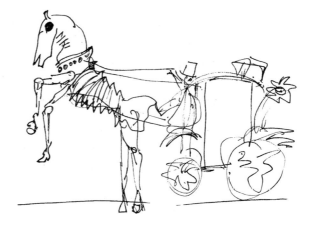

Munakata 'saku' – Japanese pilgrimage
Necklace – fence

To put my thoughts in order, on 5 December I wrote an essay which, along with our scrapbook of sketches and thoughts, was displayed in the foyer to 'deconstruct' our process.

> My father was born in 1900. He died in 1979. He was a merchant seaman captain. A commodore on the North Atlantic run. He was one of the last survivors in two open boats, in both the First and Second World Wars. He left a note on the mantelpiece telling my mother about magnetic mines and U-boats. He described himself as a God fearing man and knew he wouldn't be drowned because he was born with a caul over his head.

> He retired early with neurasthenia. When my mother died aged 62 he found risks in the betting shop and spent all his pension. Before that for a while he had a small boat called *Spray*. My best memory was going with him fishing for mackerel in a rough sea off Scarborough. It was freezing and I remember pissing warm pee in a rusty tin without a handle.

> I was born in 1938. A war baby, as they say. As we sat under our dining table or in the air-raid shelter listening to bombers droning overhead, I wouldn't go to sleep until I had heard 'Just another bomb Mummy.'

I admire the optimism of those who turn disaster into art. It would be nice to think that Hiroshima or Dresden could be reactivated as mere sparklers the size of tower blocks. Huge silver Christmas trees where the cremated corpses were only temporary rag dolls hanging for a while at advent to remind us of what we are capable, and then put away in a box under the floor ready for the next Christmas. In researching for *Sand*, I read the most chilling book ever. *Ordinary Men* by Christopher Browning describes reserve police battalion 101 and the Final Solution in Poland. In a day-by-day analysis, we follow the horror of the butcher, the baker and the plumber called up to exterminate Jews. Manipulated with propaganda and fearful of letting down their mates, they shoot hundreds of Jews. Ordinary blokes like me and my dad do the killing. I fear I would have done it too. And I fear it could happen in Ulverston. Given an evil climate we could slaughter strangers too, despite Dickensian Christmases and fake urchins.

Sand was not a closed fantasy. It was an open-ended, playfully imagined art work drawn from the collective creativity of five artists. It offers an art of conscious pretending but hopefully without manipulative deceit. For nearly all the first week, we 'sketched' inside the Barn, placing fragments and objects at different locations to gain a plastic sense of scale and sightlines. Then, in the second week, the whole team made it a furiously accelerating organic process. Specific 1999 triggers for me were the Killing Fields of Cambodia, which I visited in October. The sun was shining and the rice fields were bright green, but underfoot, where 22,000 people were poleaxed just two decades ago, human rib bones still stick through the earth. In Tuol Sleng, victims were tortured in a modern secondary school in tiny cells crudely fabricated with breeze blocks and lumpy cement. Here, in a dark corner, was a small enamelled bowl, a flash of colour, a small treasure in a darkness unfortunately only too easy to imagine.

A friend of mine makes regular trips to Ypres to see the war graves. 'I go to weep,' he says, 'as an atonement to apologise to the dead. I'll keep going until I can't cry any more. There are 2,500 graveyards in France and Flanders. All those men and boys turned into stones. You just can't imagine what it was like, it's beyond imagination. I have never seen so many butterflies. Scores of varieties, and sloes. As many as grains of sand. My mate is a Welshman and there are many buried there. At my feet there were fragments of bone. Imagine that. The blood

Cherub with wings, *Sand,* 1999

243

and the bone of Welshmen nurturing the sloes. I won't tell him all the details, but I'll give him a bottle of sloe gin for Christmas.'

On 20 March 1983, I wrote:

> The first day of spring
> On one time-scale an interval year.
> Fifteen Springs ago Welfare State International started.
> After fifteen more Springs the year 2000
> A time for reflection.
> A time for stories.
> And if the stories are seeds for action, what kind of action should
> they provoke?

My daughter Hannah, then twelve, had given me a present, a book, *The Day of the Bomb* by Karl Bruckner. Written in 1961, it describes the dropping of the first atom bomb as seen through the eyes of a four-year-old girl. In 1961 there were a thousand hydrogen bombs waiting in readiness around the world. Thirty years later, in November 2001, in Barrow-in-Furness, *Vengeance*, the fourth Trident nuclear submarine, was launched. Each of its twelve missiles has a firepower greater than Hiroshima. The one before this was launched by Lady Di, who helped to ban land mines.

Sand, Part Two: 'New Journeys', 6–21 January 2000, took off literally from the edge of 'Letting Go'. Inside the Barn, Vivien Mousdell, our artist-in-residence, had made a hundred fragile life-size shoes with sand and a little cement. These paraded across the floor rather randomly to the big glass doors. A six-year-old boy on a school visit spent quite some time on the floor, taking in all the shoes. 'You see they are the shoes of everyone who has drowned, and the sailor must gather them all together.' As darkness came, we lit candles inside them and on closing the installation each evening we extinguished the candles one by one, always leaving the last one for a few moments.

For 'New Journeys', the shoes of sand were transformed into ice (by Carl Binstead, a local glass sculptor), so that outside and across the courtyard, to the sound of our opened river, they danced off to a dark and burned forest we had made with eighty discarded Christmas trees. In the centre of the torched trees was a little cairn supporting a tiny garden of moss and yellow and purple crocuses. Springing above them on fifteen-foot-high poles were mobiles, weathervanes and small colourful flags flapping like dragonflies in a child's kaleidoscope.

We had originally planned to remove *Sand*, Part One – just leaving the excellent digital cartoon version by Simon Byford on our website – but then, partly through sentiment and laziness but also because the two installations worked so well together, we left it until late January. Coming out of the sombre interior Barn space – where some visitors would spontaneously burst into tears – the garden exit into the elements was refreshing and joyous.

There were many pleasures. On 21 January, the last day, with a full moon rising, Richard Greenwood, a young classical cellist, played Bach in the centre of *Sand*. He also took the risk of improvising, which he had never done in public before. The cello echoed in the resinous beams of the Barn, which Dan started to 'play' with percussive sticks and blocks. I joined in with a reedy low drone on my melodeon. As the full earthy sound resounded in the dark Barn, it became the living ribcage of a forest animal. Just then, the full moon came up, unplanned but on cue, to shine directly through the central window of the clerestory. Old friends gathered. Gilly Adams, a key partner in our Celebrants' Wing, gave us performance guidance. Rob Hill, who had been responsible for all the electronic wizardry in Satellite House, returned to create more wonders, with tiny space stations in the roof. Even Jamie Proud, the original Lancelot Quail from 1972, came 'home' to clown with disturbing childlike illusions.

From old laths the colour of the shacks, he made a wooden toy railway truck. Obsessively and systematically, he stuffed it to suffocation with fifty balls of crumpled newspaper. Then, after pulling it through the sand, he crashed it under the avenging shadow angel of Auschwitz. Here, he released fifty sprung paper flowers from the carriage which lay on the grey sand until the New Year. He then transformed into a NASA scientist to launch a home-made three-stage rocket, hunting for a toy mirrorball. I had to explain to the afternoon throng that he had worked for years on the Manhattan Project (the research group led by Oppenheimer which designed the atom bomb), but the strain was too much for him. Now, even in his woolly dressing-gown and idiosyncratic knotted handkerchief, Matron allowed him out some afternoons. Today, he was old and toothless and a danger only to himself.

Nativity of the Beasts

This installation was a gentle but unsentimental evocation of animal farming and slaughtering which ran in November–December 2001. An elegy to the death of animals, it was also another creative response to foot and mouth's decimation of

Cumbrian farming; a sculptural song of hope celebrating birth and fresh growth and another attempt to invest our Cruck Barn with the ambience of a secular sacred space and for us an even more advanced and innovative fusion of traditional and electronic media. A number of complex and sometimes contradictory themes ran through the work: farming, factory farming, slaughtering, butchering, the manufacture of 'pedigree' Christmas pork pies and the birth of a calf, to name a few.

Dan worked on it again. Hannah couldn't, as she was being a full-time new mother, but Caroline Menis and Martin Brockman were part of the team. I had been trying to arrange for them to work together for about five years. Created by seven artists in a month, *Nativity* was presented in a twenty-minute cycle. It was a mixed-media work, fusing electronically generated animation, video, sculptures made with elemental and basic materials – willow, clay, paper, wood, fire, charcoal, lighting and music. It was possibly our purest work yet, with a relatively small number of monumental sculptures carefully placed with video projections and stereophonic sound. The admixture of time-based work with static sculptures was tricky, but we solved it by a sophisticated lighting cycle which animated the static works.

Caroline used lantern-making techniques, drawing immaculately in willow to depict a three-dimensional flying ass and a life-size pregnant cow with a lantern calf foetus. Martin constructed another braying ass and a tormented bull, virtually life size: animal kilns, first fired in our courtyard and then ferried inside on a fork lift to rest on circular charcoal beds. Digital video captured the drama of the firings and then re-created them in a new form where they were shown on computer screens inside the body of the fired clay animals.

Witnessing the birth of a calf was made difficult by farmers' very real concerns about allowing people on to their land following the foot and mouth epidemic. The birth, which was filmed in the middle of the night by Alec Bell, took place in September on the Isle of Arran. The dramatic pixillated blue-greys of half-light and the flashes of a storm lantern reminded me of El Greco's storm in *View of Toledo*. A cartoon digital video by Simon Byford depicted the journey of a farmed pig through the slaughterhouse to multiple pork pies. Simon pitched this very carefully to avoid both gratuitous melodrama and bland sentiment.

The cycle of lights, sounds, animation and video was run from a PC through Macromedia Director. The software played the media elements in a pre-programmed order and sent cues, via midi, through to the lighting desk. As the audience sat in a stall with their feet in straw, they could hear Stuart Oetzmann talking to them through their headphones. He is one of the few remaining Norfolk farmers who has never adopted any 'modern' farming methods and who runs a pie-making factory using rare-breed meats, wild game and organic crops.

Meanwhile (from an amplified old-fashioned tape recording), the late Jack Teasdale, a Cumbrian farmer, chanted the numbering of his sheep in a rich Cumberland dialect. Spindly shadows from a slowly spinning mobile of wire sheep leaped on the white barn walls. Finally, as a warm yellow glow suffused all the animals in turn, particularly the lantern calf foetus in the willow cow, a lilting flute and harp lifted our spirits in a light but joyous anthem. Then the cycle returned to the beginning. I wrote in the programme:

> As the moods shift, there is space for meditation and time for silence. As in real life, there is no fast forward button, but in the midst of the everyday maelstrom there can be a pause for contemplation.

Nativity of the Beasts, 2001

Wishbone House

One third of the way through writing this book, September 11th happened. On that day, our grandson Reuben, who was coming up to his first birthday, saw live television for the first time. As the twin towers burned, he tapped the screen with sticky fingers, trying to hold that burning ball which to him was a rose, a pink cauliflower or smoking candyfloss. In the face of such uncertainty, my concern continues to be: what are the lessons we can pass on to him, and what have we learned on our epic journey that can be of any use to him?

I am back where I started, in the beach hut, looking east with a different mist rolling in. This time, though, behind the spiky branches of our ash tree, the tide is going out and the clumps of mallard zooming past signal a new and expansive horizon. Soon there will be a new year. In the evening, the tangle of sparks on our log fire intertwine with festoons of street lights across the bay. Christmas cards already dangling on red ribbons give messages; this child is autistic, that couple have separated, this person has died and, by the way, how do we enjoy being grandparents?

In this way, the big sea, the whole bay and our perception end up on the same hearth. The local cannot be separated from the monstrously large and incomprehensible. Behind the English grey that Constable painted are two nuclear power stations and a nuclear submarine factory. That feathery slipstream of an aeroplane ploughing so delicately overhead might just be hijacked to jack-knife in seconds on to Windscale.

I recently read Andy Kershaw's shocking account of children in Iraq deformed by the depleted uranium shells left behind by the USA and Britain after the last war in the Middle East.[1] Incredibly, Blair and Bush seem to be planning another invasion.[2] If nuclear radiation triggered by insider or outsider terrorism were to creep from behind that curling mist, then where would our Reuben be? How long would he even have fists left to playfully pummel that TV screen?

The isolation of the beach house and the vista of the bay are an anchoring point to contemplate global issues from a backyard perspective. Here, sometimes, it is possible to balance outer and inner landscapes. The subtle interconnectedness of the ecology of Morecambe Bay is an awesome lesson. Winter waders, migrating shellducks, lug worms, invertebrates eating each other, cockles, shrimps and dabs all depend on the cycle of the tides. They survive overfishing; rampant spartina grass (originally brought to Plymouth on the prow of Yankee schooners); a silting channel that heaves across the bay on an eighty-five-year cycle; global warming (a quarter of the world's population, mostly in the USA, consumes 80 per cent of its energy); and random pollution from sewage, animal and bird droppings, heavy metals and plutonium from nearby factories and power stations.

In their book *The Allotment*, David Crouch and Colin Ward explain that we achieve a kind of freedom, a sense of the world, identity and self-image through escaping into a symbolic and practical sub-culture (such as allotment gardening) where we try to balance the outer and the inner.[3] I think our epic journey, our steps in rehearsing Utopia, has been this. We have surfed umpteen tides and with our own consciously adopted sub-culture have projected many dreams, leaving behind a set of tangible, if not concrete, stepping stones. These may still indicate directions for the continuing journey. As with the tides, there have been discernible, sometimes overlapping, cycles of transition and transformation.

In both the tidal shifts of Morecambe Bay and our wanderings, there are recurring patterns. Time for most of us in the Western world is seen as linear progress. Accordingly, we never live in the present, but build on the past and oblige the funding bodies by pretending we have planned exactly what we are going to do in the future.

Other cultures more conscious of the inevitable cycles of birth and death that are integral to the natural world conceive of time quite differently. Also, more than many, the artist, the dreamer, the shaman, the musician, the fool and the child seek to live in the eternal present and may in the moment achieve a timeless state associated with creativity and ritual. Apollo and the priest need fixed codes and order, whereas Dionysus and the artist/fool thrive on and promulgate chaos. The first major cycle was establishing our nomadic village of caravans and parachuting like seed-pods into the temporary soil of international festivals. The second began a growing rootedness, when, in the communities of Barrow and Ulverston, we activated regeneration on the Furness Peninsula. In the third, we discovered death and shifted energy to our rites of passage exhibitions, books and courses. This inevitably engendered a 'Flight from Spectacle'. Breaking the taboo of death first for ourselves and then for others was a radical if not revolutionary way of thinking.

The fourth cycle was the building of Lanternhouse. Here, influenced by vernacular traditions of barn building and the Arts and Crafts movement, we constructed a total art work which linked architecture, two romantic towers, studios, galleries, accommodation and furniture, and developed our refurbished headquarters as an efficient toolbox to train artists to make new and celebratory art informed by the local context. It is a place to visit for contemplation and meditation which will also, via its microwave dish, communicate with the wider world. Currently, in the fifth cycle, starting in 2002, we are researching the first years of a child's life. In partnership with our community, the project (called Birthrites) will examine the play, culture, architecture and cosmology of the early years. This is balanced by some installations and workshops away from base. My office is still a garden shed on the roof of Lanternhouse, though I think it is looking for wheels and I can hear wings sprouting in the night.

We are now planting an amphitheatre at our warehouse site where we plan to create regular performances, of seasonal mythic celebrations. Polarities always recur. In the context of the Gulf War in September 1990, after seventeen months of preparation for our extensive lantern parade in Glasgow, I wrote in an article, 'The Iris and the Lantern':

'New lamps for old. New lamps for old,' hissed Abenazar. Sometimes it seems that we are being nudged hysterically into the last decade of the century by violent old men offering new myths for old. We know that evil magicians really want the ultimate power of the genie, but they are not averse to a little gold or lamp-oil along the way. Sometimes they kill for it and will exploit the young to get it. Then a ritual battle in the wilderness becomes inevitable.

During this sacrificial encounter Aladdin and many other young bloods are trapped in the dark cave. We spectators are not sure if the conflict is real or artificially induced. Is the spectacle manipulated by arms dealers seeking to maintain the instability of the status quo or is it the self-fulfilling prophecy of the Film Industry? For long enough, surrogate gladiators have acted out our fantasies. Many an oily male muscle has been rippled in the consuming fire of latent fascism. We get the art we want.

Isolated and passive within a web of engineered violence we are easily mesmerised and marginalised by the Big Spider of Consumerism. Instead of ever increasing novelty and bigger and bigger spectacles of distraction we need participatory celebrations that enhance and encourage and Art that will surprise, involve and reveal once again. The blue irises of Van Gogh were once simple flowers celebrating the universal in the moment. Now they illuminate a secret desk in a high-rise bank. The dried petals of irises could easily be incorporated into the paper-thin skin of a simple tissue lantern.

That surface cannot be polished. It cannot even reflect the spectacular dullness of million gold bars. But within its soft candlelight even a small iris will grow and glow moderately. But Abenazar (and the Big Spider for that matter) couldn't buy it.

Eleven years later, on the eleventh day of September, the two towering 1s, the two towering look-at-me 1s in New York were, in a fit of reactive strategic hatred, literally, and symbolically demolished. Tragically, the same old ritual of conflict continues and will almost certainly accelerate. The West might win a battle but the war will continue. The irises are still locked away of course, but at least their energy is simmering in another tower as yet undemolished. Painted when Van Gogh was not far from madness, the art and the irises are of another world. Maybe they or their fragile tissue will still help us get by.

The battle now is for power and oil, of course, but it is also for ideas and ways of life. And ideas usually win. So we, the artists, the unwilling holders of some understanding of the nature of the creative soul, must project our own understanding of art as a mode of knowledge. If we don't, others will. We all need to belong somewhere or we shall be forced to rally round the flag of the club of some outmoded quaintness, such as God, or the Monarchy, or the Market economy.

I am inspired by Thoreau living in solitude by Walden Pond (isolated, apart from the visits of his mother, who kept bringing him cookies).[4] If only there was one simple arc of a fish or a dab of thistledown on the ripples to seize my attention. But he never saw the shadows of airliners reflecting on his reverie or his pond. So where do we find peace of mind? Finding peace of mind, to me, means continually connecting and reconnecting with our talents and potential and trying to humanise work. Striving to generate a creative and equal society where work need not mean economic conscription and where the imagination of the many may be as significant and free as the indulgence of the few.

There is an awesome moment in *Moby Dick* when Ahab realises the White Whale is chasing him. How relevant to current massive capital expenditures on art emporia. There's little we can do to stop it. We are as much caught in the mutual chase of our times as was Ahab in the nineteenth century or Cortez in the sixeenth. Just as Cortes was obliged to burn pagans in the name of Catholicism, or George Bush has to smoke out alleged terrorists, we condone more concrete in the name of more artistic product (we often pretend it will be process), which has little to do with the creativity of a wider society, but everything to do with power products, investment, distraction and insecurity.

Top-down funding lines, art politics, the sanctity of property, the capitalist inevitability of one-way consumerism (with no exchange or reciprocity) are all so embedded in our institutions, our institutionalised culture and our psyches that a Whale Change is inconceivable. But a Great Whale Change is what we need, except the whale is inside us all. I don't exclude Welfare State International. We gratefully built our own million-pound centre and believe passionately of course that we will train thousands of cultural activists in our celebratory oasis of chaos. But then naturally enough we have always believed we were doing the right thing, whichever White Whale we were chasing.

Joseph Conrad wrote about the artist (in 1921):

> It is in the impartial practice of life, if anywhere, that the promise of perfection
> for his art can be found, rather than in the absurd formulas trying to prescribe this
> or that particular method of technique or conception. Let him mature the strength
> of his imagination amongst the things of this earth, which is his business to cherish
> or know.

Over the next fifty years, the questions we must address are profound. How will we continue in the luxury of despair when seven tenths of the world is dispossessed? How can we justify our Western life-style and our ageing population when so much creativity has been removed from the poor? Why are we alive and how do we cope without work and religion and other drugs?[5] And will we use genetic engineering to rediscover or cauterise our souls?

Marshall McLuhan's *The Gutenberg Galaxy* falls off the shelf in a cloud of old dust, but he talks of the transition from the Renaissance to the modern being a shift from roles to jobs:

> The inhabitant of a ROLE is a person whose work is an expression not only of his distinctive powers or gifts but of his place in a global conception of the universe, of the 'right' way for him to be ... A JOB is, has to be, 'alienated' labour, since it is an arbitrary direction for the employment of one's talents rather than a vocation that inserts those talents, means and ends, into a total sense of existence.

> The world of play is necessarily one of uncertainty and discovery at every moment, whereas the ambition of the bureaucrat and the systems builder is to deal only with foregone conclusions.

Here is where artists may still lead culture.[6] Pathologically optimistic this may be, but it could still be a useful catalyst for the growth of a creative and artistic society, where life-style, gainful occupation, communal well-being, playful expression and new energy go hand in hand; where we don't separate economics and art; where humanitarian principles may be examined and shared and hypocrisy outlawed. Where we may decide to live more simply and easily and have more fun outside the relentless whirlpool of the White Whale.

While I am still thinking about such a remote sixties icon as McLuhan and still seriously deconstructing the origins of *Eyes on Stalks* and wiping away dangerously nostalgic dust from my eyes, here's another. Between the sixties and the seventies, Albert Hunt was the committed inventor of project teaching in the complementary studies department of Bradford Art College. Apart from giving me my first job

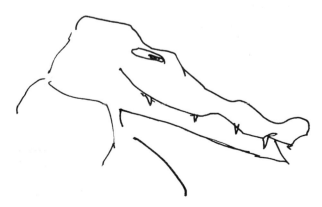

(which is why Welfare State International started with students in Bradford), he wrote a brilliant book, *Hopes of Great Happenings*, which is still visionary and inspirational.

Albert talks about the gap between awareness and reality. He was, of course, writing long ago when, incredibly, successive United States administrators were carpet-bombing millions of Asian peasants in Vietnam, Cambodia and Laos.

The gap springs not so much from a lack of knowledge – people in our society know, in a superficial and clichéd way, far more about what is going on in the world than any society has ever known – as from a failure of the imagination.

Paradoxically too much of a particular kind of knowledge leads to a slackening of the imaginative grip. It is like the effects of pornography – the kicks lessen with familiarity. In such a situation what is needed is not more of this controlled kind of knowledge but the ability to put what is known to social use. This demands, in the first place, an act of the imagination. When you are trapped inside a room in which all the windows are distorting mirrors, it's no good looking in the mirror and describing more and more of what you see. You have got to make some kind of imaginative leap to get yourself out of the closed room, to be able to look at your situation from some kind of distance.

Reuben's naming ceremony, *Wishbone House*, 2001

I would like to finish with something simple, to give some kind of distance outside the infernal box of distorting mirrors, something in the language of wonder and something with the unstilled passion for Utopia. Back to the beach hut and Reuben's naming ceremony. There is distance and here is the future. I shall only write a short description, because if this book has worked at all, your imaginative juices should by now be flowing to the point where you will create your own celebratory events and ceremonies. And if your juices are not flowing, you will doubtless guess the kind of clown poetry I would love to surprise you with.

Imagine a sunny day on a wide beach, the tide out, on 2 September 2001. Reuben is to be named. His father, Duncan Copley, a poet in wood, has constructed *Wishbone House*, a portable ceremonial space the size of a small, delicate pavilion, made from a pair of large oak cruck wishbones engineered to lean away from each other. Shelter is provided by ten oak ribs which support an undulating willow wall, draped to the skeletal shape, which has weathered and darkened. Double benches of burr elm, bleached and scrubbed, nestle you inside the curve, with the wishbones above. *Wishbone House* is parked up in the tide race, next to the shingle beach.

Families gather at the beach house. Hannah has prepared small personal copper boats with tiny sails. On each of these we write wishes, floating our boats on a pond inside a large metal dish on legs. This cauldron, which looks like a satellite dish, made by slicing the end off a rusty old shipyard boiler, is now enhanced with a blue silk sail embroidered with all Reuben's names. Reuben Horatio Ashburner Fox Copley, Horatio after my sea-captain father, and Ashburner after his great-grandfather, who is eighty-six and here today. Reuben nestles gleefully in his brawny arms, which once made bricks.

Gilly, our celebrant friend, brings us together for speeches and toasts. Naughty children fall in a muddy hole – and so does the celebrant (but we don't admit to that). We have to admit, though, that the sea took hold. The night before, there was a storm. We had calculated the exact height of the tide, but it rose too high on the wind. *Wishbone House* floated and slewed to the north. Previously it was on an east/west axis. It ended stuck on spartina grass in thick mud on a north/south axis. So the direction of the journey shifts.

References

New Lamps for Old

1. Roger Coleman, Alison Fell, Sue Fox, John Fox, Jamie Proud, Jane Durrant, Steve Gumbley, Lizzie Lockhart, Roy Dodds, Rosemary Timms, Chris Timms, Nigel Leach, Rick Parker and Ken McBurney (plus others).

2. MailOut – 87 New Square, Chesterfield, Derbyshire, S40 1AH. Tel: 01246 207070. Of many significant English groups working with the community, my favourites are the Satellites, Andy Burton and Gill Bond, Slaithwaite, West Yorkshire, Emergency Exit in Greenwich, London, Jubilee Arts in the West Midlands, Whitewood and Fleming in Brighouse and Ulverston, DARTS in Doncaster, Same Sky in Brighton, Strange Cargo in Maidstone, Bill and Wendy Harpe at the Blackie in Liverpool, Pete Moser's More Music in Morecambe and David Boyd's "Beat Initiative" in Belfast. Community plays are another matter altogether. John Rust, Jon Oram and Ann Jellicoe are key players. See Ann Jellicoe's book, *Community Plays* (Methuen, 1987).

3. The community arts movement is particularly strong in Australia. Most of the key players have worked with Neil Cameron and Faridah Whyte. See Neil's book *Fire over Water* (Currency Press, Sydney). John Carroll and Bill Blaikie run a pathfinding degree course on community celebration at Charles Sturt University in Bathurst, New South Wales. In Canada, Shadowlands of Ward's Island, Toronto, Clarke Mackay of Queen's University, Kingston and Peter and Joan Oliver in Shelburne, Nova Scotia are important. In the USA, Peter and Elke Schumann's Bread and Puppet Theatre in Vermont and Sandy Speiler's In the Heart of the Beast puppet and mask company in Minneapolis are inspirational. Methuen publish *The Bread and Puppet Theatre* Volumes One and Two (by Stefan Brecht) and the University of Minnesota Press produced (1999) an exciting book about In the Heart of the Beast.

4. Herbert Marcuse, *One Dimensional Man – Studies in the Ideology of Advanced Industrial Society*, (London: Routledge, 1964).

5. Radical information is in SchNEWS, c/o On-the-fiddle, PO Box 2600, Brighton, East Sussex BN2 0EF. www.schnews.org.uk. Red Pepper (redpepper@redpepper.org.uk – mark your message 'Attention Tessa Swithinbrook') and the *New Internationalist*, Tower House, Lathkill Street, Market Harborough LE16 9EF, UK.

6. A saint's relic or a good joke? On 12 April 2002, *Sun* readers were invited to lay hands on a large front-page picture of footballer Beckham's injured foot and all pray at noon for his recovery.

7. *Our Word Is Our Weapon*, selected writings by Subcomandante Insurgente Marcos (Seven Stories/Serpent's Tail).

8. Unpublished notes from a conference at Yale University, New England, October 1998, organised by Paul Collard.

9. *No Logo* by Naomi Klein (HarperCollins), *Captive State* by George Monbiot (Pan), *Rogue States* by Naom Chomsky (Pluto Press).

10. *Casualty Figures on 11 September 2001*

Number of people who died of hunger on that day	24,000
Number of children on the planet killed by diarrhoea	6,200
Enduring terrors	
Annual average number without access to safe drinking water	1,100 million
Annual average number of people killed by drought and famine	73,606

Source: *New Internationalist* (NI 340), November 2001

Cheap Art

1. In the mid-sixties, John Arden and Margaretta d'Arcy, the radical playwrights, lived in Kirbymoorside in North Yorkshire. They produced a Festival of Anarchy and sent their children to Hawnby school where Sue Gill (then Sue Fox) was the head teacher. They also taught occasionally at Bradford School of Art (where I was a tutor librarian). Here Albert Hunt had turned the Complementary Studies Department into the country's most progressive theatre workshop. Our most extreme adventures with the Ardens were working with art students and CAST to create an instant junk open-air fairground for their *Harold Muggins is a Martyr* at the Unity Theatre, London in 1968.

2. Peter and Joan Oliver are the unsung heroes of alternative theatre. In the sixties and seventies they transformed Oval House, a conventional youth club opposite Lord's cricket ground in London, into an amazing experimental venue which in 2002 is still hosting dynamic work. They found audiences for the People's Show, Interaction, Action Space, Bread and Puppet Theatre, Mike Figgis, Jeff Nuttall, us and scores of other companies, bands and performers. Many owe their success to the selfless support and risk taking of the Olivers. Radical as ever, they now live in Nova Scotia.

3. Interview with Peter Schumann, *Tulane Drama Review*, Volume 12, Number 2, Winter 1968.

4. Pete Moser has worked with Welfare State International for over twenty years. He first turned up in Sunderland in 1981 looking for work as a rigger. We soon discovered he was also an outstanding musician, composer and community animateur. Consequently he worked on scores of our shows and his input has been immense and irreplaceable – especially in

Barrow. Also on two milestone productions, *On the Loose*, a touring band show, and *Nutcracker*, a joint project with Bagamoyo College in Tanzania (which are not covered in this book). Pete is now the director of More Music in Morecambe, a pioneering and acclaimed community music project.

5. *What is Cheap Art?*, Bread and Puppet Manifesto. (Available from Bread and Puppet Theatre, RD#2, Glover, Vermont, 05839, USA. Tel: 001 (802) 525-3031; 525-6972):

'. . . during the last six years (starting about 1980), Bread and Puppet has produced several hundred pounds of art work on cardboard, masonite, wood, newspaper, newsprint and fabric that has been offered to the general public for popular prices, ranging from 10 cents to $20.

The Cheap Art exhibits and sales are not considered a sideline secondary to theatre work, but originate in the same conviction which started Bread and Puppet in the early 60s in New York City: art is bread, art must be accessible like bread, and – just as the degenerate tastebuds of the fluffy-white-bread-eaters (who inherited that dessert-like stuff which fattened Louis XVI from the French Revolution) must be challenged with rough old sourdough rye, crusted with the smell of pine and cedar coals which bake it – so the elitist art consumer must be provoked and the educated misconception of art as a privilege of the underfed, emotionally disturbed, apolitical members of interior decorators' clubs must be challenged – not in order to persuade them to a new cause but in order to start off new art-eaters with the right ingredients.

On behalf of these truths and in the spirit of Kurt Schwitters's Merz manifesto (. . . *wir fordern die sofortige Beseitigung aller Uebelstaende* . . .), Bread and Puppet has organised numerous exhibits and shops to provide practical cures for the ills of the deceived art-consumer as well as the no-art consumer and as an answer to the unabashedly money-obsessed Zeitgeist . . .'

6. Howie Steward is a friend of Pete Moser. Howie knows about alternative markets, has his own stall and has worked WOMAD festivals for years with a van full of Spanish rugs and fine ethnic objects. His shop is in Milford-on-Sea, near Leamington.

Rehearsing Utopia

1. Al Beach also started the Northern Open Workshop in Halifax in 1970 and continued as a champion for new art with the Hebden Bridge Festival in Yorkshire in the early seventies. This was part of a series of New Activities events steered round the country by the Arts Council Drama Department, which focused, in a small way, on the rising wave of innovative and alternative theatre.

2. Jamie Proud, who played Lancelot Quail for many years, is now a remarkable teacher working with children in Longley School, a special school in Huddersfield. In 2001 they won a *Guardian* prize for creativity, 'My Dream School'.

3. Jenny Wilson and Ruari McNeill continue to be supporters of Welfare State International and advocates of new art. Jenny is the director of the Dumfries and Galloway Arts Association and Ruari is an arts consultant. Their support in 1972 was a crucial factor in our survival.

4. A 16mm film of the tour is in the Arts Council Film archive and with Welfare State International. Directed by Jonathan Lewis, then a student at the National Film School.

5. 'A procession is a jubilant articulation of ownership, demonstrating a right to be on the streets, transforming and subverting the routine of production, consumption and habitation;

social space is transformed into ritual and ludic space.' Gavin Carver on Welfare State International, *Dictionary of Literary Biography*, vol. 245, British and Irish Dramatists, University of Reading.

6　The Russian clown, Slava Polunin, has courted anarchy with his revolutionary Ship of Fools and the Moscow Theatre Olympics 2001. *Total Theatre*, vol. 13, issue 3, Autumn 2001. Article by Emi Slater.

7.　*What shall we do with the children?*, by Catherine Kiddle, (Spindlewood, 1981, 70 Lynhurst Avenue, Barnstaple, Devon EX31 2HY. ISBN 0 907349 05 6. Out of print).

Inventing the Language

1.　See also *Engineers of the Imagination*.

2.　Lol Coxhill, fabulous jazz soprano saxophonist and along with Mike Westbrook, Lou Glandfield, Luk Mishalle, Boris Howarth, Greg Stephens, Pete Moser, Tim Fleming, Chris Hobbs, Chris Jordan, Peader Long and Dan Fox, one in a line of our brilliant music directors. Lol made many recordings. The one with WSI on Virgin Records (C1514 1975) is deleted. Early recordings of our street and theatre music are available from WSI.

3.　Adrian Henri's book *Environments and Happenings* (Thames and Hudson 1974 – out of print) gives a good historical overview.

4.　There are, however, many people and groups even in England who do work outside and sometimes inside the mainstream with strong physical and visual traditions. The magazine, *Total Theatre* (Total Theatre Network, The Power Station, Coronet Street, London N1 6HD) is an excellent information source for contemporary work. By 2002 Performance Art and Live Art are well established with their own international festivals and many practitioners. Other exceptional visual performance innovators include: Roland Miller, Shirley Cameron, John Darling, Jeff Nuttall, Bobby Baker, Rose English, Tim Etchells, Geraldine Pilgrim, Graeme Miller, Mike Pearson, Ken Campbell, John Wright, Julian Crouch, Phelim McDermott, Steve Gumbley, Lizzie Lockhart, Dave Wheeler, Paul Burwell, Ken Turner, Mary Turner, Kathryn Hunter, Lindsay Kemp, the opera designer John McFarlane and Peter Brook. Companies like Complicité, DV8, Forced Entertainment, the People's Show, IOU, Forkbeard Fantasy, Horse and Bamboo, Kneehigh, Footsbarn, Test Department, Station House Opera, Improbable Theatre, Emergency Exit, Strange Cargo, Told Like an Idiot, Faulty Optic, the Beat Initiative (Belfast), the Carnival Collective and Hillbilly (Hannah Fox's company) are visually strong.

　　There are scores of well-practised British street acts, some with a strong sculptural and/or visual component. Many of the companies described by Bim Mason in his excellent book *Street Theatre* (Routledge, 1992) can be seen at umpteen street theatre festivals. I admire Avanti Display, IOU (especially their giant walking Leech), the Chipolatas, with Sam Thomas (the son of Taffy Thomas, the story-teller who did so much on our Barn Dance tours), Big Rory, Boneshaker (Dan Fox's highly energetic percussive stilt-walking), Natural Theatre, Whitewood and Fleming's amazing Dora's Dangerous Do nut (the only Do-nut in the world that transforms into a Hotrod Motorbike) and exploding Hot Dog Caravan (both designed by Andy Plant) and Bim Mason's The Big Heads and the Whalley Range All Stars. Standards and awareness of Street Theatre and New Circus are rising, partly under the influence of foreign troupes such as Cirque du Soleil and through the Millennium Dome, the Circus Space and

Circomedia's foundation school in Bristol directed by Bim Mason and Helen Crocker, and the dissemination of ideas through conferences organised by Total Theatre. The Arts Council of England is at long last recognising these Arts (see their Strategy Report, March 2002).

Much outside work in 2002, apart from that of Dodgy Clutch (who are one of the few companies who also understand the political nature of true carnival provocation), and perhaps Desperate Men and occasionally Improbable Theatre in, for example, *Sticky*, is based on ambient busking, circus skills or interactive role play; where entertainment predominates. Some of this, such as Scarabeus and Piano Circus, collaborating on Italo Calvino's *Invisible Cities*, is very imaginative, but I haven't seen much extended narrative street theatre performance for a large static audience. Other intriguing work, such as Paul Mishkin's *Ontological Street Theatre* operates in theory 'where all awareness of artifice and distance can be removed and art becomes life'.

5. By Kate Westbrook – singer and outstanding painter of complex lyrical imagery.

6. We appeared at the De Lantaren Theatre in Rotterdam and the Schaffy Theatre in Amsterdam. Ben Mangleschotts made a strong 16mm documentary called *Bungalow*.

7. After a show, Albert Hunt, a sharp theatre critic, a Burnley football supporter and my first employer (see Wishbone House chapter) who said, 'I have never seen a telephone box smashed so thoroughly, so quickly and so ritually'.

8. Bob Frith is the artistic director of Horse and Bamboo company who with masks, puppets, live music, caravans and horses create some of the best visual theatre in Europe.

9. There are exceptions. Mike Mould of Bruvvers (with his Zapatista play) in Newcastle-upon-Tyne (2001), Pam Sandiford and Alec Bell (from Ulverston) with their Burma Play (2000-3) exposing the excesses of the military dictatorship, and playwrights David Hare, David Edgar and Caryl Churchill. In the less reactive climate of 2002 where style and box office predominate it is easy to forget that in the seventies there was much didactic if not confrontational work. Albert Hunt with the Bradford College of Art Theatre Troupe, the late John McGrath with 7:84 in England and Scotland, Red Ladder, Belt and Braces, Gay Sweat Shop are just a few of the politically motivated companies. See *The Moon belongs to Everyone* Elizabeth MacLennan (Methuen) and *A Good Night Out* by John McGrath (Eyre Methuen, 1981).

10. Other examples: *The Fiesta for Life against Death* - an audacious carnival intervention against the arms trade in Docklands, by coincidence on 11 September 2001 in Docklands (www.disarm-trade.org). The organisation Reclaim the Streets (now labelled as a terrorist organisation) and the Greenpeace invasion of the Cabinet room April 2002. The *New Internationalist* 338, September 2001 lists many international carnivals against capital 'that are turning the world upside down.' See also *The Politics of Performance*, Baz Kershaw (Routledge); *Radical Street Performance*, Jan Cohen-Cruz (Routledge); *The Radical in Performance* Baz Kershaw (Routledge).

11. Boris Howarth's life and work would make a wonderful book. As associate artistic director he took over Welfare State International when Sue and I went to Australia in 1979. We worked together in a very creative and equal partnership from 1972 to 1984. Boris and his wife Maggie Howarth were a huge influence on WSI. Boris invented the big fire shows, Maggie the big puppets and both of them the sculptural gardens which are hardly referred to in *Eyes on Stalks*. There is a woeful omission in the theatre history books of the extraordinary

events they organised in Lancaster in the mid-sixties. This was to my knowledge the first proper community art in Britain. Focused around seasonal occasions and working with local children and youths, they built bonfires, ran street drumming bands, made dragon ships and drove cars on fire into the River Lune. Dangerous, innovative and well before anyone was getting a wage for being a community artist, they did it unpaid from the back room of their terrace house. Many events in WSI's portfolio were under Boris's direction, works such as *Homage to Meister Eckhart* (1974), *Harbinger* (1975), *Uppendown Mooney* (1978), *Volcano Junction* (1979), *Stillpoint* (1980) and were very important. Although I have chosen in *Eyes on Stalks* to write about my own journey I would like to acknowledge their immense contribution.

12. Pierre Schwarz was a remarkable artist and blacksmith/sculptor, accordion and bagpipe player who lived on the Dutch–Belgian border with Henni his wife and children. Their company, Het Flupf Ju Bedrijf (since 2000 Het Bedrijf v/h) featured marvellous edgy spiky metal puppets with which they told childlike elemental tales in landscapes and shopping precincts. Pierre died fifteen years ago. Henni kept the family (and the puppet show) together.

13. Founder and artistic director of the Theatre of Fire who died in an accident at his factory in 1999.

14. Andy Plant is an extraordinary inventor and engineer/artist who can make anything (see also *Scarecrow Zoo* and *False Creek* in On Tour). His speciality is animated sculpted clocks, which may be seen in many shopping centres such as Newport. Tim Hunkin is another highly skilled inventor, engineering artist and cartoonist who for many wonderful years wrote and drew the *Rudiments of Wisdom* strip in the *Observer* Colour Supplement.

15. There is a description of *Parliament in Flames* at Catford in Bim Mason's book *Street Theatre* (Routledge, 1992, p.133).

16. Greville White is a superb artist and inventor who makes models and wonders from cogs, elastic bands and washers. As well as creating small-scale animated objects (such as twenty metal piranha fish robots for two videos we made for Border TV) he also constructs big sculptures as he did for Ulverston Raft Race, *Scarecrow Zoo* (Bracknell) and *False Creek* in Vancouver and others.

17. Andy Burton is a gentle clown and travelling visual poet who composes and plays soaring tunes for the fiddle and who can do conjuring story-telling for children at the drop of a hat. Both Andy and Gill Bond (his wife) were major contributors to many of our shows and ceremonies up to about 1990. Welfare State International's street shows were particularly enhanced by Andy's lyrical and clear style. At Christmas they produce recordings of their wonderful simple songs with and for children.

18. As Graeme Dunstan – who had organised the original Aquarius Festival – put it in an article in *Simply Living* (1980): 'The process of a living culture is facilitated by shared ritual ceremonies and celebrations . . . one cannot experience community cohesion without agreed ceremony and celebration that both heal differences and proclaim unity. But one cannot agree on ceremony unless one agrees on the sacred. The sacred exists all of the time of course and people have their icons and rituals and many small and large and unconscious ways of genuflecting. But what John and Sue were seeking and Nimbin needing were ceremonies and celebrations that were real, relevant and alive to myth making, post

industrial possibilities.' My account of the work in Nimbin owes much to Graeme Dunstan.

19. The *Nimbin News* (quoted from *How to be a Survivor* by Dr Paul R. Ehrlich): What would happen if people were to abandon the ethic of Mammon in favour of the spirit of love and remembrance? If one felt the desire to give someone a material gift, what a pleasant surprise it would be to receive something which had been hand-made and had some of the personality and the spirit of the giver. Some people, especially children, already follow and enjoy this custom. Perhaps when most of us feel free to express our emotions more openly, the spirit of gathering together to celebrate a joyous occasion might supplant the need for material symbols of our feelings.

20. Before Sue and I left Burnley to go to Australia in 1979 there was a prolonged and draining dispute over issues of leadership and artistic direction. Some wanted a collective. I thought I was the boss . . . There was a generation gap, too. Some wanted to produce more rarefied fine art, and I was looking to work more in the community and so on, on the advice of Peter (Lord) Feversham. We split the company, split the grant, and IOU was born and off to a good start. By April 2002 it is still flourishing and most of us are good friends again.

21. Another key ingredient of our theatre 'language' is celebratory food. On scores of occasions we have brought together performance and feasting. There are fourteen pages in *Engineers of the Imagination* with descriptions, scenarios, instruction and recipes covering everything from setting up a field kitchen and how to avoid a bortsch and spare ribs riot in a Liverpool youth club (the answer is to serve hamburgers).

Some of my most dramatic memories are connected with food and celebration. When Sue Gill and I were adolescents, we eloped to Paris. Sitting on a pavement, at 2 a.m., scoffing our first ever onion soup at a market café next to Les Halles, we were unexpectedly surrounded by huge men with knives in bloodstained aprons emerging from their shift for a shot of brandy. Twenty years later, we were touring with Dan and Hannah in the village of Sawan in north Bali. At a festival, gangs of men cut the throat of a pot-bellied pig, and immediately on a vast wooden block, chopped up the carcass into tiny pieces. Their many clattering knives ensured no tapeworm would survive. Simultaneously teams of women modelled pink and green rice flour into towering offerings as delicate as lace. To celebrate our twenty-fifth wedding anniversary, we trekked through a remote mountain district of northern Portugal, where pilgrims traditionally brought roof tiles and carnations for the August feast of St John. An ancient chapel stood on a small volcanic plateau. Round its paved exterior, penitents crawled on their knees. In the gloomy interior, many wax replicas of human body parts hung over dark altars. These yellow thank-yous for potentially healing miracles were strangely counterpointed by piles of barbecued chicken thighs stacked outside. As the sky turned cobalt, Romany men in battered trilbys poked charcoal which was glowing in oil drums sliced in half. Scores of celebrants feasted at trestle tables laid with cream paper, crusty bread and earthenware jugs of wine. A perfect communion of flesh and spirit.

I love cooking. It is the perfect antidote to the heady world of arts management, with all its fundraising and abstract planning. It gives me a rare opportunity for meditation and hands-on solo creation. Surrounded by obsessive consumerism as we are, it also offers the chance to satisfy basic needs in a real context, a place to prepare, show and nurture. The work of chefs and site-specific theatre directors can be similar. Find an occasion to celebrate. Invent new recipes which build on traditional techniques. Select, prepare and if appropriate, slaughter fresh ingredients, gather guests comfortably in a conducive atmosphere (with candles and a breeze on linen and wood). Dress up and serve in style some unspeakable innards larded with flesh and subtle sauce. Receive accolades and cash. Wash up. Scrub, sleep, curse and begin again. Peter Schumann has always emphasised that his puppet performances should be as fundamental as bread, so he serves fresh rye loaves at all his shows, which he bakes on site in a brick and clay oven.

The study of food and theatre merits its own book, but there is a parallel between fast junk food and fast junk entertainment. Both poison our systems. The growing and preparation of food is increasingly dominated by agri-industry and is no longer taught at school. Communal food preparation at home and feasting with the family are declining in the West, another celebratory and vernacular event to connect us with our own hands, other people, the land, water and other species is disappearing.

On Tour

1. For Barn Dances – see *Engineers of the Imagination,* pp. 151–64.

2. *Tempest on Snake Island.* Ron Grimes's article is reprinted in *Engineers of the Imagination* pp. 164–81.

3. Welfare State International is recharged by people who arrive with new skills and ideas. David Clough who worked with us for over a decade up to 1989 brought pyrotechnics. Some of our most daring and memorable effects in for instance *Tempest on Snake Island, Parliament in Flames, The Wasteland and the Wagtail, Raising the Titanic* and the *Town Hall Tattoo* in Barrow (to name a few) would have been nothing without his dedication, skill and invention.

4. Mike Barrett, the British Council man on the ground, was an experienced boatbuilder who jigsawed all the wooden skeletons.

5. Ali Wood who had the responsibility of constructing the giant King Lear, had never made such a puppet before, but she had been well taught by Maggie Howarth, for whom she deputised. She more than rose to the occasion. She now plays trombone with the Peace Artists, a fervent street band.

6. PIA magazine (Japan) wrote that we were the best theatre event in Japan in 1983.

7. See *Engineers of the Imagination* and the documentary film made for Channel 4 directed by Alan Ravenscroft.

8. Tony Lewery was a key member of the Welfare State International team for over ten years up to 1983. He designs maritime exhibitions and theatrical pageants, paints lettering on canal boats, writes books on popular art, canal book painting and sign writing (published by Charles and Charles). He also gives lectures on popular and vernacular art. Les Sharpe is a visual adventurer, performer and artist who we met via one of our summer schools. He is also founder and artistic director of Emergency Exit Arts.

9. Luk Mishalle is one of the best soprano and tenor saxophonists and composers in Northern Europe. He worked with us as an administrator in the seventies but as his music developed, he created many bands – often with a hundred musicians – on a spectrum between jazz, rap and multi-ethnic street orchestras based in Belgium.

10. (Potlatch) Angus Alfred, Alert Bay 1980.

11. There were state management problems. We only had access to the space from 10 p.m. to

4 a.m. during the production period, so we had to work a nightshift, then go home to sleep as construction crews started up outside our accommodation. There were other shows in the same space during the day and every night it took two hours to de-rig to clear all our props, scenery and staging into an outside truck. The back stage space, was so small and the doors so tiny that the Cadillac of the final denouement had to be constructed to fold to fit in and be assembled in silence backstage during the first part of the show. Andy Plant was probably the only genius who could have found a solution and maintained a fabulous sense of humour throughout.

12. Mike White, in *Making Sense of Experiential Learning* edited Weil/McGill (Open University Press 1988).

The Barrow Years

1. Baz Kershaw, *Politics of Performance* (Routledge).

2. Joan Trent – a talented Barrow performer who sang and wrote music-hall style songs. See also Kevin Fegan (Weflare State International's writer in residence for *Shipyard Tales*) whose performance poem *Matey Boy*, (Iron Press, 1991) gives a strong sense of Barrow as a 'Wild West Town' at the end of a cul-de-sac.

3. Adrian Mitchell's script of *King Real* is published in *Peace Plays* (Methuen, 1985, out of print).

4. As our development director for three years between 1987 and 1990 Mike helped formulate many of our ideas of vernacular art. He has since steered much of Gateshead Council's acclaimed Arts policy and also invented and driven new thinking on the relationship between the arts and primary health care.

5. John Angus is a silk screen artist, poster maker to many theatres and arts companies, and instigator of outstanding exhibitions in Lancashire. Alison Jones worked with us in our mid-term years and had a major effect on the Lantern Parade. A visual artist, with an interest in arts and health, she is the artistic director of her own art centre in Bentham (near Lancaster).

6. Sam Samkin worked on a few gigs in the eighties, in particular *Parliament in Flames*, *Wildfire* and the Barrow *Tattoo*. The unusual and extensive daylight pyrotechnic display over Barrow Town Hall was partially his invention.

7. Baz Kershaw, *Town Hall Tattoo*. See *Engineers of the Imagination* and *The Politics of Performance*.

8. Tony Liddington is a peripatetic director who was once the artistic director of Wakefield Opera House. Also a member of the touring, singing group *The Pierotters*.

9. Mandy Dyke is one of the few, but increasing number of women pyrotechnicians (Hilary Hughes – see Lanternhouse – is another). Mandy's work is very personal and particular. As well as rescuing the Ulverston Dragon (Ulverston chapter) she designed all the water-borne mines in *Trawlers at Peace* (Rites of Passage chapter) and all the blueprints for alternative industries which were projected 20 feet high on our theatrical submarine sheds in *The Golden Submarine*.

10. Dougie Nicholson is an artist/sculptor/engineer who has created many pyrotechnic specials with us mainly for the Finale of the Ulverston Lantern parade. Working with the late Duncan

McGregor he also designed the explosive climactic end of the Barrow Years with the pyrotechnics for *The Golden Submarine*. His own company, External Combustion, is in great demand.

11. (i) *The Shipyard Tales* is given a full account in Baz Kershaw's *Politics of Performance*, (Routledge pp. 224 – 42).

    (ii) Granada TV's arts programme *Celebration* made a fiery and political screen equivalent of Shipyard Tales (1990). Sarah Miller's bluesy and gutsy song cycle, *Getting Out*, about women trapped in manipulative employment, came over well. When it was shown, Barrovians did not complain about the strong depiction of the economic exploitation of women, but about the portrayal of local girls' alleged sexual habits behind the chip shop.

12. *Building the Trident Network – A Study of the Enrolment of People, Knowledge and Machines*, by Maggie Mort (MIT Press, £22.50).

The Flight from Spectacle

1. Robert Hewison's books including *Culture and Consensus*, (Methuen, 1997) provide good food for thought.

2. There is an intriguing account of *Glasgow All Lit Up* by Baz Kershaw in *The Politics of Performance*, (Routledge).

3. In the early nineties many other companies were energetically and imaginatively creating spectacle on national and international circuits. Some like Emergency Exit (director Les Sharpe), Dodgy Clutch (director Ozzie Riley), Strange Cargo (director Art Hewitt), IOU, Whitewood and Fleming, Same Sky (director Pippa Smith) and Kneehigh Theatre Trust (director Sue Hill) had worked with us or been on our summer schools. John Wassel for example, was our dynamic production manager on The Golden Submarine and the director of *Glasgow All Lit Up* before he and Liz Pugh bought a Norwegian ferry, converted it to a theatre ship Fitzcarraldo and under the name Walk the Plank created performances and pyrotechnic shows all round Britain.

    Other English companies making fire shows were Paboom, the commercial Dragonfire, Industrial and Domestic in Devon, Test Department and Bow Gamelan. Meanwhile, European companies such as El Comediants, La Fura dels Baus, Malebar, Royale de Luxe, Archaeos, Urban Sax, Tietra Nuclear, Michel Jarre and many others have developed fire and firework spectacles and extravaganzas in tents and streets.

    My favourite was Dogtroep in Holland, founded by Warner van Wely in 1975 (after he had been resident with us for a year). They create daring site-specific visceral theatre with machines and clowns who fearlessly transform dry docks, beaches, parks and opera houses with performances for thousands of people. Our children, Hannah and Daniel (when they were in their twenties) independently of us and each other, worked with them for about five years during the time the company were producing some of the most amazing theatre in the world. Warner, restless genius that he is, left to form another extraordinary street theatre troupe called Warner and Consortium. Warner's inspirational book, *The Art of Wild Theatre*, published in Dutch and English, was published in 1992 by Vitgeverij International Theatre and Film Books and Dogtroep, (ISBN 90 6403 300 5).

4. Essay entitled 'Surgery for the Novel – or a Bomb' (in *Phoenix – the posthumous papers of D. H. Lawrence*, Edward D. McDonald (ed.), (London: Heinemann, 1936, pp. 517-20).

5. I was very influenced by the views of Sir Herbert Read. His *Art and Society* – originally published in 1936, was reprinted in 1967, just before we started Welfare State International. In this he argues for art as a "mode of knowledge".

6. Published by Pluto Press.

7. Definition of Vernacular Art (from Ivan Ilich, *Shadow of Work*, 1981).
   'Vernacular is a Latin term that we use in English only for the language that we have acquired without paid teachers. In Rome it was used from 500 BC to AD 600 to designate any value that was home-bred, home-made, derived from the commons, and that a person could protect and defend though he neither bought not sold it on the market. I suggest we restore this simple term 'vernacular' to oppose commodities and their shadow, i.e. commodity culture.'

8. 'Plea for Poetry' available from Welfare State International. As a final provocative polemic I suggested (among many 'wild ideas') that poets should do cabinet placements, that theatres and aircraft carriers should be converted into centres for new ceremonies, that there should be "salon" bars with attached art schools in every town, and that Arts Council officers would be obliged to write poetry every Monday. One person at The Arts Council reacted strongly to this suggestion and soon after our revenue grant was cut by £30,000!

Ulverston

1. Health and Safety caution: lanterns can catch fire. They must be used only outside. On parades it is necessary to have sufficient stewards with fire extinguishers and fire blankets. Participants should not wear plastic or nylon clothing.

2. For Dougie Nicholson (see *Golden Submarine* in Barrow Years). I have known Caroline Menis for over thirty years. She is a brilliant artist who draws perfectly and creates stunning sculptures, inspiring lanterns and pyrotechnic gardens. The *Finale of Glasgow All Lit Up* 1990 and *The Nativity of the Beasts* 2001 were just two events where her work was supreme. Roger Bloomfield has directed the Lantern Finale on a number of occasions. He is an all round sculptor who works with wood, mosaic, fire and large willow constructions with a particular interest in shamanism and constructing sculptural environments in landscape for ceremonial celebrations.

3. Shona Watt has created hundreds of flags and banners for many international festivals. Her work was seen at the opening of the Millenium bridge over the Thames and at many WOMAD gatherings. We also work with her brother Angus Watt, whose work is equally stunning.

4. Welfare State International constructed a fine dragon for the summer carnival parade; it is brought out every year and danced by different teams of strong sportsmen and women. A sculpted Ulverston Georgian street trips along its serrated scaly green back, and above its nostrils is a model of the Hoad Lighthouse. My most embarrassing Ulverton moment was at its dress rehearsal. It crept out looking like a collapsed camping holiday. Speedy repairers Mandy Dyke and Russ Dean rescued it and everyone, including the stony-faced carnival committee, was happy. I was happy not to be driven out of town.

Lanternhouse

1. Such as Luis Valdez's theatrical actions with Campesino grape-pickers in California in the sixties, the San Francisco Mime Troupe, John McGrath's *The Cheviot, The Stag and the Black, Black Oil* (Methuen) or Peter Schumann's many strong street actions and performances against the American involvement in the Vietnam War. Also John Arden and Margaretta D'Arcy and Albert Hunt's work at Bradford College of Art, Augusto Boal's Forum Theatre, Armand Gatti in France, and Dario Fo in Italy.

2. Hilary Hughes, our project director on *Glasgow All Lit Up* (1990) inspired us to develop the 'House' idea at our base in Ulverston. This was a simple but transforming idea typical of Hilary. Hilary is a regular member of our team and her input on many major gigs has been crucial. She was a key member of the Design Forum that set up Lanternhouse. Hilary made a massive contribution to the *Lord Dynamite* tour, and to *On the Street*, an important community art work we created in and around one multi-ethnic street in Bolton, Lancashire, for the 1994 Manchester City of Drama (which she directed).

3. Workshopped and edited by Tanya Peixoto, an artist and maker of books who runs her own bookshop (Bookart, 17 Pitfield Street, London N1 3HB. Tel: 020 7608 1333). As the diarist of Lanternhouse, Tanya made two elegant and eloquent art books about the process of building. These may be seen at Lanternhouse.

4. *Lantern Arcade (Winter Solstice Runway) – The Scenario*. Welfare State International and Acme will create, within the Tramway, a landscape of illuminated lanterns, mobile structures, projected light and collaged sounds. Designed to coincide with the Christmas and Pantomime season and to open on the evening of the Winter Solstice (21 December), the Lantern Arcade will be a colourful and spacious installation constructed with paper figures, four-wheeled towers, constellations of lanterns and dominant moving shadows. It will contain echoes of distant grottoes.

   Each tower will represent a different world (with its own traditions, logic and metaphysics), be mounted on a flanged wheeled truck and located on a single set of tramlines. Four towers on four sets of rails will move independently and in parallel with each other. Only occasionally will there be any contact of one world with another. When this does occur it will be random and comic; snowstorms, cow bellows and dynamite whoopie cushions sometimes do disturb the most twinkly Chagall evening.

   High in the roof, balanced on horizontal cogwheel constellations, unattainable moons and stars will move intermittently. Movement will be triggered by the towers passing underneath their orbits.

   Large silhouette shadows from all moving structures will be projected on to the perimeter walls giving the effect of a fluctuating seascape of dreams and occasional nightmares.

   Although quotations from traditional seasonal celebrations may occur, the intention is to discover new patterns (or re-work old ones). These will be informed, laterally, by current political and ecological tensions.

   The Lantern Arcade will be a place to escape to: a home-made, low-tech environment where the spirals of party music, dancing shadows and fragile lanterns will conjure up memories and hopes. Between old towers a delicate runway will materialise and a new New Year will take off.

5. Chris Coates, who also selected the oak trees, is a versatile all round performer/carpenter/builder and author who seems to recur in our life at ten year intervals. One evening he was in the front row of a performance of *Hollow Ring*. The next moment he was the site manager of our Barn project and then the crucial and influential convenor of our Artists' Forum, which steered Lanternhouse to its successful conclusion. Chris has always been interested in visions of Utopia and his own book, *Utopia Britannica* (Volume 1) published by D and D in 2001 illustrates British utopian experiments from 1325 to 1945.

6. Gilly Adams is ex-drama director of the Welsh Arts Council and ex-artistic director of the Made in Wales Stage Company. In 2002 a BBC Radio Drama Producer in Wales, Gilly is one of our major artists. She chaired our Executive Committee for thirteen years, steering us through a bad period to our Lottery success. Having been a researcher and teacher of our rites of passage work and a celebrant, she is now pioneering new forms of digital story-telling with the photographer Daniel Meadows.

7. Derek Pearce was the leader of a wild sixties folk band called Roaring Jelly. He now makes even wilder sculptural furniture where nothing is ever as it seems.

8. Hilary Hughes and Gill Gill with Susan Clarke run Beavers Arts, a well-established and powerful theatre collective based in Newcastle-under-Lyme. They work with both the local community and communities in central Europe; often with asylum seekers. Gill is also an experienced writer, theatre director and the editor of our *Dead Good Time Capsules* book. Susan Clarke runs our Street Comedy workshops.

9. There is an illustrated description of Lanternhouse in *Pride of Place*, published by the Arts Council of England, March 2002.

Rites of Passage

1. Graeme Gilmour was a member of ACME, the Scottish company, which grew out of *Glasgow All Lit Up* (1990) and with whom we had also worked on *Fragile Gift* (1992) and *Lantern Arcade* (1993). He was also part of the design team with Julian Crouch, Phelim McDermott and Jo Pocock, who created the very successful *Shockheaded Peter* which in 2002 is still running in London's West End. Max Orton is from Ulverston. An all-round welder, fitter and demon worker who is part of many teams, including that of Andy Plant and Walk the Plank.

2. See *Vigor Mortis – The End of the Death Taboo*, Kate Berridge (Profile Books Ltd., 2001).

3. Steve Gumbley was a founder member of Welfare State International and IOU, with whom he still works. He is also a freelance artist and exhibition/installation designer and maker. Recent collaborations with Jane Revitt include EXPO 2000 and The Earth Centre.

4. It is easy to forget that as early as 1962 Peter Cheeseman was running a community-based theatre in a converted cinema in Stoke-on-Trent.

5. See *Beyond Boundaries*, the speech he gave at the National Portrait Gallery on 18 March 2002. He maintains that The Arts Council of England (ACE) has a new-found capacity for innovation and states 'if support for the arts becomes too controlled and prescriptive, it will kill off the very creativity it is meant to set free and we must establish a right to roam ... we need artistic capacity spread throughout our society and its many communities to provide us with the depth and diversity of imaginative capital to make sense of, and the most of, the complex world we live in.' (ACE, 14 Great Peter Street, London, SW1P 3NQ ISBN 0 7287 0872 8).

6. The catalogue for *Hatch, Match, Dispatch,* 2000, available from Welfare State International, price £2.

7. The catalogue for the *Dead* exhibition, 2001 (with essays) is available from Welfare State International, price £3.

New Generations

1. The other artists were Rob Hill, Patsy Forde and Sharon Dippity. Rob Hill has been the lighting designer and technician on a number of our gigs – especially the Lantern Finale. He works with many other companies, such as Contact Theatre in Manchester, and is a bass guitar player. Patsy Forde is a freelance fine artist who constructs stunning installations based on domestic objects. Sharon Dippity makes personal decorative and witty hand-made books.

Wishbone House

1. *Independent*, 1 December 2001.

2. Article by John Pilger, *Daily Mirror*, 5 April 2002. Within our so-called democracy it is hard to take a stand outside centralist propaganda. One way is to seek to divert our taxes from war and armaments through 'Conscience', The Peace Tax Campaign, Archway Resource Centre, 1b Waterlow Road, London N19 5NJ Tel: 0207 561 1061/0870 777 3223 www.conscienceonline.org.uk/info@conscienceonline.org.uk

3. Published by Mushroom, 1994.

4. *Walden* (1854) and *Civil Disobedience* (1849). (Reprinted in Penguin Classics 1986).

5. According to *Religious Trends* (2001), 27 million people live in some kind of slavery, 37,000 people a day die of curable infectious disease, attendances in church in Cumbria have dropped by a third in ten years, yet two thirds of British people still claim to believe in God and 54% of first-time weddings take place in church. Three quarters of the population have a Christian funeral and more than half believe there is a heaven.

6. *A Snake's Tail Full of Ants* by John Lane, (Resurgence, £14.95) gives an overview of cultures where the artist has a more integrated role.

★

Books by Welfare State International can be obtained from Welfare State International, Lanternhouse, The Ellers, Ulverston, Cumbria. Telephone: 01229 581127 Fax: 01229 581232 e-mail: info@welfare-state.com website: www.welfare-state.org

Books published by Welfare State and Engineers of the Imagination include *The Dead Good Funerals book, The Dead Good Time Capsules Book, The Dead Good Guide to Namings and Baby Welcoming Ceremonies, Learn about Lanterns Educational Pack.*

Roger Coleman on the Welfare State bike, 1968